American Hippies

In the late 1960s ~~~~~~~ us of thousands of white middle-class ~~~~~~~ ddenly became hippies. This short overview ~~~~~ ie social movement in the United States examines ~~~~ ovement's beliefs and practices, including psychedelic drugs, casual sex, and rock music, as well as the phenomena of spiritual seeking, hostility to politics, and communes. W. J. Rorabaugh synthesizes how hippies strived for authenticity, expressed individualism, and yearned for community. Viewing the tumultuous Sixties from a new angle, Rorabaugh shows how the counterculture led to subsequent social and cultural changes in the United States with legacies including casual sex, natural foods, and even the personal computer.

W. J. Rorabaugh is Professor of History at the University of Washington, Seattle. His numerous books include *The Alcoholic Republic: An American Tradition*, *Berkeley at War: The 1960s*, *Kennedy and the Promise of the Sixties*, and *The Real Making of the President: Kennedy, Nixon, and the 1960 Election*. Rorabaugh received his AB from Stanford University and his PhD from the University of California, Berkeley.

Cambridge Essential Histories

Series Editor

Donald Critchlow, *Arizona State University*

Cambridge Essential Histories is devoted to introducing critical events, periods, or individuals in history to students. Volumes in this series emphasize narrative as a means of familiarizing students with historical analysis. In this series leading scholars focus on topics in European, American, Asian, Latin American, Middle Eastern, African, and World History through thesis-driven, concise volumes designed for survey and upper-division undergraduate history courses. The books contain an introduction that acquaints readers with the historical event and reveals the book's thesis; narrative chapters that cover the chronology of the event or problem; and a concluding summary that provides the historical interpretation and analysis.

Titles in the Series

American Hippies

W. J. RORABAUGH
University of Washington

CAMBRIDGE
UNIVERSITY PRESS

32 Avenue of the Americas, New York, NY 10013-2473, USA

Cambridge University Press is part of the University of Cambridge.

It furthers the University's mission by disseminating knowledge in the pursuit of education, learning, and research at the highest international levels of excellence.

www.cambridge.org
Information on this title: www.cambridge.org/9781107627192

First published 2015

Printed in the United States of America

A catalog record for this publication is available from the British Library.

Library of Congress Cataloging in Publication Data
Rorabaugh, W. J.
American hippies / W. J. Rorabaugh.
   pages   cm. – (Cambridge essential histories)
Includes bibliographical references and index.
ISBN 978-1-107-04923-9 (hardback) – ISBN 978-1-107-62719-2 (pbk.)
1. Hippies – United States – History.   2. Youth – United States – History –
20th century.   3. Counterculture – United States – History –
20th century.   4. United States – Civilization – 1945–   5. United
States – History – 1961–1969.   I. Title.
HQ799.7.R66   2015
305.5'680973–dc23   2014049553

ISBN 978-1-107-04923-9 Hardback
ISBN 978-1-107-62719-2 Paperback

Contents

vii

FIGURE I. In October 1967 two hippies stood on Haight Street in San Francisco.

Charles W. Cushman Collection: Indiana University Archives (P15596).

Introduction

Suddenly, in 1966 there were hippies, thousands of them, then tens of thousands, and within a couple of years, hundreds of thousands, or even millions of long-haired youth of both sexes dressed in tight-fitting jeans or bright-colored pants accompanied by colorful tie-dyed T-shirts with or without printed slogans, or, in the case of a goodly number of women, wearing Victorian "granny dresses" either out of the attic or from a chic store. The clothing, by contemporary standards, was outrageous. For men, slender pants flaunted sexuality in a traditionally repressed culture, while hip-swinging bejeaned women turned men on by wearing low-cut blouses and going braless. Hippie men and their "chicks" gave heightened display to the body from the red bandannas they wrapped around the forehead, to beads or Indian jewelry draped around the neck, to thick homemade leather belts with gigantic steel buckles, to sockless sandals made cheaply from recycled tires and imported from Mexico. As visibly different from mainstream culture as possible, they could not be ignored.[1]

The hippie counterculture is historically important for several reasons. First, this counterculture was a significant part of the

---

[1] Gene Anthony, *Magic of the Sixties* (Salt Lake City, UT, 2004), 12, 86–7, 98–102, 178–83; Charles Perry, *The Haight-Ashbury* (New York, 1984), 6.

massive upheavals of the 1960s, which included civil rights, Black Power, feminism, and gay liberation, as well as looser sexual mores, the end of censorship, street protests, political radicalism, and environmentalism. Collectively, these movements profoundly changed the United States. Second, the hippie counterculture was large. Hundreds of thousands of young Americans were, at least for a time, hippies, and millions adopted some if not all hippie beliefs and practices. The numbers mattered. Third, hippie values represented a generational break with traditional middle-class culture. When hordes of people concentrated in a single youth generation simultaneously adopted new thoughts and behaviors, mainstream culture was forced to pay attention. In the long run, hippies played a significant role in transforming American society.

Why did the hippie counterculture emerge in the late Sixties? That is one main question that this book addresses. Related questions also need to be answered. What antecedent subcultures or countercultures shaped the hippie counterculture? Hippies both emerged from and were in opposition to mainstream society. They were young, white, and middle class, but they were never a majority of young Americans. Nonwhites rejected being hippies. The emergence of this counterculture during the 1960s owed a great deal to the large size of the "baby boomer" generation, as well as sharp generational differences between boomers and their parents, and the decade's economic prosperity. The bulk of this book, however, is about what might be called the counterculture's internal dynamics. Drugs, rock music, and a spiritual quest played a big role in the rise of hippies. So did new sexual attitudes and practices that were spreading throughout the society. The hippie relationship to politics was complicated and tangled. Eventually, many hippies settled in communes. Finally, the hippie legacy flowed in many directions.

Before exploring these issues, it is necessary to define a few terms. Every modern complex society has a *mainstream culture* that includes huge numbers of people, probably a majority, and that dominates the overall society to such an extent that those who adhere to different values and ways of living are said to belong to a *subculture*. Members of a subculture may choose to keep particular beliefs or practices that are outside the mainstream but otherwise participate in mainstream culture either wholly or in part. For example, Italian immigrants might have a strong devotion to opera that sets them apart from other Americans, but attending operas does not impede subscribing to mainstream practices. However, when members of a subculture hold beliefs or engage in practices that are opposed to or radically different from mainstream values or practices, so that adherents to the subculture either cannot or do not wish to function inside the mainstream, then the subculture can be called a *counterculture*.[2]

Hippies, like other counterculture followers, rejected mainstream society and its culture. Hostile to the norms that the establishment tried to impose through public opinion and legal sanctions, hippies particularly resented pressure to conform concerning hair, dress, sex, drugs, and work. They celebrated nonconformity. In this sense, hippies expressed an anarchistic or even libertarian view. Such an attitude was consistent with hedonism, which was another hippie value. Mainstream authority was perceived to be the source of virtually all social, political, and economic ills, ranging from racism to the Vietnam War, corporate power, and oppression of hippies and their lifestyle. Hippies looked askance at the nation-state, its gargantuan size, its use of brutal force, and its enthusiastic militarism, as evidenced by Vietnam. This was no way, hippies concluded, to run any society.

During the past century several prominent countercultures appeared in the United States, beginning with Greenwich Village in New York during the early 1900s. These bohemians, as they were called after the characters in Puccini's opera, *La Boheme*, rejected ordinary jobs, marriage, and social norms. In the 1940s Harlem's black jazz musicians defied mainstream norms

---

[2] In 1960 Milton Yinger invented the idea of contraculture, which quickly became counterculture. Fred Davis, *On Youth Subcultures: The Hippie Variant* (New York, 1971). See also Theodore Roszak, *The Making of a Counter Culture* (Garden City, NY, 1969).

by using illegal drugs, especially heroin. At the same time, the Beat writers, primarily Jack Kerouac, Allen Ginsberg, and their friends, created another counterculture. After the war, poets who had been interned in Oregon as conscientious objectors in World War II gathered in North Beach in San Francisco. During the 1950s, Kerouac and Ginsberg bridged the Beat communities in San Francisco and New York. Smaller oases developed in the French Quarter in New Orleans, in Venice in Los Angeles, and in a few other places. As late as the mid-1950s, only a few thousand bohemians lived in the United States. What differentiated the hippie counterculture of the 1960s from these earlier groups, more than any other aspect, was sheer numbers.[3]

To understand the sudden emergence of "hippies," it is helpful to trace the origin of this somewhat enigmatic word. The fact that the singular was spelled both "hippy" and "hippie" in the Sixties suggests complex origins. Virginia Pope, the fashion editor of the *New York Times*, promoted the "hippy" look in high fashion from 1945 into the Fifties. Pope applauded postwar skirts worn low on the hips to accentuate hyperfemininity. One of the traits of the period was to make women look more womanly, which hippy skirts did. This use of the word *hippy* within haute couture continued sporadically throughout the 1950s; the main effect was to give the public familiarity with the sound of the word. Any connection to the Sixties counterculture was merely coincidental.[4]

A few scholars have suggested an African origin for the word *hippie*, but the evidence is thin. What is certain is that *hippie* is related to *hip* and *hep*. Both terms appear in the jazz musician *Cab Calloway's Cat-ologue: A Hepster's Dictionary*, a pamphlet on Harlem jive talk first published in the late 1930s. Calloway defined *hip* as "wise, sophisticated" and "hep cat" as "a guy who knows all the answers, understands jive." According

[3] Gerald W. McFarland, *Inside Greenwich Village* (Amherst, MA, 2001); Phil Ford, *Dig* (New York, 2013); John Tytell, *Naked Angels* (New York, 1986; orig. 1976).

[4] E.g., Virginia Pope, "From the Big Six," *New York Times*, September 9, 1945, 103.

to the *Autobiography of Malcolm X*, jazz musicians, especially bebop artists, called themselves "hipsters" during the 1940s, either because they swung their hips to the music, or because they kept drug stashes on the hip under the belt. In the Forties *hipster*, *hip*, and *hep* all circulated among whites in New York, originally applied to black jazz performers and then later to jazz artists and fans of all races. African American musicians used *hippie* as a putdown for young white followers who startled performers by unexpectedly attending all-black clubs and copying jive talk. The *Autobiography* became a bestseller in late 1965 and helps explain the media's sudden interest in the term.[5]

Some additional evidence about "hippies" dates from the late 1950s and early 1960s. Most of the references are elliptical, clearly refer to a counterculture, and primarily suggest a small group of misfits. In 1957 the *New York Times* published a list of current jazz hipster slang. *Hippy* meant, "Generic for a character who is super-cool, over-blasé, so far out that he appears to be asleep when he's digging something the most." The next year *Playboy* dropped a mention. The comedy album *How to Speak Hip* (1959) included a booklet defining a *hippy* as "a junior member of Hip society, who may know the words, but hasn't fully assimilated the proper attitude." In 1960 the entertainment columnist Earl Wilson referred to the pop singer Bobby Darin as "a hippie from New York City" who had "conquered all the New York hippies." When Darin sang, girls swung hips in their seats. In 1961 the *New York Times Magazine* ran an article complaining that Greenwich Village was being overrun by "hippies from Forest Hills and South Orange," that is, by middle-class tourists who pretended to be bohemians on the weekend.[6]

---

[5] David Roediger, "Guineas, Wiggers, and the Dramas of Racialized Culture," *American Literary History* 7:4 (Winter 1995), 663–4; Cab Calloway, *Cab Calloway's Cat-ologue: A Hepster's Dictionary* (N.p., circa 1938); Malcolm X with Alex Haley, *The Autobiography of Malcolm X* (New York, 1965), 95. See also Perry, *Haight-Ashbury*, 5; Lewis Yablonsky, *The Hippie Trip* (New York, 1968), 28; Davis, *On Youth Subcultures*, 14, note 7.

[6] Elliot Horne, "For Cool Cats and Far-Out Chicks," *New York Times Magazine*, August 18, 1957, 14; Herbert Gold, "What It Is – Whence It Came," *Playboy*, February 1958, 84; *How to Speak Hip* (1959), booklet accompanying the

In 1963 the white Philadelphia rock singer Freddy Cannon, a regular on the afternoon television dance show *American Bandstand*, released "Do What the Hippies Do." Cannon's hippies swung hips and danced. Around the same time the pop culture columnist Dorothy Kilgallen wrote, "New York hippies have a new kick – baking marijuana in cookies." In 1964 the *Village Voice* referred to "baby beatniks" as hippies, and *Time* reported on "hard-shell hippies" living improbably in Darien, Connecticut, a wealthy suburb. Jean Shepherd, a bearded radio talk show host on WOR, broadcast from a Village coffee house on Saturday nights. Off-air, he mused, "And the little old grandmother from Circleville [Ohio] can really be a hippie." The dance teacher Killer Joe Piro, who taught café society the frug, the watusi, and other fast rock dances, said that New Yorkers wanted to be "hippies" and never "square."[7]

When *The Rolling Stones, Now!* (1965) was released in the United States in February, Andrew Loog Oldham's notes on the back cover observed the "hippy" presence in London and then described the Stones: "Their music is Berry-Chuck and all the Chicago hippies." Oldham, who served as the band's manager, was acknowledging his group's debt to the black rock 'n' roll artist Chuck Berry, but the inverted name had a double meaning. By using a technique common in African American jive talk, Oldham suggested a close familiarity with the black hipster world. At the same time, the jive inversion could be read as a putdown of Berry's influence on the Stones, because an inversion suggested that the opposite was true. The cited Chicago hippies were whites who liked black music, or more accurately grooved

---

album; Earl Wilson column, Colonial Heights, VA, *Progress-Index*, June 8, 1960, 4; David Boroff, "An Appeal to Save the Village," *New York Times Magazine*, May 7, 1961, 77.

[7] Freddy Cannon, "Do What the Hippies Do" (1963); Dorothy Kilgallen, "The Voice of Broadway," New Castle, PA, *News*, June 15, 1963, 20; Sally Kempton, "Baby Beatniks Spark Bar Boom on East Side," *Village Voice*, September 10, 1964, 6; "Darien's Dolce Vita," *Time*, November 27, 1964, 60; Bernard Weinraub, "Jean Shepherd Leads His Flock on a Search for Truth," *New York Times*, December 6, 1964, X17; Gay Talese, "Killer Joe Piro," *New York Times*, December 13, 1964, 88.

on rock, including the Stones. In effect, Oldham redefined hippies: youthful whites opposed to mainstream values, hippies pursued casual sex, took drugs, especially psychedelics, and listened to rock music.[8]

Hollywood was one of the first places to identify hippies, which became a term used inside the trade as early as 1964 to describe a new category of young filmgoers. Hippies liked arty foreign-language films, watched the French New Wave, were intrigued by Britain's angry young men, and admired the comedy *Tom Jones* (1963), the first non-American film to win the Oscar for best picture. They flocked to see Peters Sellers in *A Shot in the Dark* (1964). By 1966 hippies were being noticed more widely. When the black entertainer Sammy Davis Jr. promoted his new television variety show, he vowed, "The show won't be for hippies only." That same year the folksinger Joan Baez did a concert in which she sang her brother-in-law Richard Farina's ballad, "The House Un-American Blues Activities Dream," which contained a "hippy, hoppy" reference in its lyrics. Shortly afterward, a *New York Times* reporter denounced "hippie dippies" who were "lisping, prancing, cursing" on Macdougal Street in Greenwich Village. The *Times* also found hippies in Los Angeles and Berkeley.[9]

There is a related but alternative explanation for how the word *hippie* developed on the West Coast. In the late 1950s San Francisco's North Beach and New York's Greenwich Village were the nation's only important counterculture communities. They remained relatively isolated from each other. The Beats came of age during or just after World War II, and by the late Fifties a

---

[8] Rolling Stones, *The Rolling Stones, Now!* (1965), back cover notes by Andrew Loog Oldham.

[9] Philip K. Scheuer, "Film Audience Hippy, Hooray," *Los Angeles Times*, September 27, 1964, B1, B4; Bernhard Weinraub, "A Long Day's Journey with Davis," *New York Times*, January 2, 1966, 91; "Joan Baez Success at Philharmonic," *New York Times*, March 14, 1966, 37; "City Cleanup of Macdougal Street Is Called a Failure," *New York Times*, May 30, 1966, 24; Peter Bart, "Bohemian Newspapers Spread across Country," *New York Times*, August 1, 1966, 30; Ben A. Franklin, "A Showdown Is Expected in Strike at Berkeley," *New York Times*, December 4, 1966, 85.

new, younger counterculture generation became visible. The *San Francisco Chronicle* columnist Herb Caen called the Beats' young followers "beatniks." Caen played upon audience familiarity with "sputnik," but he was also drawing upon Yiddish, where the –nik ending meant the diminutive, that is, beatniks were little Beats, which referred to their youthful status. Interestingly enough, Caen in 1958 described a hip teenager as a "hippie." Beatnik, however, became the standard term, probably because beatniks faithfully copied Beat clothes, slang, and love of jazz.[10]

A new word was needed when the hip young dropped jazz for rock. In 1959 an Australian rock musician produced a single, "Hippy Hippy Shake," which became a local hit. The song urged dancers to shake their hips. Although the recording was sold only in Australia, a traveling Australian disc jockey later gave a copy of the record to a San Francisco disc jockey. Never heard on the radio, the record was played at parties, which promoted the word *hippy* in San Francisco. In 1961 the local critic Kenneth Rexroth alluded to youthful "hippies." By the mid-1960s, a younger rock-loving counterculture generation had to be distinguished from the jazz-oriented beatniks. The musical switch was connected to the rise of the psychedelic drug lysergic acid diethylamide (LSD). Michael Fallon, a reporter for the *San Francisco Examiner*, used the words *hippie* or *hippies* twelve times in a four-part series in September 1965. Focusing on the Haight-Ashbury, he defined hippies as "the outer fringe of the bohemian fringe" and noted connections to the arts, homosexuals, and marijuana. "Hippies" gained broader notice in 1966, when Caen used the word in his *Chronicle* column, which had more than one hundred thousand daily readers.[11]

---

[10] W. J. Rorabaugh, *Berkeley at War* (New York, 1989), 133; Herb Caen column, *San Francisco Chronicle*, June 17, 1958, 15.

[11] Richard Neville, *Hippie Hippie Shake* (London, 1995), 10; Kenneth Rexroth, "What's Wrong with the Clubs" (1961), in *World Outside the Window* (New York, 1987), 194; Michael Fallon in *San Francisco Examiner*: "A New Paradise for Beatniks," September 5, 1965, sec. 1, 5 (quote); "A New Hip Hangout," September 6, 1965, 14; "Bohemia's New Haven," September 7, 1965, 1, 8; "Are Beats Good Business?" September 8, 1965, 17; Herb Caen column, *San Francisco Chronicle*, December 22, 1966, 27; William

Except for the *Chronicle* and the *New York Times*, mainstream newspapers barely mentioned hippies until 1967, which produced frenzy. From 1967 to 1970, newspapers ran hundreds of stories about the counterculture, but the slant depended upon the paper. The *Chicago Tribune* linked hippies to crime with such headlines as "2 Hippie Types Rob Brink's." In reality, the robbers, who may or may not have been hippies, were identified as such because they were longhairs. The *Los Angeles Times* tied hippies to drugs, and most drug references included the word *addict*. The *Seattle Times* sent reporters to talk to hippies about why they believed and acted as they did. So did the *Washington Post*, which published Nicholas von Hoffman's thoughtful fifteen-part series. The establishment *New York Times* rarely interviewed hippies. Instead, the paper's reporters discussed hippies with psychiatrists and sociologists, a method that stressed deviance. The *San Francisco Chronicle* was unique in employing hippie sympathizers, notably the columnist Ralph Gleason.[12]

Hippies looked to the new underground press weeklies for information about their own communities. The *Berkeley Barb*, founded by political radicals in 1965, gradually shifted toward hippiedom. Its youthful reporters routinely talked to San Francisco's numerous hippies. The *San Francisco Oracle*, an avowedly hippie newspaper, appeared sporadically and only published twelve issues in seventeen months (1966–8) before disappearing. Like other hippie publications, its LSD-influenced graphics and typography became distorted and bizarre. In New York, the *Village Voice*, founded in 1955, covered the counterculture, but its vision was not youthful. Hippies preferred the *East Village Other*, which never matched the *Barb*'s vigor. Other important counterculture papers included the *Los Angeles Free Press*, which covered cultural events extremely well; the Boston

Hedgepeth, *The Alternative* (New York, 1970), 17; Barney Hoskyns, *Beneath the Diamond Sky* (New York, 1997), 37.

[12] "2 Hippie Types Rob Brink's of $29,000 in Cash," *Chicago Tribune*, March 8, 1968, B2; Nicholas von Hoffman series, *Washington Post*, October 15–29, 1967. Online searches were conducted for all of the newspapers except the *San Francisco Chronicle*, which was read on microfilm.

Avatar, which was swept into the Mel Lyman cult; the salty and sardonic Austin *Rag*; and the militantly radical Detroit *Fifth Estate*.[13]

The hippie social movement is not always easy to document. Sources are a problem. Hippies were not very articulate and often spoke in vague terms, for example, "groovy" or "far out." This counterculture was about the expression of feelings; it was openly anti-intellectual. Hippies blamed reason and linear thought for most of the world's troubles. Unlike the Surrealists of the 1920s, no hippie Andre Breton issued a guiding manifesto. There were no hippie membership organizations. The hippie counterculture lacked the philosophical underpinnings that Albert Camus and Jean-Paul Sartre gave to the French Existentialists. Whereas the Beat writers in the Fifties had critiqued existing society and offered a literary vision for the future, hippies produced no significant literature. They did produce some art and impressive rock music. In addition to the music, the main sources for studying hippies are statements by older gurus such as Ken Kesey and Timothy Leary, media coverage, social science field research, medical reports (which often stress deviance), and later hippie memoirs. A vast secondary literature is crucial.[14]

Ironically, hippies disliked being called hippies, which both the public and the media used derogatorily. Long-haired protesters and criminals were called "hippies," which conflated all young male longhairs, whether or not they shared hippie values. When the press queried the public, interviewees often spat out the phrase "dirty hippie." Counterculture adherents preferred to be called the "love generation," "heads," or "freaks" and contrasted the "freak" and "straight" worlds. (In this book "freak" and "hippie" are used interchangeably.) Or they used "flower children," which evoked nature and peacefulness, a benign phrase that separated hippies from violent thugs or political radicals.

[13] John McMillian, *Smoking Typewriters* (New York, 2011). The microfilm of the Underground Newspaper Collection remains indispensable.
[14] Joseph Conlin, *The Troubles* (New York, 1982), 229–30; Greil Marcus, *Lipstick Traces* (Cambridge, MA, 1989).

Others said that they belonged to a counterculture or a new culture, and still others said that they were part of a new society or a social movement to remake the world. Hippies cared little for labels, which they disdained as media hype. The absence of a common descriptive term from within the counterculture shows the movement's sprawling diversity. So the word *hippie* stuck, and so did the counterculture's word for the mainstream, that is, *straight*.[15]

Three themes run through this book. One is *authenticity*. Hippies stressed the need for authenticity in one's personal life, relationships, and the larger social structure. When they found a society filled with hypocrisy, consumer gluttony, status seeking, and power politics, they fled to create space in order to live a life true to the self. In daily life and in work, hippies believed that each person needed to be true to the self in order to succeed, be fulfilled, and be happy. One way to express authenticity was through spontaneity. Hippies lived for the moment. Rejecting any concern for the future, they held that present experience was all that mattered. The focus on the present could be seen in the emphasis upon drugs and instant sex, as well as rock concerts and festivals, or theatrical displays that were brilliant but ephemeral. Washable body paint and chalked sidewalk paintings left no lasting impressions. The whole idea was to do what you wanted right now.

The search for authenticity often involved a spiritual quest. Because hippies saw mainstream culture as hopelessly rotten, they had little use for Western civilization or the Judeo-Christian tradition, both of which were associated with mainstream cultural oppression. Americans, like Europeans, had oppressed "other" peoples all across the globe, and particularly Native Americans in what was now the United States. But the establishment had also oppressed the self. The hippie spiritual quest celebrated the primitive, especially American Indians, and elevated the "other" to a place of esteem. Foreign spiritual gurus were common. Psychedelic drugs, yoga, and meditation often

---

[15] Barry Miles, *Hippie* (New York, 2005), 9.

constituted spiritual practice, which was usually conducted within a community setting. Hippies borrowed spiritual or religious practices willy-nilly from Native American rites, Hinduism, Buddhism, or Taoism.

Hippies also embraced *individualism*, that is, the right of the individual to be fulfilled through personal belief and discovery apart from any societal constraints, but this penchant for individualism was not truly libertarianism, because it was not developed in any ideological or systematic way. The distrust of ideas and education, which was seen as part of the establishment's desire to control the individual, left freaks disinterested in rooting individualism in any philosophical tradition. Each person ought to follow his or her own instincts. Expertise was highly doubted. Hippies expressed a fierce pride in being independent, living one's own life, and learning even the most basic skills from personal experience. This rugged individualism was matched by hippies looking to the western frontier for ideas about how to behave so as to carve out a space of one's own. The West was romanticized as a place where free people might still settle as if they were pioneers.

One curious aspect of this yearning to reproduce pioneer individualism was a tendency toward nostalgia. In a culture that routinely celebrated newness, hippies yearned to live in old houses, become farmers, abandon flush toilets for outhouses, acquire secondhand furniture, wear Victorian clothes, or reject doctors for midwives and replace medical prescriptions with home remedies. Because they believed that mainstream society was too sick to be healed, they were determined to retreat to a more primitive past that lacked current ills. Opposed to their own parents, hippies often embraced their rural grandparents' values. The fascination with nature, the primitive, or the only recently departed western frontier expressed a Freudian inversion: they sought to go forward from the unacceptable mainstream present by reverting to a pastoral past where a heroic individual created personal space. This process, like the use of psychedelic drugs, was supposed to cleanse away cultural inhibitions as hippies boldly remade the self and thereby resolved to create a new social order.

Finally, hippies expressed a deep yearning for *community* with the like-minded. The idea of community was perhaps a necessity for a counterculture in which the search for authenticity and individualism might tend toward both social and personal disintegration. This desire for community set hippies apart from the Beats, who lacked the critical mass to create a numerically significant community. Badly outnumbered, the Beats projected sullen despair as pariahs. In contrast, the hippie search for community could be seen from the beginning in early rock concerts, Be-Ins, and festivals. These large-scale events validated the existence of the counterculture, affirmed its huge size, and warned the establishment that it was so big that it would have to be accepted or at least tolerated. The communal ideal took a tangible and systematic form in the development of communes, cooperative stores, underground newspapers, and other collaborative projects. Rural communes, in particular, enabled hippies to work out the meaning of the counterculture.

These three themes will recur in most of the book's five chapters. The first three chapters emphasize authenticity and individualism. Chapter 1 examines the origins of the hippie counterculture, including the key role of the Beat writers. Chapter 2 shows how psychedelic drugs, particularly LSD, helped launch hippies in the mid-Sixties. At the same time, the Grateful Dead invented a new kind of drug-influenced rock music, and spiritual-seeking grew. Chapter 3 takes up the sexual revolution, including hippie free sex, new gender relations, the rise of feminism, and gay liberation. Chapter 4 looks at the complex relationship between hippies and political radicals. Politically, the search for authenticity was in tension with the desire for community. Chapter 5 considers why hippies moved to rural communes to seek self-sufficiency, find spiritual satisfaction, and live in harmony with nature. Communes were primarily about community. The conclusion explores the numerous legacies of the hippie counterculture, ranging from more casual attitudes about sex and drugs to the development of the high-tech industry.

The inspiration for this book goes back to walking along Haight Street in San Francisco in the Sixties. I was, however, a student who stayed in college, not a hippie who dropped out. However, my high school friend, the late Ken Culver, did drop out to join the counterculture. As his wife said decades later, Ken made a thirteen-year detour before resuming normal life. He told me that he had taken LSD more than five hundred times. During one period he did so daily. I asked Ken if he regretted those years, and he answered that he did not regret one minute. Upon reflection, I realized that my question was a poor one: it would be difficult for anyone to admit that a thirteen-year adventure had been a mistake. There were other reasons to write this book. A short overview about the hippie counterculture has been needed, and, as a social historian, the upheavals of the Sixties in the United States have long interested me. Finally, today's college students, some of whom are the grandchildren of hippies, show a great deal of curiosity about the Sixties counterculture.

A number of people aided making this book possible. Professor Lynn Thomas, chair of the History Department at the University of Washington, as well as Dean Judy Howard and Dean Robert Stacey helped arrange a paid leave to write. I owe much to the Cambridge University Press team, including my editor Lewis Bateman, the series editor Donald Critchlow, and Shaun Vigil. I would also like to thank Bren Bovee, Stanford Microform Library; Nicolette Bromberg, University of Washington; Coi E. Drummond-Gehrig, Denver Public Library; my friends Roland Guyotte and Barbara Posadas; my friends Kurt and Gladys Lang; and Nicholas Meriwether, University of California, Santa Cruz. Several people provided photographs and permissions for photographs: Molly Lannon, Getty Images; Tim Noakes and Mattie Taormina, Stanford University; Jessica Henderson at the Wylie Agency, which manages the Allen Ginsberg photographs; Jadeen Young, Oakland Museum of California; the photographer Lisa Law and Pilar Law; Benjamin Formaker-Olivas and Simon Elliott, UCLA; Lisa Marine, Wisconsin Historical Society; Lance Neckar; and Bradley D. Cook, Indiana University.

W. J. R.
Seattle
August 2014

I

Origins

In the 1960s hippies were in revolt against mainstream American culture, its values, and its practices. Naturally, they borrowed from other countercultures that preceded them, especially from the Beat writers Jack Kerouac and Allen Ginsberg, but the big hippie idea was self-emancipation from the larger culture. To understand that revolt, it is necessary to begin with a brief discussion of mainstream values as they existed after World War II. During the Fifties it was widely held that American society had reached a mature age of consensus in which conformity to mainstream values and practices was all but universal. Most World War II veterans and their wives valued conformity, and those who dared to disagree often found themselves ostracized or denounced as communists, communist sympathizers, or dupes. Nonconformists could be committed for life without trials to mental hospitals, where they often received involuntary shock treatments. Political conformity was matched by calls for artistic and literary conformity. Abstract artists were suspected of subversion, and magazines or books that pushed against cultural norms risked prosecution or being banned from stores.[1]

What, then, did most Americans believe in the Fifties? They believed in God, country, work, and family. They practiced those

[1] For an overview see David Halberstam, *The Fifties* (New York, 1993).

beliefs by attending churches and synagogues in record numbers, although attendance fell by the end of the decade. Religion was traditional, especially among the quarter of Americans who were Roman Catholics. Living within a pre–Vatican II worldview that encapsulated nineteenth-century values, they sent their numerous baby boomer children to conservative, nun-dominated church schools. While Catholics and Jews were joining the middle class in large numbers, many suburbs, country clubs, and colleges practiced open anti-Semitism. White ethnic tensions had subsided, but they still existed. Mainstream white Protestants – Episcopalians, Presbyterians, Lutherans, and Methodists – had large numbers, enjoyed high social standing, and appeared frequently on radio and television, whenever clergy were sought for interviews. The Fifties would be the last decade in which mainstream Protestants dominated the culture, as they had since the country's founding. Nonwhites were 10 percent of the population and usually lived such segregated lives that they were invisible to most whites.[2]

Americans were intensely patriotic in the Fifties. They fervently believed that the United States was the greatest nation on earth. Concluding that isolationism had led to both world wars, Americans were determined not to make that mistake again. World War II veterans promoted the American Legion and the Veterans of Foreign Wars, both of which gained enormous political influence and sponsored patriotic parades, picnics, speeches, and essay contests. Being religious, Americans despised godless communism, and they embraced anticommunism. When North Korea invaded South Korea in 1950, Americans backed President Truman's decision to send in U.S. troops. Even after the war became a frustrating stalemate, there were few protests. Young Americans accepted being drafted into the war, and after the war ended, the only peacetime draft in the nation's history drew no opposition. Walt Disney glorified Davy Crockett's death at the Alamo, and millions of ten-year-olds bought imitation

---

[2] On ethnicity see Richard D. Alba, *Blurring the Color Line* (Cambridge, MA, 2009).

coonskin caps. To call a young man unpatriotic in the Fifties was one of the quickest ways to start a fistfight.[3]

After the unemployment of the Thirties and the sacrifices of World War II, Americans loved the postwar economic boom. Millions used the G. I. bill to go to college, and these new graduates generally prospered. The government also aided veterans with home loans, which set off a postwar housing boom, including migration to the suburbs. By 1960, one-quarter of American homes had been built in the past decade. City bus riders became suburban auto commuters, and by the later Fifties, the two-car family was common. Auto production soared. New factories opened, and without effective foreign competition, labor unions won unprecedented high wages and benefits, while companies made record profits, partly due to increased sales to high-paid workers. In the mid-Fifties nearly a quarter of the workforce was in manufacturing. Almost everything Americans bought, except coffee and bananas, was made in the United States. Overtime work, however, often left factory workers frazzled, while white-collar workers in big corporations felt that they lived in the "rat race." Individual proprietorship was in decline, and start-up companies were rare.[4]

High wages meant that couples married at an early age – in the Fifties men were marrying at twenty-two and women at twenty. While large numbers of women started college, 60 percent dropped out to get married. For women, college was mostly about finding a husband. Given high male wages, married women usually did not need to work, while discrimination, public opinion, and tax policies discouraged married women from holding jobs. Married women gradually entered the workforce, but they often worked part-time and were rarely paid the same as men doing identical work. Becoming pregnant usually meant

---

[3] Stephen J. Whitfield, *The Culture of the Cold War* (Baltimore, 1991); Tom Engelhardt, *The End of Victory Culture* (New York, 1995).

[4] John K. Galbraith, *The Affluent Society* (Boston, 1958). Housing statistic is in Theodore H. White, *The Making of the President, 1960* (New York, 1961), 219. On the workforce see U.S. Bureau of the Census, *Historical Statistics of the United States, Colonial Times to 1970* (Washington, DC, 1975), 139.

forfeiting a job. African Americans participated in this boom, too, but with less success due to discrimination, limited education, and a decline in unskilled work. The Great Migration from the rural South to the industrial North continued after the war, but jobs for low-skilled migrants became increasingly difficult to find.[5]

The key to the Fifties was the family. In no other decade have Americans been so focused on home life. Television featured family-based comedies, including *I Love Lucy* (1951–7). Lucille Ball turned her real-life pregnancy into an on-air season, and the show even had Lucy and Ricky move from a city apartment to a suburban home. The postwar baby boom was a product of prosperity. Living standards for average Americans went up almost 50 percent from 1947 to 1960, and this unexpected windfall led many parents to have an extra child or two beyond what they originally had planned. In 1960 children born after 1945 were almost one-third of the population. When the masses of boomers hit the schools in the Fifties, class sizes soared, and so did new schools staffed with inexperienced teachers. In these overcrowded schools, everything was standardized, from rows of desks laid out on the gridded linoleum block tile floors to fill-in-the-bubble tests to military-style physical exercises. Conformity was the most important school value, and woe to the backside of the defiant child.[6]

There were, however, undercurrents of anxiety about the family during the Fifties. Many wartime marriages had failed, and the divorce rate throughout the Fifties, although low, remained higher than one might have expected considering the cultural

[5] Elaine T. May, *Homeward Bound* (New York, 1988), 76–7, 81–3, 87–8; Susan M. Hartmann essay in Joanne Meyerowitz, ed., *Not June Cleaver* (Philadelphia, 1994), 84–100. On marriage age see U.S. Bureau of the Census, *Historical Statistics of the United States, Colonial Times to 1970*, 19. The college dropout rate is in Betty Friedan, *The Feminine Mystique* (New York, 1964; orig. 1963), 12.

[6] May, *Homeward Bound*, 135–42, 158–61. Living standards are in U.S. Bureau of the Census, *Historical Statistics of the United States, Colonial Times to 1970*, 164. Number of children is in Peter Wyden, *Suburbia's Coddled Kids* (Garden City, NY, 1962), 49.

placidity and prosperity. By the late Fifties, millions of mothers of older boomer children were bored. Family life seemed to be a dreary stream of laundry, cooking, and driving children to events broken only by shopping sprees, home decorating, or vacations. As men advanced in careers, women could advance only to the next level of shopping. For many women consumer culture was not satisfying. In 1963 Betty Friedan labeled this "The Problem with No Name." While Friedan conceded that working-class and minority women had different issues, the problem for white, educated, middle-class women was that they had no personal identity. The solution to this identity crisis, Friedan wrote in *The Feminine Mystique* (1963), was to envision a career, earn a degree, acquire a job, and achieve sufficient earnings to put marriage upon a basis of female financial independence.[7]

By 1960 the world of the Fifties was badly frayed. Religious restlessness was in the air, as church attendance fell, and the new Pope John XXIII called for reform of the Catholic Church. The civil rights movement had propelled Martin Luther King Jr. and other African American preachers into the limelight, and King in particular spoke with a moral fervor that made the tepid views of mainstream Protestants seem increasingly irrelevant. In a diverse country, Protestant leaders had used blandness to assert maximum influence while holding society together. This strategy worked only so long as the country believed in consensus. Norman Vincent Peale's *The Power of Positive Thinking* (1952), a bestseller that argued for confident projection of the self, represented the best of mainstream thought, but it was not adequate to cope with the urgency of King's plea for racial equality. At the same time, placid mainstream Protestants faced a serious challenge from Billy Graham, a charismatic white Baptist evangelical on the edge of the mainstream whose star was rising.[8]

[7] On divorce see May, *Homeward Bound*, 4–8, 185–6; James T. Patterson, *Grand Expectations* (New York, 1996), 360–1. On women's anxiety see May, *Homeward Bound*, 102–13, 162–82. For a different interpretation see Joanne Meyerowitz essay in Meyerowitz, ed., *Not June Cleaver*, 229–62.

[8] Taylor Branch, *Parting the Waters* (New York, 1988); John Andrew, "The Impending Crises of the 1960s: National Goals and National Purpose," *Viet Nam Generation* 6:1–2 (1994), 30–41.

The Cold War between the United States and the Soviet Union also entered a new phase. When Richard Nixon ran for president in 1960, he discovered that his fervent anticommunism, which had been his greatest asset in previous campaigns, no longer energized his base. Disinterested in Nixon's stale rhetoric, young people were captivated with John Kennedy's call for the Peace Corps, even as Kennedy promised to be as militant an opponent of communism as Nixon. After the disaster at the Bay of Pigs in 1961 and the near-disaster of the Missile Crisis in 1962, Kennedy began to turn toward a new foreign policy in 1963 with his call for international cooperation at American University and with the Nuclear Test Ban Treaty. Recognizing Cold War weariness, Kennedy wanted to turn patriotism from war to global nation building with the Peace Corps and glorification of American greatness with the project to land an American on the moon by the end of the decade. At the same time, he continued to meddle in Vietnam, a problem that blew up in Lyndon Johnson's face.[9]

By 1960 the postwar boom was beginning to play out. Manufacturing employment was dropping as automation began and as foreign competition, especially from Japanese textiles and German automobiles, intensified. Good jobs increasingly required college degrees, and the age of marriage began to rise. For millions of African Americans who had fled violence in the South, which was now in the throes of a revolution in race relations, jobs were harder to find than ever. In 1963 Martin Luther King Jr. led the March on Washington for Jobs and Freedom. Just as these trends were underway, the oldest baby boomers crowded into the labor market and colleges in record numbers in 1964. Size matters. In fast-growing California, where many young veterans had settled after World War II, the number of high school graduates went up 41 percent from 1960 to 1965. Where would they all go after high school? It was hard to see either enough jobs or enough spaces in college.[10]

---

[9] W. J. Rorabaugh, *The Real Making of the President* (Lawrence, KS, 2009); Richard Reeves, *President Kennedy* (New York, 1993).

[10] David F. Noble, *Forces of Production* (New York, 1994); 41 percent is in U.S. Bureau of the Census, *Census of the Population: 1960, V. 1. Characteristics of the Population, Pt. 6, California* (Washington, DC, 1963), 6:471.

Declining religion, a weaker economy, and poorer prospects for the young did not bode well for the family. Out-of-wedlock births were rising. The more the older generation, sensing impending social disaster, imposed tougher rules, the more the youngsters joyfully expressed defiance. Unruly boomer children, knowing that they had numbers on their side, became increasingly restless. They were confident that their considerable energy could outwit and outlast the exhausted elders. Had not Elvis Presley already found a way to swing his hips on national television? Patriarchy was in decline, as Betty Friedan knew when her book, *The Feminine Mystique*, became a bestseller in 1963. Churches, schools, and families could no longer contain the boomers. Change was in the air, the actors were in place, and when teenage hormones kicked in for millions of boomers in the mid-Sixties, the direction of that change became clear – a sex-charged counterculture was about to be born.[11]

But that is only part of the story. The hippie counterculture also owed a great deal to earlier countercultures, and especially to the Beat Generation. Hippies and Beats shared a desire for authenticity and an ethos of individualism. In 1944 Jack Kerouac (1922–69), who had dropped out of Columbia University to be a novelist, met Allen Ginsberg (1926–97), an aspiring poet, at Columbia. Kerouac was Catholic, a native French speaker, athletic, commanding, shy, the son of a small-town printer, and a former college football player; Ginsberg was Jewish, near-sighted, insecure, gregarious, the son of a high school English teacher, some sort of leftist, and a brilliant, eccentric literature student. The two quickly became acquainted with William Burroughs (1914–97), an older well-read Harvard graduate from a wealthy family in St. Louis and a would-be writer. This threesome, along with a few minor characters, set out to use writing to challenge mainstream American culture, which seemed to be globally dominant when World War II ended.[12]

---

[11] Regina G. Kunzel essay in Meyerowitz, ed., *Not June Cleaver*, 304–31; James B. Gilbert, *A Cycle of Outrage* (New York, 1986); May, *Homeward Bound*, 100–2, 208–26.

[12] Allen Ginsberg, *Composed on the Tongue* (San Francisco, 1980), 69–74; Jack Kerouac, *Selected Letters, 1940–1956*, ed. Ann Charters (New York, 1995),

In December 1946 the group gained a new adherent when Neal Cassady (1926–68), accompanied by his sixteen-year-old wife LuAnne, arrived in New York. A Denver street tough who claimed to have stolen more than five hundred cars for joy rides, he exuded charm, independence, intellect, raw energy, low morals, and explosive enthusiasm. In thought and deed, he was committed to authenticity. While the self-educated Cassady could hold his own intellectually, he was also a noble savage, a primitive "other" who possessed keen knowledge about the underworld that middle-class bohemians could exalt. He boasted of numerous sexual conquests of women but also occasionally engaged in random homosexual acts. "I know I'm bisexual," he stated, "but prefer women...." In 1947 Ginsberg fell in love with Cassady, who mostly proved unresponsive. Cassady and Kerouac became fast friends and took a series of trips that became the basis for Kerouac's novel, *On the Road* (1957). In the Sixties Cassady would drive Ken Kesey's Merry Pranksters across the country in their famous bus.[13]

The Beats believed that everything was rotten. The starting point for this thesis was World War II, the Holocaust, the atomic bomb, and the Cold War, all of which alarmed Kerouac, Ginsberg, and Burroughs. In 1945 the great slaughter ended, but this disaster was being replaced not by peace but by threat of nuclear death raining on everyone. Nor did industrial capitalism's consumer culture have any appeal. "I don't believe at all in this society. It is evil," Kerouac wrote. "It will fail. Men have to do what they want." Kerouac always expressed a belief in individualism. No one was more disgusted than Burroughs. "Repressive bureaucracy," he declared, "is a vast conspiracy against life." He blamed liberals. "The word liberal," he wrote, "has come to

76, 89–90; Steven Watson, *The Birth of the Beat Generation* (New York, 1995), 35–53.

[13] Neal Cassady, *The First Third and Other Writings* (San Francisco, 1971), 1–80, 105, 129; Carolyn Cassady, *Off the Road* (New York, 1990), 4, 16, 18–19; Tom Clark, *Jack Kerouac* (San Diego, 1984), 73–86, 92; William Plummer, *The Holy Goof* (New York, 1990; orig. 1981), 36, 41–2, 44. The quote is in Allen Ginsberg–Neal Cassady, *As Ever*, ed. Barry Gifford (Berkeley, 1977), 17.

stand for the most damnable tyranny, a snively, mealy-mouthed tyranny of bureaucrats, social workers, psychiatrists, and Union officials." Not that he had any use for business. He confided, "I would not hesitate to defraud a company if I could."[14]

Concluding that the United States and Western civilization were fundamentally violence prone and unsound, the trio used writing to define themselves and to challenge society through development of an oppositional subculture. Their goals were authenticity and individualism. Recognizing their own tiny numbers, the Beat writers expressed pessimism, even despair, and often recommended withdrawal from the world rather than reformation. At times they evoked libertine anarchism. Kerouac drew inspiration from African American jazz musicians, especially Charlie Parker, Dizzy Gillespie, and other proponents of fast-paced bebop music; Ginsberg was attracted by Walt Whitman's democratic vision; and all three were drawn to the French avant-garde writer Arthur Rimbaud, as well as other experimental writers. They became known as the Beat Generation, a phrase coined by Kerouac, because, he said, they were beaten down by mainstream culture, were interested in the musical beat aspect of jazz, and sought perfection in both writing and life with a beatific attitude.[15]

Avowedly experiential and experimental, the Beats embraced jazz because it was an African American art form that had developed apart from white middle-class culture in a society that had systematically tried to crush any cultural productions that the establishment could not control. Rhythm expressed feelings, the individual jazz artist improvised, and the player and the audience shared the performance. By the mid-1940s many musicians and patrons adopted a particular style of flashy dress, jive talk, and cocky attitude. They called themselves hipsters.

[14] Kerouac, *Selected Letters*, 193; William S. Burroughs, *The Letters of William S. Burroughs, 1945–1959*, ed. Oliver Harris (New York, 1993), 125, 61, 79.

[15] Watson, *Birth of the Beat Generation*; James Campbell, *This Is the Beat Generation* (London, 1999); John Tytell, *Naked Angels* (New York, 1986; orig. 1976). See also Jack Kerouac, "The Origins of the Beat Generation," *Playboy*, June 1959, 42, 79.

The black jazz-hipsters impressed the Beats. "You ain't known nothing about the new hipness in America," wrote Kerouac, "till you've dug the younger Negroes who call New York the Apple." Kerouac used jazzlike riffs to write his first novel, and Ginsberg's poetry began to show a looser style, a longer line, and a more open and frank expression of emotion.[16]

Jazz led the Beat writers to a second insight. Heavily influenced by jazz improvisation, Cassady called for spontaneous writing. Adopting his own version of this idea, Kerouac argued that conventional writing techniques lacked the authenticity of lived experience. In spontaneous prose, the author wrote only out of personal events and poured words onto the page without revision. "There is nothing to do but write the truth. There is no other reason to write," Kerouac declared. Respect for truth required that the writing not be revised. To retouch prose enabled mainstream culture to contaminate the writing. As Ginsberg later put it: "First thought best thought." Spontaneous music and writing formed a larger pattern of spontaneous living. If society was rotten and corrupt, then its rules were putrefying and immoral. Only by freeing oneself from all rules could one free oneself from the evils of society. Spontaneity, which expressed authenticity, was the first step in purification on the road to freedom.[17]

At the heart of the Beat Generation was a spiritual quest. This quest was also based on authenticity. Casting aside tradition, they sought what Kerouac called a New Vision. They decided to find this New Vision through writing. To begin the process, they immersed themselves in "otherness," beginning with jazz. Taking drugs and freely indulging in sex showed defiance, but drugs also aided finding a spiritual center. Rejecting the Judeo-Christian worldview, they looked east to Hinduism and Buddhism. Kerouac expressed an early enthusiasm for Buddhism, but the

[16] Kerouac in Arthur Knight and Kit Knight, eds., *The Beat Diary* (California, PA, 1977), 138.
[17] Kerouac, *Selected Letters*, 248; Ginsberg in Donald Allen and Warren Tallman, eds., *Poetics of the New American Poetry* (New York, 1973), 350.

discipline clashed with Kerouac's impulsiveness, and by the Sixties Kerouac had returned to the Catholicism of his childhood. Sin and forgiveness were perhaps concepts that he needed. Ginsberg shed Judaism and, after decades of study and practice, became a Buddhist. Burroughs and Cassady remained aloof from organized religion.[18]

Allen Ginsberg's alienation from the mainstream came from the war and the Holocaust; from his mother's communism and the Cold War; from nasty political arguments between his mother and his father, a socialist; from his problematic status as a Jewish student at Columbia, which discriminated against Jews; and from his own conflicted sexuality. Did his homosexual desires mean that he was sick, as Freudian psychiatrists told him in the late 1940s, or was he just born that way? Perhaps he had inherited a family disease. For years Ginsberg suffered the agony of doubt, a doubt that was heightened when his insane mother was institutionalized. Following a sudden and inexplicable deep spiritual epiphany in 1948 that came after reading William Blake, Ginsberg tried unsuccessfully to recreate that moment with exotic travel and drugs, including hallucinogens that he took during the Fifties.[19]

Settling temporarily in San Francisco, Ginsberg burst into fame in 1955 with a public reading of "Howl," a powerful poem that defied existing poetic and cultural conventions to embrace individualism, ecstatic homosexuality, and a denunciation of the existing social, political, and cultural order. Other readers that night included the poets Gary Snyder and Michael McClure; the latter would be identified with the hippies a decade later. At the reading Kerouac passed around a bottle of red wine and, as Ginsberg recited "Howl," gave a rhythmic "go" after each line. The performance electrified the audience and left Ginsberg in tears. McClure explained the emotional release. "We had gone

[18] Stephen Prothero, "On the Holy Road: The Beat Movement as Spiritual Protest," *Harvard Theological Review* 84:2 (April 1991), 205–22.
[19] Ginsberg, *Composed on the Tongue*, 81–2; Barry Miles, *Ginsberg* (New York, 1989), 99–104; Michael Schumacher, *Dharma Lion* (New York, 1992), 94–9.

beyond a point of no return," he observed later, "and we were
ready...." The end of the Korean War and the fall of Senator
Joseph R. McCarthy influenced McClure, who continued, "None
of us wanted to go back to the gray, chill, militaristic silence ...
we wanted vision."[20]

Using spontaneous prose, Kerouac typed his second novel,
On the Road, in three weeks in 1951 on a 120-foot scroll of
cheap paper aided by coffee, cigarettes, red wine, and Benzedrine
tablets ("speed"). Stripping away sanctimonious middle-class
propriety, he celebrated self-emancipation from traditional culture and vicarious personal experience. When published in 1957,
the book struck a chord, sold three million copies, established
Kerouac's fame, and inspired a younger generation. "Kerouac,"
said Burroughs, "opened a million coffee bars and sold a million
Levis." *On the Road* transformed its readers. In Minnesota Bob
Dylan recalled, "It changed my life...." In Texas Janis Joplin
read about Kerouac in *Time* magazine: "I said 'Wow!' and split."
Kerouac's novel drew Ed Sanders to New York, where he became
a leading counterculture poet and later cofounded the rock band
the Fugs. Kerouac led the writer Ken Kesey from Oregon to
North Beach. Also inspired was John Lennon; the later Beatles,
originally Beetles, paid tribute to the Beats with their name.[21]

Of the Beat writers, Burroughs was the oldest, the boldest,
and the most troubled. Born into a prominent St. Louis family, he
lived off a family trust in return for the promise to stay away. His
writing career went nowhere, because, he later concluded, he was
trapped inside mainstream culture; its language was the basis for
culture's control of the individual. Deeply alienated, he became a
heroin addict. This addiction led to his first book, *Junkie* (1953).

---

[20] Michael McClure, *Scratching the Beat Surface* (New York, 1994; orig. 1982),
11–24 (quote at 13).

[21] Clark, *Kerouac*, 164–5, 173; Gerald Nicosia, *Memory Babe* (New York,
1983), 556–9. Burroughs in Steve Turner, *Angelheaded Hipster* (London,
1996), 17; Dylan in Turner, *Angelheaded Hipster*, viii; Joplin in Wini Breines
essay in Meyerowitz, ed., *Not June Cleaver*, 392; Sanders in Sohnya Sayres,
et al., eds., *The Sixties, without Apology* (Minneapolis, 1984), 240; Kesey
in Linda Gaboriau, "Ken Kesey," *Crawdaddy*, no. 19 (December 1972), 37;
Lennon in Turner, *Angelheaded Hipster*, 20–1.

He moved to Texas with his wife Joan to grow marijuana, was charged with possession, and avoided a long prison sentence by fleeing to Mexico, where he accidentally shot Joan (both were drunk) during a game in which he fired at a liquor glass that she had placed on top of her head. The bad spirit made him aim too low, he said. Escaping from Mexico to Tangiers, Burroughs used his trust fund to buy heroin and Arab boys. He wrote *Naked Lunch* (1959), a mélange of sexual visions so offensive to mainstream American culture that it could not be printed in the United States. Eventually, Burroughs's friend Brion Gysin got the writer into a methadone program in England. By then the two had innovated a new writing method that they believed allowed prose to be freed from mainstream culture.[22]

The original Beats were white, but their openness toward all races enabled a tiny number of African Americans to break the color line and join the movement. The most prominent were the poet Bob Kaufman, a fixture in San Francisco's coffee houses and bars, and the New York playwright LeRoi Jones, who during the 1960s left the counterculture, embraced black power, and changed his name to Amiri Baraka. During his Beat phase, Jones was married to a white woman. In the Fifties interracial couples were rare, and while the Beats accepted LeRoi and Hettie Jones, the two often got stares from tourists in Greenwich Village and could not leave the neighborhood without risk of violence. Beat culture had little appeal to African Americans because, as Baraka later complained, it was overwhelmingly rooted in the white world. Photographs of Beat events show Jones, Kaufman, or other African Americans performing before audiences that were virtually all white. Although tolerant, Beats were not multiracial.[23]

The Beat Generation's quest for a New Vision included widespread use of drugs. They all smoked marijuana. "If it wasn't for

[22] Barry Miles, *William Burroughs* (New York, 1993); Daniel Odier, *The Job* (rev. ed., New York, 1970; orig. 1969).

[23] Hettie Jones, *How I Became Hettie Jones* (New York, 1990). See photos in Elias Wilentz, ed., *The Beat Scene* (New York, 1960); Fred W. McDarrah and Gloria S. McDarrah, *Beat Generation* (New York, 1996).

you, Mr. Marijuana, noblest of intoxicants," Ginsberg confided in his journal, "we'd all be lying in a drunken bloodynose stupor in a gutter." To the extent that society outlawed or disdained drugs, these nonconformists felt a duty to defy the ban. In keeping with the spirit of spontaneity, a drug might be taken on a whim, to achieve a desired result, or out of curiosity. Much drug taking was experimental. The Beats sought drugs that challenged the existing culture by opening new insights into the human condition. "It was necessary," recalled Ginsberg, "to go through a long period of change of consciousness before people could be liberated from the hypnotic hallucination that they'd been locked in." Few Americans knew about mind-altering drugs before the 1950s. Burroughs proved the most adventuresome, which led to his heroin habit. Kerouac loathed needles, ingested various substances, smoked pot, and drank heavily. Ginsberg did a great deal of sampling.[24]

To the mainstream, the most disturbing aspect of the Beats was the attitude toward sex. Beats had rejected marriage as an antiquated institution that did not allow for the free expression of the self. To the Beats, consenting adults ought to be able to engage in sex at any time. This included partner-swapping, bisexuality, homosexuality, and group sex. "I am definitely interested in going to bed with everybody," wrote Ginsberg. Personal desire was all that mattered. "Laying a woman, so far as I am concerned is O.K.," stated Burroughs, "if I can't score for a boy." Kerouac and Cassady claimed to be basically heterosexual, and both belligerently denounced anyone who suggested otherwise, but each also had homosexual encounters, including brief flings with Ginsberg. Society was uptight, and the breakdown of traditional barriers imposed by cultural norms was a necessary reform to bring about the restructuring of society and its culture. As soon as each person was free to love every other person, then society would be cured, culture healed, and crime, violence, and war would vanish.[25]

---

[24] Quotes from Allen Ginsberg, *Journals Mid-Fifties, 1954–1958*, ed. Gordon Ball (New York, 1995), 216; Ginsberg, *Composed on the Tongue*, 76.
[25] Ginsberg in Cassady, *Off the Road*, 185; Burroughs, *Letters*, 88.

Treatment of women was condescending and crude. To the Beat writers, women were sex objects; even in that role, women sometimes had to compete with men. While parents rarely minded a son moving to the Village to try out the Beat lifestyle, they vehemently opposed a daughter taking the same course of action. During the Fifties respectable middle-class young men could do things that young women could not do without being considered sluts or prostitutes. Parents might even try to commit a sexually promiscuous daughter to a mental institution. Beat gatherings had a big gender gap. Only a handful of Beat women, including the poet Diane di Prima, achieved fame. Talented women found it difficult to be accepted in a subculture ruled by highly competitive male poets, some of whom degraded or denigrated women. Public performances of poetry before largely male Beat audiences also inhibited women. Women like di Prima, the poet Denise Levertov, or the painter Joan Brown were rare.[26]

Kerouac, Ginsberg, and other Beats quickly drew a youthful following when they burst upon the literary scene in the late 1950s. Both read poetry in clubs, while Ginsberg toured campuses, and Kerouac appeared on television. Beat poetry was sometimes performed with jazz accompaniment. The impoverished Beats had dressed in secondhand clothes, and youthful followers created the Beat look: men adopted beards, berets, and sandals, while women dressed in black leotards, wore long hair, and avoided makeup. The media soon dubbed the followers "beatniks," or little Beats, due to youth, and the name stuck. Beats and the more numerous beatniks, amounting to a few thousand people in Greenwich Village in New York or North Beach in San Francisco, hung out in coffee houses, jazz clubs, avant-garde art galleries, and bars. Beatniks spread to Venice in Los Angeles and college towns such as Madison, Wisconsin and Lawrence, Kansas. Beats and beatniks shared the same values. Members of both groups liked jazz and smoked marijuana, an

[26] On women see Diane di Prima, *Memoirs of a Beatnik* (2nd ed., San Francisco, 1988; orig. 1969); Brenda Knight, *Women of the Beat Generation* (Berkeley, 1996).

act of outlaw defiance that separated them from mainstream culture.[27]

The producers of popular culture could not resist the beatniks, although Hollywood portrayals were so lurid with sex-crazed violence that none of the films achieved prominence. Television did better. The popular series 77 *Sunset Strip* (1958–64) featured a lovable long-haired parking lot attendant, Kookie, whose beatnik values invariably impeded his romantic pursuits. The most interesting beatnik character was the aptly named Maynard G. Krebs (a play on crab lice likely to be contracted through sexual promiscuity), who was the best friend of the straight Dobie Gillis. In *The Many Loves of Dobie Gillis* (1959–63), Gillis always succeeded by rejecting Krebs's bad advice to accept responsibility. Gillis, not Krebs, got the girl. A major ongoing theme in the series had the lazy Krebs spend inordinate energy to remain unemployed. He appeared to believe that work might be fatal.[28]

In many ways Greenwich Village was the heart of the beatnik world. The Village had housed an important counterculture since the early 1900s, and the locale was merely building upon its own past. Writers, avant-garde artists, jazz musicians, actors, political activists, and radicals had long been drawn to the neighborhood. The Cedar Bar had become a hangout for abstract artists, who when they were not painting, were drawn to drunkenness and fistfights. Many cafes in the neighborhood featured folksingers, who enjoyed a revival in the late 1950s. Downtown jazz performances brought black performers into the neighborhood in a city that was otherwise largely segregated. The Eighth Street Bookshop carried many paperbacks and specialized in

---

[27] On jazz-poetry see *Village Voice*, March 18, 1959, 1, 7; James J. Farrell, *The Spirit of the Sixties* (New York, 1997), 70–1. On looks see McDarrah and McDarrah, *Beat Generation*, 1–7, 213; Ronald Sukenick, *Down and In* (New York, 1987), 41, 57, 137; di Prima, *Memoirs of a Beatnik*, 126–7; John A. Maynard, *Venice West* (New Brunswick, NJ, 1991). On college towns see Paul Buhle, ed., *History and the New Left* (Philadelphia, 1990), esp. 67–84, 217–18. On Lawrence see Beth L. Bailey, *Sex in the Heartland* (Cambridge, MA, 1999).

[28] Vincent Terrace, *Encyclopedia of Television* (New York, 1986), 1:126–7, 391.

small-press and radical publications seldom available elsewhere. The *Village Voice* began publication as a counterculture weekly newspaper in 1955. It covered both radical politics and the emerging beatnik counterculture.[29]

The other great beatnik center was North Beach in San Francisco. The focal point was City Lights Books, owned by the Beat poet Lawrence Ferlinghetti, who published Ginsberg's *Howl and Other Poems* (1956), even though the book faced legal problems. The foundation was laid when a number of pacifist-anarchist poets who had been conscientious objectors in Oregon during World War II moved to San Francisco at the end of the war. Enjoying support from Kenneth Rexroth, an older poet and influential critic, they invented public poetry readings. In 1949 the Pacifica Foundation, a pacifist-anarchist organization, launched a noncommercial radio station, KPFA, in Berkeley. The station gave voice to the pacifist poets, as well as to Rexroth and Alan Watts. Watts, a former Episcopal minister, had settled in the Bay Area to promote Eastern religions. In the mid-Fifties Gary Snyder moved from Reed College to Berkeley to study Asian language, culture, and religion. After spending eleven years in a Zen Buddhist monastery in Japan, Snyder returned to California as a Buddhist-inspired environmentalist poet.[30]

Other signs of the crumbling of the old order occurred in the Fifties. While McCarthyism had been mostly about using state power to harass communists or their sympathizers, the majority of "security risks" who had been dismissed from federal employment in the early 1950s had been homosexuals. Previously considered a sign of willful moral perversion, homosexuality in the Fifties, among enlightened people who embraced that decade's Freudianism, was rebranded as a mental illness. Whether

[29] On Greenwich Village see McDarrah and McDarrah, *Beat Generation*; Dan Wakefield, *New York in the Fifties* (Boston, 1992).

[30] Neeli Cherkovski, *Ferlinghetti* (Garden City, NY, 1979); Barry Silesky, *Ferlinghetti* (New York, 1990); Michael Davidson, *The San Francisco Renaissance* (Cambridge, UK, 1989); Matthew Lasar, *Pacifica Radio* (Philadelphia, 1999); Gary Snyder, *Earth House Hold* (New York, 1969), 31–53.

immoral or sick, gay men and lesbians found little acceptance and few good jobs during the aggressively enforced conformism of the Fifties. As a result, Harry Hay and other leftist gay friends in Los Angeles founded the Mattachine Society in 1950, while Del Martin and Phyllis Lyon, a lesbian couple in San Francisco, organized the Daughters of Bilitis in 1955. Created in response to the decade's oppression, these self-help groups had much in common with Alcoholics Anonymous in the early years. Only later did the focus shift to civil rights. Both groups, as well as other similar small entities, had chapters in San Francisco and New York. Homosexual organizations challenged the promarriage attitudes and practices of mainstream society in the Fifties, and they resonated with Beat demands for openness about sexuality.[31]

During the Fifties the guardians of mainstream culture refused to talk about sex or allow any public discussion. Nothing could be said about homosexuality, and NBC News banned the use of the words "rape" and "abortion." In some parts of the country, conservatives found the word *pregnancy* too embarrassing to be mentioned in conversation. The stork was said to be coming, or women were said to be "in the family way." Out-of-wedlock births were so scandalous that pregnant teens vanished for months, moved into homes for unwed mothers, gave birth, put babies up for adoption, and then returned home with reputations sullied after having "visited Aunt Sally." Frequently, these young "ruined" women had to move to a different community to resume normal life. The double standard prevailed. While young men were expected to seek sex with women of easy virtue or prostitutes, young women were watched. Some parents insisted that daughters live at home until marriage. Colleges paid no attention to male students but required female students to be locked in at early hours every evening; in 1965, 75 percent of single female college graduates were virgins. At the coeducational University of Richmond the dean of women nightly raised

---

[31] John D'Emilio, *Sexual Politics, Sexual Communities* (Chicago, 1983).

the drawbridge that provided access to the female part of the
campus on the far side of the lake.[32]

But cultural change was in the air. In 1953 Hugh Hefner
founded *Playboy* magazine, featuring a topless centerfold. Grace
Metalious's steamy novel, *Peyton Place* (1956), sold millions of
copies, and Helen Gurley Brown's *Sex and the Single Girl* (1962)
urged women to seek sexual pleasure outside marriage. Lenny
Bruce, a stand-up comic, simulated masturbation of the micro-
phone in his club performances and spewed a steady stream of
obscenities. Even in tolerant San Francisco, Bruce's performance
caused large numbers of patrons to walk out, and the culturally
conservative police filmed his raunchy show in order to prose-
cute him for violating the obscenity laws. The purpose of Bruce's
performance was to challenge the establishment attitude about
sex. Bruce believed that Hitler, World War II, and the Holocaust
had been caused by repressed sexuality. If people screwed more,
they would fight less.[33]

Julian Beck and Judith Malina's Living Theatre, established by
two anarchists in New York in 1951, challenged the mainstream
in other ways, primarily by drawing the small audience close to
the performance in intimate space and occasionally surprising
patrons by making them into part of the production. Ad-libbed
lines and performances without scripts allowed cultural presump-
tions to be questioned. The audience for different shows was primarily drawn from the same four hundred avant-garde devotees,
and the effect on the audience was to build self-confidence to
take on the mainstream, which was the entire purpose of the
Living Theatre. In a show titled *The Brig*, which was filmed in
1963, Beck and Malina reenacted the regimentation, cruelty,

[32] Beth Bailey, *From Front Porch to Back Seat* (Baltimore, 1988); May, *Homeward Bound*, 114–34; NBC News in David Brinkley, *Memoirs* (New York, 1995), 141–2; Beth Bailey, "Sexual Revolution(s)," in David Farber, ed., *The Sixties* (Chapel Hill, 1994), 241–6; 75 percent virgins in Annie Gottlieb, *Do You Believe in Magic?* (New York, 1987), 239.

[33] *Playboy* and Metalious in Halberstam, *Fifties*, 571–80; Brown in Bailey, "Sexual Revolution(s)," 248–9; Bruce transcripts are in Lenny Bruce, *The Essential Lenny Bruce*, ed. John Cohen (New York, 1967).

brutality, and lack of humanity inside a U.S. Navy prison. By use of repetition, marching, and harsh lighting, the audience came to feel that they, too, were in the brig. The brig's furnishings evoked images of a camp at Auschwitz, and the guards were Nazi-like. The main point was to suggest that conformist and regimented American society in the Fifties had become a large-scale version of a prison trapping both rulers and inmates in unnatural and unhealthy relationships.[34]

Among the Village avant-garde devotees was Yoko Ono, who later became John Lennon's wife. A young Japanese-born artist who had moved to New York to escape the suffocation of traditional Japanese culture, Ono began to stage events in her combined apartment/art studio in the early Sixties that became known as "happenings." Leafleting the Village brought large numbers of young people to the event, where interactions could be strange. In one happening, participants entering Ono's loft moved into a curved plywood shelter that narrowed to a closed point, whereupon they were forced to return to the entrance and reemerge as performers facing the audience gathered to undertake the same task. In a happening, everyone performed, and everyone was the audience. The goal was authenticity and the enlightenment of the individual.[35]

In the visual arts the break with postwar Abstract Expressionism came from Jasper Johns and Robert Rauschenberg in the late 1950s. Incorporating collage, found objects, and thickly painted representations into their paintings, both reintroduced the object and representation of the object and thereby challenged the prevailing theory of abstract art. Claes Oldenburg, often considered the founder of happenings, also used found objects and opened the Store in 1961, where he sold small cheap sculptures based on everyday objects, including nonfattening slices of pie and cake.

[34] Sally Banes, *Greenwich Village 1963* (Durham, NC, 1993), 40–3; Daniel Belgrad, *The Culture of Spontaneity* (Chicago, 1998), 150–6; Bradford D. Martin, *The Theater Is in the Street* (Amherst, MA, 2004), 49–85; *The Brig* (1964 film), directed by Jonas Mekas.

[35] Thomas Crow, *The Rise of the Sixties* (New York, 1996), 124–5; Sukenick, *Down and In*, 127–8, 137–8, 150–1.

Those who disapproved of sweets could buy a ceramic baked potato. This rising critique of consumer culture found its master in Andy Warhol. After offering a biting commentary with his Pop Art soup can paintings, he satirized celebrity with his Marilyn and Jackie silkscreen portraits. Quickly bored with visual art, Warhol opened the Factory, where he made experimental films and created a rock band, the Velvet Underground, which he filmed in the world's first rock videos.[36]

Affluence in the Fifties led to the production of unprecedented numbers of avant-garde films. Although seen only by a small number of people, these underground films were important for challenging the formulas that the Hollywood studios had long imposed upon cinema. The directors expressed their own authenticity and individualism devoid of commercial considerations. Cultural assumptions were questioned ruthlessly. The key figure in New York was Jonas Mekas. In his column in the *Village Voice*, Mekas promoted films that stressed spontaneity, honesty, and youth and that operated outside normal consumer culture. Nude or lewd films could not be shown in ordinary theaters, where they risked seizure by police. Eventually, Mekas created a filmmaker's cooperative, which fitted the emerging democratic, non-hierarchical ethos. Leading new directors included Warhol, Stan Brakhage, and Robert Frank. In 1959 Frank filmed Kerouac's *Pull My Daisy*, a poetic tribute to the Beats which featured many of the Beat writers playing themselves or other Beats.[37]

Hollywood was ready to cash in on the newly emerging attitudes and the decline of establishment power over cultural norms. Throughout the Fifties, American films were still governed by the prewar Motion Picture Code: no nudity, no double beds, and short kisses. Americans who wanted to see risqué films had to seek out art houses that showed foreign-language pictures. Police and local censors who screened and made cuts to Hollywood

---

[36] Crow, *Rise of the Sixties*, 18, 34, 36, 84–92, 128; Barbara Haskell, *Blam!* (New York, 1984), 17, 68–87; Bob Colacello, *Holy Terror* (New York, 1990).
[37] Banes, *Greenwich Village*, 73–8, 236–7; Sukenick, *Down and In*, 144–6; Nicosia, *Memory Babe*, 583, 585.

FIGURE 2. In 1959 the Beat writers Jack Kerouac and Allen Ginsberg conferred on the set during Robert Frank's filming of Kerouac's screenplay, *Pull My Daisy*.

Photo by John Cohen/Hulton Archive/Getty Images.

productions usually ignored the imports because they had small audiences. A few Hollywood directors tested limits. Because Alfred Hitchcock's *North by Northwest* (1959) was a suspense film, he got away with one of the sexiest scenes ever shown in a mainstream movie. Then came Hitchcock's *Psycho* (1960), which drenched viewers with sex and violence in an unprecedented way. Billy Wilder upped the ante with cross-dressing in *Some Like It Hot* (1959) and corporate hanky-panky in *The Apartment* (1960), which won the Oscar for best picture.[38]

The courts aided the overthrow of censorship. Both Ginsberg's *Howl*, in a trial court in San Francisco, and Burroughs's *Naked Lunch*, in the Massachusetts Supreme Court, were approved as art. At first, the liberal majority on the U.S. Supreme Court held that magazines, books, and films could not be banned or censored if they were acceptable to the average member of a community. Under the community standard doctrine, actual sales of an item prior to the attempt to stop sales became proof of community acceptance. Tired of hearing cases challenging the vague community standard idea, the high court concluded in 1966 that the only items that could be banned were child pornography (because of the exploitation of children in creating it) and sexually explicit material that had no redeeming social value. Art, it turned out, was in the eye of the beholder, which is what all the countercultures had been arguing all along.[39]

Another challenge to mainstream culture in the Fifties came from the growing use of drugs throughout American society. The Beat writers had used amphetamines ("speed") to aid typing, and by the mid-1950s truck drivers popped uppers to aid long distance driving. Suburban housewives calmed themselves with Miltowns. Teens might slip a few pills to experiment, just as they did with parents' cigarettes and alcohol. In the Fifties prescription drugs were easy to get, and multiple prescriptions allowed

---

[38] Robert Sklar, *Movie-Made America* (New York, 1994).

[39] On the *Howl* case see Allen Ginsberg, *Howl: Original Draft Facsimile*, ed. Barry Miles (New York, 1986), 169–74; Silesky, *Ferlinghetti*, 70–9. On the *Naked Lunch* case see Miles, *Burroughs*, 84, 95, 106; Watson, *Birth of the Beat Generation*, 282–4.

uppers and downers to be taken in interesting combinations. Tobacco and alcohol remained the drugs of choice, and both were marketed aggressively on television. Cigarettes were associated in advertising with glamour and success, and after the first alarming reports about cancer in the early Fifties, filter cigarettes were associated with good health. Beer companies reached young men with commercials on sports programs that suggested that beer drinking was about manliness and sexual prowess.[40]

Then there were the hallucinogens. In 1943 Albert Hofmann, a Swiss researcher, had accidentally discovered lysergic acid diethylamide's (LSD's) mind-altering properties. During the Fifties the U.S. Army and the Central Intelligence Agency experimented with LSD as a truth serum or as a substance that could induce psychosis in enemy soldiers. Psychiatrists, lacking any effective medications for psychoses at the time, tried LSD to treat schizophrenia and other serious disorders. Also investigated were the related hallucinogenic substances, mescaline, derived from the peyote cactus, and psilocybin, which was chemically manufactured to be identical to the active ingredient in "magic" mushrooms. In 1953 Dr. Humphry Osmond, a Canadian psychiatrist, gave mescaline to the writer Aldous Huxley (1894–1963), who was living in Los Angeles. Profoundly affected by the trip, Huxley wrote *The Doors of Perception* (1954) and, following his first LSD trip in 1955, *Heaven and Hell* (1956). He argued that hallucinogens could provide new insights into the self and the cosmos. Concluding that these related drugs needed a more inspiring name, Osmond proposed "psychedelic," which Huxley accepted.[41]

Much of the early LSD research was performed either in Canada, by psychiatrists connected to Osmond, or in California.

---

[40] On drugs in the Fifties see David T. Courtwright, "Mr. ATOD's Wild Ride: What Do Alcohol, Tobacco, and Other Drugs Have in Common?" *Social History of Alcohol and Drugs* 20 (2005), 105–24.

[41] On early LSD see Martin A. Lee and Bruce Shlain, *Acid Dreams* (New York, 1985); Jay Stevens, *Storming Heaven* (New York, 1987). Sybille Bedford, *Aldous Huxley* (New York, 1985; orig. 1973–4), 525–7, 537–45, 588, 597–8, 605.

Medical experimenters in Los Angeles administered the drug either to psychiatric patients or to curious celebrities. Among those who tripped were the film star Cary Grant, the diarist Anais Nin, the writer Gerald Heard, the *Time* publisher Henry Luce, and his influential wife Clare Boothe Luce. Another research group at Stanford conducted LSD experiments at a nearby Veterans Administration hospital in 1959. Allen Ginsberg volunteered. Finding his own consciousness to be merged with the universe, he noted, "This drug seems to automatically produce a mystical experience. Science is getting very hip." At the time Ginsberg believed, like Huxley, that psychedelics would alter consciousness, change society, and eliminate war and competition, as individuals turned inward to seek peace and self-satisfaction. Drugs promoted authenticity and individualism.[42]

Huxley personally found psychedelics, and especially LSD, so potent that they would cause individual users to rethink the meaning of life, recalibrate personal relationships, and challenge existing power structures. How the state functioned would be reinvented. Many of the myths that bound society together and allowed elites to exercise power would dissolve. Huxley imagined this world in his novel, *Island* (1962). Having spent his entire life in influential circles, the author felt that the establishment would respond to this challenge by moving aggressively to ban these drugs, because they threatened existing power arrangements. To avoid this outcome, Huxley concluded that psychedelics had to be spread slowly in a stealth campaign that retained a medical model. So long as hallucinogens were only available through highly reputable physicians, and so long as they were prescribed only to elite patients, the state would take no interest. A great deal more needed to be learned about psychedelics before there could be wider use.[43]

[42] On Los Angeles see Sidney Cohen, *The Beyond Within* (New York, 1965). Grant, Nin, and the Luces are in Lee and Shlain, *Acid Dreams*, 57, 62, 71, 89. On Heard see Bedford, *Huxley*, 562. On Ginsberg see Miles, *Ginsberg*, 141–2, 192, 260 (quote), 262, 269–82.

[43] Bedford, *Huxley*, 604–5, 713–20.

Ginsberg found Huxley's argument unconvincing. Having only recently won his suit against the attempt to ban *Howl*, Ginsberg keenly understood the power structure's desire to destroy unwanted innovation. At the same time, Ginsberg was offended by Huxley's undemocratic model, which would leave psychedelics under the control of a tiny elite experimenting on an equally narrow group of "patients." Ginsberg also believed that these drugs might have different effects upon different types of people. Certainly LSD tests on psychiatric patients did not predict how normal people would be affected, and celebrities often used LSD only for thrills. A shallow motive was unlikely to produce much insight. In 1960, Ginsberg traveled to Peru to take yage, a liquid psychedelic potion brewed from a vine. He followed the path of William Burroughs, who had taken yage in 1953. On his first yage trip, Ginsberg saw colored designs, insects, and snakes. Then a small black dot appeared, and Ginsberg's soul entered it. He felt intimacy with the universe. On the third trip "the whole fucking Cosmos broke loose around me." Yage was more potent than LSD.[44]

In 1960 Ginsberg learned that Timothy Leary (1920–96), a psychologist only recently recruited to Harvard, had begun to conduct psilocybin experiments. Leary did so immediately after taking his first mushrooms in Mexico. "In four hours by the swimming pool in Cuernavaca," he later wrote, "I learned more about the mind, the brain, and its structures than I did in the preceding fifteen as a diligent psychologist." During a trip at Leary's house in Newton, Massachusetts, Ginsberg telephoned Jack Kerouac to announce, "The revolution is beginning. It's time to seize power over the universe and become the next consciousness." Believing that creative intellectuals might have unusually perceptive trips, Ginsberg and Leary decided to give the drug to artists, jazz musicians, and writers. The first four volunteers were the artists Willem de Kooning and Franz Kline and the jazz musicians Dizzy Gillespie and Thelonious Monk.

---

[44] William S. Burroughs–Allen Ginsberg, *The Yage Letters* (3rd ed., San Francisco, 1988; orig. 1963), 57–69 (quote at 60).

Results, however, were inconclusive. Ginsberg and Leary then gave psilocybin to Kerouac. Questioning whether any drug could absolve sin, Kerouac sneered at the psilocybin, yelled, drank wine, and smoked cigarettes. He declared, "Walking on water wasn't made in a day." Years later Leary concluded that Kerouac was "an old-style Bohemian without a hippie bone in his body." Kerouac's favorite drug remained alcohol.[45]

While Leary disagreed with Huxley's elitist approach and shared Ginsberg's interest in giving psychedelics to writers, artists, and musicians, Leary also found Ginsberg's approach too narrow. The true potential for these drugs could only be learned if they were taken by many different types of people. In 1961–2 Leary gave psilocybin to Massachusetts prisoners, Harvard psychology graduate students, and nearby theologians and theology graduate students. Richard Alpert (1931–), a Harvard assistant professor, became Leary's main collaborator. Ginsberg urged Leary to try LSD, a far stronger substance, but Leary resisted until December 1961, when Michael Hollingshead offered Leary a dose from his famous mayonnaise jar. Taking LSD was the most "shattering experience of my life," wrote Leary about his stunning first trip. Ginsberg had been correct that LSD was much more potent than psilocybin. From then on, Leary devoured LSD.[46]

Early on, Leary had shrewdly concluded that the likelihood of a successful trip depended primarily upon "set and setting." By "set" Leary meant the mind-set that the potential user brought to the occasion. The person needed to be stable, calm, receptive, adventuresome, and looking for a positive outcome. But the "setting" also mattered. A trip under bright lights in a sterile laboratory agitated. Instead, a trip should be taken with a guide in a warm, cozy place with comfortable furniture, interesting

---

[45] Timothy F. Leary, *Flashbacks* (Los Angeles, 1983), 33 (quote); Don Lattin, *The Harvard Psychedelic Club* (New York, 2010), 57; Miles, *Ginsberg*, 276–82 (quotes at 278, 281); Robert Greenfield, *Timothy Leary* (Orlando, FL, 2006), 127–30, 133–8.
[46] On Leary's democratic attitude see Leary, *Flashbacks*, 45–6. On Leary's first LSD trip see Greenfield, *Leary*, 165–70 (quote at 167).

artwork, and friends. Because psychedelics enhanced sensory perceptions, there should be good food, drink, and music. Leary's home turned out to be much more comfortable for tripping than the lab. Leary had one other insight: it was natural to have sex during a trip, and bad trips occurred when the user lacked either a spiritual motive or a partner.[47]

To Leary, Alpert, and the theologians that Leary had dosed, psychedelics appeared to be primarily about spirituality. If that was true, then Huxley's medical model was inappropriate. Indeed, it was doubtful that physicians should administer psychedelics. While on a trip, the user might feel dissolution of the ego, the oneness of everything, and the interconnectedness of all creatures and inanimate objects. Many trippers reported seeing trees that breathed and living rocks. This religious sensibility, Leary came to believe, was similar to that described in certain Buddhist or Hindu texts. He recommended the *I Ching* and prepared a psychedelic interpretation of the *Tibetan Book of the Dead*. While the Judeo-Christian tradition emphasized the uniqueness of the individual soul, Eastern religions were more likely to explain the individual as a particle flowing through the great river of life that contained all. In this view, God was everywhere – or, indeed, could be gods. For Leary, this polytheism promised to overthrow both the theology and political theory upon which Western civilization and the United States had been based. Psychedelics, as Huxley had predicted in *Island*, would lead to a new kind of universal religion, which in turn would produce a new global political, social, and economic system.[48]

Ginsberg partially agreed with Leary's analysis about the significance of the drugs. Like Leary, Ginsberg believed that psychedelics, and particularly LSD, offered a chance to gain spiritual insight, and Ginsberg also respected the way that these drugs mirrored nondrug methods such as yoga, meditation, or chants

---

[47] On set and setting see Lattin, *Harvard Psychedelic Club*, 70–2. On bad trips see Greenfield, *Leary*, 133.

[48] Timothy F. Leary, *High Priest* (New York, 1968). On spirituality see Lattin, *Harvard Psychedelic Club*, 73–82. On texts see Greenfield, *Leary*, 187, 208–9, 214, 240, 334.

that were used in Eastern religions to achieve egoless harmony with everything. But Ginsberg did not necessarily subscribe to the notion that LSD would do more than change individuals one at a time. Individual consciousness was more important to Ginsberg than to Leary. Having lived in India and after having a transformative spiritual experience in 1963 while traveling without drugs on a train in Japan, Ginsberg had begun to realize that LSD might offer a tool for a novice to understand spiritual enlightenment through a drug-induced trip, but he also concluded that real spiritual enlightenment had to come from great personal effort unaided by chemicals. That was the only kind of enlightenment that would last. Drug trips were temporary, and the subsequent enlightenment was ephemeral.[49]

Huxley also disagreed with Leary. Widely read in science, Huxley was deeply interested in brain science. To him, the actual way that acid worked inside the brain was the most interesting question. While he did not doubt that LSD trips could be spiritually inspiring, he mused that the inspiration, deep down, was a matter of chemistry. Perhaps all religion, he noted, was nothing more than a particular arrangement of chemicals inside the brain. As for LSD changing the entire world through some sort of massive global spiritual change, Huxley doubted that the existing establishment would ever allow acid to be used by very many people. In any case, it was necessary to build a much stronger case, he thought, before trying to launch LSD in the global marketplace. Only limited use by elites could do that, he concluded. Leary heaped scorn upon Huxley's position and began to see himself, by the early Sixties, as a guru for a religious crusade, sometimes privately comparing himself to Christ. LSD may have dissolved a great many egos, but it certainly never dissolved Timothy Leary's ego. In 1963 Leary, Alpert, and their followers left Harvard, and after a brief sojourn in Mexico, relocated to the Millbrook estate in upstate New York, until it was raided in 1965.[50]

[49] For Ginsberg's views on drugs and spirituality see Miles, *Ginsberg*, 260, 270–4, 301–5, 309–18, 325–7; Lee and Shlain, *Acid Dreams*, 58–61, 110–13.
[50] On brain science see Bedford, *Huxley*, 540, 714–15. For Huxley's views on LSD see Lee and Shlain, *Acid Dreams*, 75, 78, 96; Bedford, *Huxley*, 543–4,

While Huxley, Ginsberg, and Leary were debating the significance of acid, Ken Kesey (1935–2001), a novelist who achieved fame with *One Flew over the Cuckoo's Nest* (1962), had reached his own conclusions about LSD. A rugged individualist born into a hardscrabble rural family that embraced frontier values, Kesey had been a champion wrestler as well as a magician, actor, and playwright at the University of Oregon. After failing to make it in Hollywood as either an actor or screenwriter, he decided to become a novelist. In 1958 he won a graduate fellowship to Stanford University, started to write a novel about Beat life in North Beach in San Francisco, and moved with his wife Faye to the swingers' counterculture community on Perry Lane near Stanford. In 1960 Kesey participated in trials of psychedelic drugs at the local Veterans Administration hospital. "I'm high out of my mind," he told the tape recorder on one LSD trip, adding that he saw "wild color images." He found that color and sound intermingled. Later, he recalled, "It was discovering a hole down to the center of the earth."[51]

Psychedelic trips jolted Kesey; they were the most profound experiences he had ever had. LSD led him to question cultural assumptions. Like Huxley, Kesey felt that acid could bring universal enlightenment. What should be done with this magic potion? A libertarian and an egalitarian westerner, Kesey wanted everyone to share the experience. "When we first broke into that forbidden box in the other dimension," he mused, "we knew that we had discovered something as surprising and powerful as the New World when Columbus came stumbling onto it.... We were *naïve*. We thought that we had come to a new place, a new, exciting, free place; and that it was going to be available to all America." Kesey promoted psychedelic drugs among his neighbors on Perry Lane, which soon became a miniature drug utopia. They used a great deal of peyote, which was easy to obtain by mail.[52]

588–9, 713–17. On Leary leaving Harvard for Mexico and Millbrook see Lattin, *Harvard Psychedelic Club*, 86–118, 131–3.

[51] Rick Dodgson, *It's All a Kind of Magic* (Madison, WI, 2013), 15–37, 43–5, 58, 61, 67–120 (quotes at 117, 118).

[52] Ibid., 119–23, 134–5 (quote at 121).

Kesey then took a job at the VA hospital to get material for *Cuckoo's Nest*, write the novel late at night, and steal psychedelic pills for friends on Perry Lane. The idea for the novel came to Kesey while he was high on peyote, and he made Chief Bromden, a Native American, the narrator of the story. The portrayal of an Indian in this fashion jarred the literary establishment, but the novel became a bestseller largely because young readers liked the countercultural tone. In Perry Lane, in San Jose, in Santa Cruz, and in the Haight in San Francisco, as well as longtime bohemian centers such as North Beach or Greenwich Village, tiny knots of youthful nonconformists barely out of high school had discovered each other in the early 1960s. Contemptuous of mainstream culture, they hung out at coffee houses, sneered at the Cold War, denounced racism, listened to folksingers such as Joan Baez or Jerry Garcia, enjoyed poetry performances, popped uppers and downers, smoked marijuana, found occasional psychedelics, and indulged in casual sex.[53]

Kesey moved back to Oregon to research his second novel, *Sometimes a Great Notion* (1964), a libertarian tribute to the union-busting Stamper family, and then returned to Perry Lane to write and take more drugs. When Perry Lane's cottages were bulldozed in 1963, Kesey bought a house on wooded acreage in La Honda in the hills behind Stanford. In this secluded location Kesey finished his novel (often on speed), swore off further writing, and resolved to bring LSD to the masses. Heralding this "new way to look at the world," the author declared acid to be the "Neon Renaissance." Confessing that he was uncertain where the psychedelic revolution would lead, he nevertheless believed that "the old reality is riddled with radioactive poison." He sensed cultural transformation. "I can't imagine another scene, another period," he told an interviewer in 1963, "that I'd rather be living in. I think we're living in a wild and woolly time.... We're on the verge of something very fantastic."[54]

---

[53] Ibid., 135–41, 156, 161–4.
[54] Quotes from ibid., 189–190.

This notion of being on the cusp of change led Kesey to give up being a novelist. Having become a celebrity, he chose to use fame and charisma to promote the acid revolution. With high-quality LSD made by Owsley "Bear" Stanley (1935–2011), a chemistry dropout from the University of California at Berkeley, Kesey and Jerry Garcia (1942–95) began to experiment with the best sights and sounds to accompany an acid trip. After trying and rejecting jazz and folk music, Garcia created a particular style of rock music. Kesey installed speakers throughout the woods. Stanford friends, Perry Lane neighbors, Oregon fraternity brothers, and hangers on visited or camped out on the grounds. Never one to miss a party, Neal Cassady showed up. Everyone got stoned. For Kesey, the purpose of LSD was to be free and have fun. It was all about drugs, music, and sex. This close-knit group became Kesey's Merry Pranksters.[55]

In 1964 Kesey decided to visit the New York World's Fair, in part to launch his second novel. So many Pranksters wanted to come along that Kesey bought a secondhand school bus. It was painted in wild psychedelic colors, with the destination at the front labeled "Furthur" and the rear carrying a sign: "Caution: Weird load." Cassady, the hero of Kerouac's *On the Road*, drove the bus, which careened around corners at record speed. High on Methedrine, Cassady was called Speed Limit. Stuffed with Benzedrine, joints, and LSD, the space cadets on board hardly noticed. Garcia rode only a short distance and confessed being terrified; nevertheless, he honored Cassady as "a tool of the cosmos." The Pranksters stopped in New York City, where Cassady and Kerouac had a somewhat awkward reunion. Kerouac carefully folded an American flag in order to make a place to sit on a couch. The Pranksters tripped, while Jack drank. He hated the flashy Sixties as the antithesis of the cool Beat Fifties.[56]

[55] Ibid., 176–9, 186–90; Plummer, *Holy Goof*, 117–22; Tom Wolfe, *The Electric Kool-Aid Acid Test* (New York, 1969; orig. 1968), 30–2, 36–48, 51–7, 189, 210–21.

[56] Plummer, *Holy Goof*, 123–33 (Garcia quote at 127); Stephen L. Tanner, *Ken Kesey* (Boston, 1983), 89–91, 137; Wolfe, *Electric Kool-Aid Acid Test*, 60–92. See also Paul Perry and Ken Babbs, *On the Bus* (New York, 1990).

FIGURE 3. In 1964 the Beat and hippie movements came together, when Neal Cassady drove Ken Kesey's Merry Pranksters across the country in Kesey's wildly painted bus. The Pranksters traveled to Millbrook, New York, to greet Timothy Leary. Allen Ginsberg snapped this photo when Cassady and Leary, in the foreground, met briefly on board the bus.

Courtesy of Department of Special Collections and University Archives, Stanford University Libraries. Untitled photograph of Neal Cassady and Timothy Leary, dated January 1, 1964. Copyright © 1964, 2014 by Allen Ginsberg LLC, used by permission of The Wylie Agency LLC.

After receiving directions from Allen Ginsberg, the Pranksters next visited Timothy Leary at Millbrook, whose residents seemed genteel and restrained compared to Kesey's exuberant friends. At the time Leary was annoyed by Kesey's freewheeling, celebratory approach to psychedelics, which contrasted with Leary's desire to do scientific research and belief in LSD's enhancement of spirituality, but Leary later understood Kesey's point: because no one knew the true consequences of the dissemination of LSD throughout American culture, the best way to discover the result was to spread the drug as rapidly as possible. Kesey did not see how Leary's attempt to claim scientific or spiritual status would end opposition, and Kesey's idea was to spread LSD so fast that society would not only have to accept it but would also be transformed.[57]

Ken Kesey believed that if he could flood the country with LSD quickly and democratically on a massive scale, there would be a cultural revolution. During the return trip from Millbrook to California, the author turned psychedelic guru pondered how to bring about this marvelous result. Recognizing that older middle-class Americans were unlikely to be interested, he realized that the key to success was to reach the large and emerging boomer generation. A hook was needed to get them to try LSD. Based on the experiments that had already been done at La Honda with the Merry Pranksters, he calculated that rock music offered the best way to reach youth. Accordingly, he began to plan the Bay Area's drug-and-music Acid Tests, which more than any other events marked the beginning of the hippie counterculture.

[57] Leary, *Flashbacks*, 204–6; Wolfe, *Electric Kool-Aid Acid Test*, 93–6.

2

Drugs, Music, and Spirituality

During 1965 the young Americans who became known as "hippies" soared in numbers in the San Francisco Bay Area, as youthful use of still legal lysergic acid diethylamide (LSD) swept the region. Trippers also grooved on "Acid Rock" music, and many were also spiritual seekers. Drugs, music, and spirituality were at the core of the hippie movement. Acid heads believed that psychedelic drugs would transform both individuals and society. Seeking the like-minded, freaks congregated in the city's Haight-Ashbury district. In the early Sixties, white working-class families had fled the Haight for the suburbs, and the large, old Victorian homes commanded little rent. San Francisco State College students moved into the area, and so did counterculture types driven from North Beach by rising rent, crowds of tourists, and police harassment. This hippie neighborhood was bordered to the East by a commercial area, to the North by the black Fillmore district, to the South by a steep hill, and to the West by Golden Gate Park.[1]

Seeking authenticity, hippies moved to the Haight to enjoy rock music, easy sex, pot, and acid. Compared to the beatniks of North Beach, the hippies of the Haight were poorer and younger.

---

[1] The best source on the Haight remains Charles Perry, *The Haight-Ashbury* (New York, 1984).

Most were in their early twenties, and a few were teens. Many were college dropouts. Almost all were white, although the Haight was racially mixed, which was unusual for a neighborhood in an American city at that time. Too zonked to work due to frequent acid trips, freaks lacked cash and packed themselves into group homes. They shared rent, food, drugs, and each other. Sleeping on mattresses on the floor, they lived spontaneously, and, in the eyes of the mainstream reporter Michael Fallon, seemed apathetic. When Fallon asked a houseful of hippies how that night's dinner was going to be provided, one longhair answered, "A lot of us have straight friends. They bring us food." Although there was no sign of any preparation for cooking, they said that they planned to eat lasagna. Perhaps the lasagna would magically appear, or at least the trippers could imagine that they were eating lasagna.[2]

At the Blue Unicorn coffee shop, a hippie hangout, Fallon found a young woman desperately trying to locate a male hippie from New York, a transplanted New Englander who had just spent twelve hours meditating in the Zen Buddhist center, and a reclining male who was doodling eyeglasses onto the face of a woman on the cover of *Harper's* magazine. The doodler declared himself a "peacenik." He explained, "I get part-time jobs occasionally." The coffee house was a place for freaks to meet, a clearing house to find people, and a mail drop. It also offered free food to anyone willing to wash dishes, but few did so. Tripping was more important than eating. One Haight ceramic potter observed that hippies were nomads, who frequently were forced to move for nonpayment of rent. Most of what went on in the Haight only made sense if one perceived the world through a psychedelic lens. Almost every item sold in the district had a drug connection, either directly, as in the case of hash pipes and hookahs, or indirectly, as in the case of music, art, clothes, and spiritual texts.[3]

---

[2] Michael Fallon, "A New Paradise for Beatniks," *San Francisco Examiner*, September 5, 1965, sec. 1, 5 (quote); Michael Fallon, "Are Beats Good Business?" *San Francisco Examiner*, September 8, 1965, 17.

[3] Michael Fallon, "The New Hip Hangout-the Blue Unicorn," *San Francisco Examiner*, September 6, 1965, 14 (quotes); Michael Fallon, "Bohemia's New Haven," *San Francisco Examiner*, September 7, 1965, 8.

The most important fact about LSD, Ken Kesey knew, was that it profoundly distorted and heightened all the senses: sight, sound, touch, smell, and taste. Therefore, the best way to promote use was to administer the drug in an environment in which the senses were fully engaged. LSD appeared to slow down time, so the user could savor each tiny moment. Smell and taste could be accommodated with burning incense, sumptuous food, and flavorful beverages, while touch required the close proximity of attractive warm bodies. Sound meant music, especially rhythms that enhanced the other senses, and sight meant the use of projected film, slides, and the newly invented pulsing strobe light, which had been perfected by William Burroughs's friend, Bryon Gysin. The lighting obliterated normal vision by showing fragmentary snippets that the drug allowed to be savored and pondered. Sight and sound could be blended in a rich and heady brew.[4]

The key to this total drug experience, Kesey came to believe, was the music, and because LSD was a new drug, it stood to reason that a new music had to be invented. The drug experience required a music that expressed authenticity. Throughout 1965 Kesey and the Merry Pranksters conducted sound and sight experiments at his new home in La Honda, in the hills behind Stanford University. Kesey supplied the sound equipment – or at least the money to buy the parts, while Owsley "Bear" Stanley made the acid and built the sound system, and the San Jose folk-singer Jerry Garcia worked on the music. Speakers were placed on the roof of Kesey's house in order to blast sound throughout the wooded property, and later additional speakers were added in the trees. Small sculptures were sometimes placed in the trees as well. Strange colored lights were programmed to pulse on and off with the music.[5]

[4] Rick Dodgson, *It's All a Kind of Magic* (Madison, WI, 2013), 115–21, 140. On Gysin and strobe lights see Chrissie Iles essay in Christoph Grunenberg, ed., *Summer of Love* (London, 2005), 71; Matthieu Poirer essay in Christoph Grunenberg and Jonathan Harris, eds., *Summer of Love* (Liverpool, UK, 2005), 288. These two distinct volumes are very easy to confuse.
[5] Tom Wolfe, *The Electric Kool-Aid Acid Test* (New York, 1969; orig. 1968), 186–9, 219–24. See Owsley Stanley's 1991 interview in David Gans, ed., *Conversations with the Dead* (New York, 1991), 291–5.

Kesey's property attracted many visitors, some of whom came temporarily, and others of whom lived in tents in the woods. A few were fans of Kesey's first novel, *Cuckoo's Nest*, others were from Perry Lane, and still others were connected to Garcia and the Bay Area music scene or to Owsley and the seemingly endless supply of the cheap, high-quality acid that he manufactured. The parties were constant and ongoing, which provided a great test audience for the search for the correct music to accompany an acid trip. At first, the Pranksters tried jazz, but the results proved disappointing. For whatever reason, jazz did not work with LSD. Neither did folk nor classical music. The listener needed a music that worked for the individual acid head. Garcia, who was in charge of the musical experiments, then turned to rock 'n' roll, which proved fruitful after Garcia altered how it was performed. Garcia went on to found a rock band called the Warlocks, which later changed its name to the Grateful Dead.[6]

After Elvis Presley rose to fame in the mid-1950s, rock 'n' roll had become the most popular music in America. Early rock, however, had limitations. A startling break with softer and more melodic pop music songs or the brassy Big Band sound, rock 'n' roll put the backbeat front and center in a rather monotonous thump-thump-thump, while often overly simplified lyrics carried a melody in the vocal line that tended toward endless repetition. The guitar line usually repeated the vocal line, which acted as reinforcement but quickly became boring. Vocal masters like Presley, Little Richard, or Jerry Lee Lewis entertained the masses with these songs, but even top singers could not sustain interest in a particular song for more than three minutes because of pedantic lyrics, dull repetition, and insufficient variation. Simplicity made rock 'n' roll catchy, but it also limited the music's capacity to keep the audience engaged.

Kesey and zonked-out listeners in Kesey's woods, however, noted that rock 'n' roll, unlike other types of music, did penetrate their drugged state. Requesting more rock, trippers asked that the drum base line be emphasized and that the volume be

---

[6] Perry, *Haight-Ashbury*, 12–15.

turned up on the speakers. What made rock interesting was a very loud repetitive beat that crashed into the middle of an acid trip and caused drug-inspired visions to pulsate. It was this crucial intersection of the visual and aural within the drug trip that made rock so stimulating. Garcia then made an important discovery: the key to success for any particular rock song was in the guitar line. Instead of echoing the main vocal melody, which had been the mainstay of Fifties rock 'n' roll, a more interesting stimulation could be produced for the listener by playing the vocals off of variant or even contrasting guitar melodies. When the listener was on acid, the surprising interplay of the two lines built tension, teased out meaning in the contrasts, and eased tension in grand resolutions. A series of tension-building and tension-resolving sections enabled a song to last far longer than three minutes. When combined with riffs and guitar improvisations, each performance could uniquely express the mood of the moment. A song might go on for eight minutes or even longer.[7]

Lyrics were still important in this new type of rock, which became known as Acid Rock or the San Francisco Sound, but they played a different role inside the music. In older rock 'n' roll, like other pop music, lyrics had usually been about simple universal subjects, most commonly falling in love, and they had dominated the unsophisticated music that accompanied the lyrics. In Acid Rock the melodic variations and the contrasts between the vocal line and the melodic variation were the keys to the song. Musical borrowings produced exoticism that allowed the listener to retreat from the mainstream, but in doing so the counterculture remained complicit in the neocolonial policies that drove the mainstream. Lyrics still mattered, but they rode above the underlying turbulence that was the heart and soul of the music. Acid Rock suggested that listeners should trust feelings, as expressed by the guitar and beat, more than reason, as represented by the lyrics. In the new music, lyrics tended to be

[7] Garcia interview in Gans, ed., *Conversations with the Dead*, 41–3, 48–50, 54, 66–74.

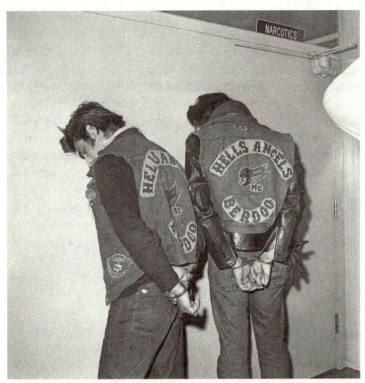

FIGURE 4. In 1964 two members of the Hell's Angels motorcycle club were arrested in a drug bust in Southern California. When Ken Kesey introduced LSD to the Angels, they proved receptive.
Los Angeles Times Photographic Archive, Library Special Collections, Charles E. Young Research Library, UCLA.

elliptical and mysterious, and songs frequently stated a problem but refused to resolve it by the song's end, although the music sometimes hinted at the ultimate resolution, which often suggested drastic change or doom.[8]

The Pranksters' experiments, Owsley's acid, and Garcia's music influenced others, some of whom got a head start on the public stage. In the summer of 1965, the Charlatans, a minor

---

[8] On musical borrowings see Nadya Zimmerman, *Counterculture Kaleidoscope* (Ann Arbor, MI, 2008), 60.

San Francisco band, performed the new rock at the Red Dog Saloon in Virginia City, Nevada. In keeping with the outlaw flavor of the music and Billy the Kid, the band and patrons wore real guns. This successful gig led the Family Dog in the fall to stage rock concerts at the Longshoremen's Hall in San Francisco. Not long afterward Chet Helms started to hold rock dances at the Avalon Ballroom. By then the Hell's Angels, the motorcycle gang who used and sold many drugs, had taken up residence at Kesey's place in La Honda. When the Angels showed up, Kesey said, "We're in the same business. You break people's bones. I break people's heads." Kesey welcomed the Angels because he wanted to learn what would happen when the macho Angels took LSD. Would it dissolve their propensity to violence? How would they respond to Garcia's new music? As it turned out, the Angels, known for drinking large quantities of alcohol as well as drugs, liked LSD. It was groovy, they said, and they liked Garcia's music, too. They did not, however, mellow out.[9]

In November 1965 Kesey staged the first Acid Test, a public event where strangers shared food, drink, LSD, avant-garde art, and the new rock music. The first test was held on private land in a rural location at Soquel, near Santa Cruz, California. Everyone got stoned. The success of this venture led Kesey to stage many more Acid Tests to turn on as many people as possible. The Acid Tests quickly moved to rented halls in San Francisco. The owners of the halls were generally clueless about the specific purpose behind these "rock concerts," which featured LSD-laced Kool-Aid. The music was the draw, but the real purpose was to spread the use of acid. The attendees, said the counterculture journalist Hunter S. Thompson, were "pathetically eager acid Freaks who thought they could buy peace and understanding for three bucks a hit." Flyers and posters advertising the concerts

---

[9] On the Charlatans see Zimmerman, *Counterculture Kaleidoscope*, 22–5. On Chet Helms see Richard Goldstein, "Hurok of Haight Street," *Los Angeles Times Magazine*, August 27, 1967, 16–18, 21. On the Hell's Angels see Hunter S. Thompson, *Hell's Angels* (New York, 1967); Wolfe, *Electric Kool-Aid Acid Test*, 150–61. Kesey quote is in Warren Hinckle, "The Hippies," *Ramparts*, March 1967, 11.

taunted, "Can You Pass the Acid Test?" The manhood question was calculated to lure college students. Kesey later said, "The need for mystery is greater than the need for an answer."[10]

Already, Kesey and Garcia, partly as native westerners and partly influenced by LSD trips, began to develop an egalitarian ethos that would surround the acid counterculture. According to this theory of equality, everyone was equal in all respects. Thus, while Garcia's band agreed to play at the Acid Tests, they refused to do so from a stage, and they insisted on being as stoned as the crowd. This did not help the performances. Sometimes multiple bands played at the same time, and some of the Acid Tests featured other entertainments, including Allen Ginsberg and others reading poems. The last Acid Test was held in Los Angeles in March 1966. By then, the events had attracted the attention of authorities, and from then on attendees generally had to supply their own LSD. Kesey sponsored the Acid Graduation Test in San Francisco in October 1966, in which he asserted that one could get high at rock concerts without acid. At the time Kesey had legal problems with a marijuana bust, and his statement should be interpreted as an attempt to placate authorities.[11]

In 1965 Bill Graham (1931–91) was the business manager for the San Francisco Mime Troupe. Graham (nee Wolfgang Grajonca) was a Berlin-born Jewish refugee who, against heavy odds, had managed to escape Hitler and flee to New York as a boy. Drawn to entertainment while a waiter in various Jewish resorts in the Catskills, he moved to California, failed to find work as an actor, and took over running the Mime Troupe. Created by Ronnie Davis, the Mime Troupe was a unique local institution that challenged the establishment by giving free performances of avant-garde plays in the public parks. The players always strived

[10] On the Acid Tests see Wolfe, *Electric Kool-Aid Acid Test*, 207–21; Christopher Gair, *The American Counterculture* (Edinburgh, Scotland, 2007), 134–5 (Thompson quote at 135); Michael J. Kramer, *The Republic of Rock* (New York, 2013), 31–66 (Kesey quote at 44).

[11] Dodgson, *It's All a Kind of Magic*, xxiv; Gair, *American Counterculture*, 132; Kramer, *Republic of Rock*, 36; Scott MacFarlane, *The Hippie Narrative* (Jefferson, NC, 2007), 24.

to express authenticity and to appeal to individuals. Arrested during one performance, the impoverished Mime Troupe needed to raise money to pay a lawyer to defend them. After Graham saw hundreds of young people waiting to gain admission to one of the new rock dances, he quickly decided to stage a benefit rock concert.[12]

He held the first benefit in a small loft on November 6, 1965, on the same night that the Family Dog sponsored a rock dance at the larger Longshoremen's Hall. Despite the competition, Graham had no trouble attracting customers, and he quickly decided to hold another dance concert on December 10. At the time, Graham was a bit naïve about the role that acid played at these events. LSD was sometimes passed out at concerts, and a high proportion of the participants were stoned. For this second benefit event, he rented the much larger Fillmore Auditorium, which had fallen into disuse because it was at the edge of an African American neighborhood. Thousands of young people filled the hall to the fire marshal's limit to dance to the Jefferson Airplane; those who could not get in formed a line that doubled around the block. At that point, Graham decided to leave the Mime Troupe and lease the Fillmore long-term to stage weekly dance concerts.[13]

In January 1966 counterculture enthusiasts caught up in the LSD craze sponsored the Trips Festival at the Longshoremen's Hall. The main organizer was Stewart Brand (1938–), a Stanford graduate with a lifelong fascination with American Indians who had gotten a job photographing reservations for the Department of the Interior. Brand had also married a Native American. He later produced the *Whole Earth Catalog* (1968). The first day of the multimedia Trips Festival was devoted to Brand's

---

[12] Bill Graham and Robert Greenfield, *Bill Graham Presents* (New York, 1992); Michael Lydon, "The Producer of the New Rock," *New York Times Magazine*, December 15, 1968, 40ff. See also R. G. Davis, *The San Francisco Mime Troupe* (Palo Alto, CA, 1975).

[13] Benefit handbills are in Paul D. Grushkin, *The Art of Rock* (New York, 1987), 113–14. On Graham leaving the Mime Troupe see Robert Hurwitt, "Mime Troupe Always Set to Shuffle," *Berkeley Barb*, July 28, 1967, 9.

"America Needs Indians," which featured projections of Brand's six hundred slides, two films, a light show, rock music, and live dancing Indians. The second day "Acid Test" presented Kesey's Merry Pranksters, Neal Cassady, Allen Ginsberg, a light show, the Grateful Dead and other rock bands, the Hell's Angels, and free LSD-laced punch. More than six thousand young people attended.[14]

Graham held his first regular weekly rock dance at the Fillmore on February 4, 1966. He filled his hall with a combination of local bands and traveling acts. Garcia's Grateful Dead made frequent appearances, often accompanied by Quicksilver Messenger Service, which did the opening set. These were referred to as the Quick and the Dead concerts. Graham imported the Paul Butterfield Blues Band from Chicago, as well as Stevie Wonder, B. B. King, and Otis Redding. One of Graham's goals was to introduce his white audiences to major black performers, who shared programs with local white rock bands. Major local bands included Moby Grape, with an unprecedented three co-lead guitarists; Jefferson Airplane, who served as the Fillmore's house band; and Big Brother and the Holding Company, who rose from obscurity after they signed Janis Joplin from Port Arthur, Texas as the lead singer.[15]

The local bands' strange names expressed the emergence of hippie culture. Garcia had picked the Grateful Dead by randomly opening an old dictionary; Quicksilver Messenger Service's name came from the odd coincidence that Mercury was prominent in the astrological charts for all the players. While the band delivered music, other messengers were known to deliver drugs. The members of Moby Grape drank a great deal of cheap red wine, which was widely believed to go well with LSD. Although Jefferson Airplane insisted publicly that the name honored Blind

---

[14] Trips Festival program and flier are in Grushkin, *Art of Rock*, 115–16; Kramer, *Republic of Rock*, 51–3. On Brand see Andrew G. Kirk, *Counterculture Green* (Lawrence, KS, 2007), 38–40.

[15] Graham and Greenfield, *Bill Graham Presents*, 174–82. On the bands see also Joel Selvin, *Summer of Love* (New York, 1994); Jack McDonough, *San Francisco Rock* (San Francisco, 1985).

Lemon Jefferson, an African American performer, many young people in the Bay Area thought that the name stood for "free trip." Big Brother and the Holding Company could only be explained as a reference to dealing drugs. Songs also celebrated drugs. The Airplane's "White Rabbit" (1967) sneered at mother's pills, because they did not alter consciousness, and ended with a drug prescription that did. Until the Doors scored a hit single with "Unknown Soldier" in 1968, the songs generally ignored the Vietnam War.[16]

Graham's concerts allowed the bands to play in a flat floor setting, which encouraged dancing. Previously, most bands had performed in auditoriums where fans were trapped in seats. Influenced by psychedelic drug culture as well as the Bay Area's rich jazz scene, the bands used riffs and improvisation. They strived for authenticity and expressed individualism. With Graham's approval, the sound systems were often experimental. Owsley, who worked with the Grateful Dead, liked to hide microphones in odd spots throughout the hall and to use feedback loops that caused eerie reverberations. Sometimes even the artists were startled by the sounds that they had created. Graham, who understood the totality of the LSD experience and the essential intersection of sound and sight, deployed hippie lighting experts to mount powerful strobe light shows. Very brief slide projections of nude bodies, marijuana plants, or flowers intermixed with swirling colors made by mixing oils complemented the flashing strobe lights. There was incense, and dancers wore body paint that glowed.[17]

In keeping with the emerging hippie philosophy, the concert-goers and the band were equal participants in the creation of the concert. Feedback from the crowd influenced improvisations, and inspired passages excited the audience. The Berkeley music columnist Ed Denson described a concert: "walls

---

[16] Jefferson Airplane name is in jeffersonairplane.com/the-band/jorma-kaukonen. Grateful Dead name is in Sandy Troy, *Captain Trips* (New York, 1994), 73–5.

[17] Graham and Greenfield, *Bill Graham Presents*, 142–6. On lights see Alastair Gordon, *Spaced Out* (New York, 2008), 49. On body paint see Mitchell Hider, "S. F. the City with Turned on Sound," *Los Angeles Times*, July 1, 1967, B9.

of dark pulsing electric blues, cooking with intermitrible [*sic*] guitar sobs, musicians wavering back and forth as they play to a darkened hall half filled with entranced hippies watching glassy-eyed and half cauldrons of energy where whirling dancers bodies become molten and flowing as the music meets their minds." Each individual could take from the concert what that person deemed most important: there was no preconceived outcome. Furthermore, the experimental nature of the experience affirmed that the event was authentic.[18]

Graham and rival promoters advertised concerts with psychedelic posters that frequently featured swirled lettering and distorted drawings. Such traits were immediately recognizable as visual representations of an acid trip. Smaller versions were circulated to stores for use in shop windows, and postcards with the same images were mailed to regular concert goers. The posters were handmade using a silk screen process that allowed multiple shaded colors to be used in one pass through the screen, and due to the handmade process, there was always some variation among individual posters. The best posters displayed deep significance. For example, the Dead were represented by a skeleton and roses to indicate death and rebirth. Leading poster artists, including Wes Wilson, Alton Kelley, and Stanley Mouse, developed unique styles that immediately identified the artist. Another important artist with an inside connection was Bonnie Maclean: she was married to Graham. Graham printed the posters on high-quality paper, and they quickly became collectable. They were generally available at no cost at outlets that sold concert tickets.[19]

The popularity of Graham's concerts drew the attention of the New York record companies. At the time, RCA and Columbia were the major record labels, and both companies sent scouts to San Francisco. The Jefferson Airplane became the first band to sign with a major label, RCA, but the recording sessions in

---

[18] Ed Denson, "Folk Scene," *Berkeley Barb*, September 15, 1967, 8.
[19] Grushkin, *Art of Rock*; Graham and Greenfield, *Bill Graham Presents*, 196; Stephen Gaskin, *Haight Ashbury Flashbacks* (2nd ed., Berkeley, 1990), 51.

Los Angeles were disappointing. The technicians, used to working with pop artists, could not conceive of a song longer than three minutes. Anything longer would never be played on AM radio. Disliking the undisciplined nature of the band, the engineers saw no virtue in riffs, improvisation, distorted sounds, or loop feedback, and obliterated all of these items. The resulting record was flat and lacked the vicarious thrill of the Airplane's live performances. Columbia did only slightly better producing Moby Grape's first record. After hearing what had happened to the other bands, Jerry Garcia held out for artistic control. The top labels refused to budge, so the Grateful Dead signed with the less prestigious Warner Brothers. Warner's Los Angeles engineers were sympathetic to the new music. It took several albums, however, before the Dead achieved on record a sound that came close to the power of a live performance.[20]

The new music quickly found its way onto radio in San Francisco. Acid Rock bands disliked Top Forty radio's three-minute song limit, and stations aimed at teens resisted playing drug-oriented songs. In April 1967 KMPX, a station with a small audience on the little-used FM dial, hired Tom Donahue to host a late night program, and he began to play long cuts from rock albums. Ratings soared, Donahue became the station manager, and hippies programmed most of the airtime with what became known as album rock. KMPX shortly had the largest audience of any radio station in the Bay Area. Eventually, the owner sold the station, and in 1968 Donahue and much of the staff moved to KSAN-FM, the new home of album rock. Within a year a good many radio stations switched to the new format in most major markets.[21]

Entwined with use of LSD in the emerging counterculture was widespread use of marijuana. Pot was used much more frequently

---

[20] Dominick Cavallo, *A Fiction of the Past* (New York, 1999), 146–50, 161, 167; Gair, *American Counterculture*, 133–4; Troy, *Captain Trips*, 95–6; Zimmerman, *Counterculture Kaleidoscope*, 188, note 13.

[21] Kramer, *Republic of Rock*, 67–93; Walter Medeiros essay in Grunenberg and Harris, eds., *Summer of Love*, 333–4. On rock on FM radio see John J. O'Connor, "FM Radio's Ear to the Underground," *Wall Street Journal*, August 27, 1970, 10.

for the simple reason that it was more widely available. It was also cheap, running ten dollars a lid, which was usually defined as an overly large ounce. While an LSD trip might last for hours or an entire day, which was inconvenient if one had business to attend, a puff or two on a marijuana cigarette could provide a mild buzz that lasted only a short time. Although one could not compare a mild marijuana high to the intensity of an acid trip, both drugs caused time to appear to be slowed, enhanced the senses, and distorted reality. Marijuana is properly classified as a euphoric, however, rather than a psychedelic, because it lacks the capacity to trigger wild visions. One sociologist who studied hippies living in San Francisco reported that of eighty hippies surveyed, all but one indicated daily pot use. A different study of female hippies in Berkeley found that 97 percent had smoked marijuana and 91 percent had dropped acid.[22]

After Ron and Jay Thelin opened the Psychedelic Shop on Haight Street in 1966, the media focused on the neighborhood as a hippie stronghold. Their store sold tickets to rock concerts as well as drug-related items. Respectable, older middle-class people who tripped only on weekends, college students trying to score drugs, and other part-time hippies began to frequent the Haight in search of drugs. By 1966 any long-haired young male walking down Haight Street was offered drug deals at least once per block. Numerous outlets sold hash pipes, hookahs, tie-dyed clothes, headbands, Mexican sandals, handmade jewelry, color-ful buttons, psychedelic posters, concert tickets, tarot cards, the Chinese *I Ching* book of divination, and the *Tibetan Book of the Dead* guide to consciousness after death. The Hell's Angels motorcycle gang policed the Haight, provided ballroom security, and sold pot and speed. Allen Cohen (1940–2004) irregularly issued the *San Francisco Oracle* as the local hippie newspaper. The Grateful Dead and the Jefferson Airplane lived in rented

---

[22] Dodgson, *It's All a Kind of Magic*, 128–31, 163–4; Robert Greenfield, *Timothy Leary* (Orlando, FL, 2006), 329; Clark Heinrich interview in Charles Hayes, ed., *Tripping* (New York, 2000), 118. On the two studies see Gretchen Lemke-Santangelo, *Daughters of Aquarius* (Lawrence, KS, 2009), 117.

Victorian mansions in the neighborhood. Both bands played numerous free concerts in nearby Golden Gate Park.[23]

In January 1967 Allen Cohen, Ron Thelin, Allen Ginsberg, and others promoted the Human Be-In in Golden Gate Park. Seeking to bridge radicals and hippies, Cohen called for "a union of love and activism." The idea was to impress authorities by attracting large numbers of young people to a big party with plentiful shared food, alcohol, and drugs, including marijuana and LSD, along with free rock music and poetry readings. "Human Be-In" was a play on *human being*, but it also meant that it was acceptable just to exist in the present. Shortly afterward, Richard Alpert announced the philosophy of "Be Here Now." Calling for a "Pow-Wow" and "A Gathering of the Tribes," the Be-In poster featured an Indian on a horse. To hippies, Indians were pure in spirit, primitives liberated from Western civilization, and true Americans. As part of the search for authenticity, the counterculture tried to gain depth by absorbing others' wisdom. On the poster the Native American carried an electric guitar, but it was not plugged in.[24]

The crowd was estimated at around twenty thousand. The Beat poet Gary Snyder officially opened the event by blowing on a conch shell, and Ginsberg chanted "om," which he had learned in India. Timothy Leary attended. Wearing white clothes with a flower in his ear, the stoned psychologist famously advised: "Tune in, turn on, drop out." Leary later explained that he wanted young Americans to tune into their feelings, get turned on by the music, and then drop out of the middle-class rat race, but most people at the Be-In thought Leary meant that they should take acid that day. Owsley Stanley passed out acid.

[23] On media discovery of the Haight in 1966 see Maitland Zane, "Trouble in the City's New Bohemia," *San Francisco Chronicle*, March 15, 1966, 1, 6; Nicholas von Hoffman, "A New Drug Culture Is Burgeoning," *Washington Post*, August 21, 1966, E1; Ed Denson, "Folk Scene," *Berkeley Barb*, November 4, 1966, 4; "The Nitty-Gritty Sound," *Newsweek*, December 19, 1966, 102.

[24] David Farber essay in Melvin Small and William D. Hoover, eds., *Give Peace a Chance* (Syracuse, NY, 1992), 15 (Cohen quote); Zimmerman, *Counterculture Kaleidoscope*, 7–10. Rick Griffin's poster is in Grushkin, *Art of Rock*, 197.

FIGURE 5. In 1967 Allen Ginsberg expressed joy by dancing at the Human Be-In in San Francisco. During another period at the Be-In he led the crowd in chanting "om."

Allen Ginsberg at the San Francisco Be-In (74_02). Photo by Lisa Law. © Lisa Law.

A good deal of LSD was consumed, and the Dead, the Airplane, and other bands played loud and long. When the political radical Jerry Rubin tried to give a speech, the crowd ignored it. Rubin's angry tone scared Garcia, who asked, "Why enter this closed society and make an effort to liberalize it? Why not just leave it and go someplace else?" Hell's Angels protected the sound system. "We had no idea there were so many of us," one attendee later said.[25]

The success of the Be-In led to an interesting philosophical discussion about the meaning of what was happening among Snyder, Ginsberg, Leary, and Alan Watts on Watts's houseboat in nearby Sausalito. The "houseboat summit" was recorded, and Allen Cohen printed the transcript in the *Oracle*. Ginsberg believed that the Be-In validated the Beat search for individual happiness and demonstrated a widespread following among the emergent hippies. He saw value in drugs, music, and community in the search for spirituality, but after his 1963 spiritual epiphany, he no longer emphasized drugs. Snyder, heavily influenced by his eleven years in the Zen Buddhist monastery in Japan, stressed the spiritual significance of the moment, and Alan Watts, the student of Eastern religions who had settled in the Bay Area, concurred. In contrast, Leary believed that LSD would change the world one stoned mind at a time. "I want no part of mass movements," he declared. "I think this is the error that the leftist activists are making." The high priest of acid sought spiritual enlightenment through drug-induced psychological transformation.[26]

[25] Helen S. Perry, *The Human Be-In* (New York, 1970); Greenfield, *Leary*, 302 (Leary quote); Gair, *American Counterculture*, 302 (Garcia quote); Herbie Greene interview in Hayes, ed., *Tripping*, 153 (attendee quote). See also "Hippies Run Wild-Jailed," *San Francisco Sunday Examiner-Chronicle*, January 15, 1967, sec. 1, 1; David Swanston, "Human Be-In's Aftermath," *San Francisco Chronicle*, January 16, 1967, 3; Ed Denson, "What Happened at the Hippening," *Berkeley Barb*, January 20, 1967, 1, 4, 7; Herbert Gold, "Where the Action Is," *New York Times Magazine*, February 19, 1967, 1, 50–2; Jann Wenner, "The Gathering of the Tribes," *Sunday Ramparts*, January 29, 1967, 4; "Dropouts with a Mission," *Newsweek*, February 6, 1967, 92, 95.

[26] *San Francisco Oracle*, #7, March–April 1967; Sherry L. Smith, *Hippies, Indians, and the Fight for Red Power* (New York, 2012), 57–69; Zimmerman, *Counterculture Kaleidoscope*, 12 (quote), 126.

FIGURE 6. Hippies in many cities copied the San Francisco Be-In. In April 1967 couples danced exuberantly at this Love-In in Los Angeles. Los Angeles Times Photographic Archive, Library Special Collections, Charles E. Young Research Library, UCLA.

The San Francisco Be-In stimulated later Be-Ins in other cities, including Los Angeles, New York, Washington, D.C., Seattle, and Detroit. Drawing much curiosity from the media, the Be-Ins marked the point where the hippie movement gained widespread public notice. Most of these outdoor events took place after warm spring weather had arrived. There was little interest in being zonked out in the snow on LSD. At this point, being a hippie seemed to be mostly about having a good time. Pot and acid were just new vehicles to achieve an altered state of being previously attained by Americans primarily through alcohol. There certainly was a generation gap, as parents wondered why their own children could not accept drinking as the normal way to get high. But while the children never truly rejected alcohol, they added these new drugs to set themselves apart as a new generation. The children also sensed that picking a new drug of choice was about more than just getting high. LSD was fun, but perhaps it was about more than having fun. Leary's advice to "drop out" expressed young Americans' discontent with the status quo, but his quotable quip did not in itself state the logical next point, which was a spiritual quest.[27]

They were called the *love generation*, a label they accepted. "We assert the right to enjoy ourselves," wrote one enthusiast, "which is the right to love." The *San Francisco Oracle* called for "the freedom of the body, the pursuit of joy, and the expansion of consciousness." Life, liberty, and the pursuit of happiness were being transformed. Tuli Kupferberg (1923–2010) of the Fugs rock band declared, "Sensory gratification and love are the first desiderata." What was needed was "a revolution of love." The young were hated because they "love more, fuck more, take more drugs." But all of the talk about love may have been camouflage. "The call for love is a cry for help," Margot Adler's father warned his daughter. *Sgt. Pepper's Lonely Hearts Club Band* (1967) affirmed that the Beatles saw love as the antidote to loneliness. Bob Dylan, too, waged war against the lonely self. Middle-class white youth felt the self was a void; they tried to fill the empty space with the blues, black language, Indian mysticism, nostalgic clothes, and American Indian shamans.[28]

Kupferberg noted, "Man's true life is inside." He later elaborated, "The real revolution is the revolution that occurs within you." This concern for the interior, derived from psychedelic experiences, permeated the counterculture. In 1968 the Hornsby College art students in London issued a counterculture manifesto: "Revolution of thought and feeling is the only permanent revolution. A structure can only work so long as it grows out of

---

[27] Other Be-Ins are in Francine Grace, "A Groovy Time at Human Be-In," *Los Angeles Times*, March 1, 1967, E8; Willard Clopton Jr., "The Be-In," *Washington Post*, April 2, 1967, B2; "Hippies Turn Out for Be-In," *Seattle Times*, April 2, 1967, 3; Scott Salsenek, "Love-In," Detroit *Fifth Estate*, May 15, 1967, 1, 5. On the New York Be-In see Bernard Weinraub, "10,000 Chant Love," *New York Times*, March 27, 1967, 1, 24; Don McNeill, "Central Park Rite Is Medieval Pageant," *Village Voice*, March 30, 1967, 1, 20.

[28] Jerry Rosenfield letter, *Berkeley Barb*, March 17, 1967, 6 (first quote); *Oracle* quoted in Troy, *Captain Trips*, 95; Tuli Kupferberg, "The Love of Politics and the Politics of Love," *Berkeley Barb*, April 14, 1967, 8; Margot Adler, *Heretic's Heart* (Boston, 1997), 202; Nicholas K. Bromell, *Tomorrow Never Knows* (Chicago, 2000), 77, 110, 130.

feeling." Citing "imagination" as the key, the students declared, "Anyone, anywhere, can create this revolution." The revolution in feelings caught the attention of John Sinclair, the radical manager of the MC5 band. "We have to establish a situation on this planet," he wrote, "where all people can feel good all the time." Rock music was always about feelings. Only the lyrics were about understanding, and they were less important. The call for a revolution in feelings suggested that the counterculture was more of an offshoot of the mainstream than it ever wanted to admit. Affirmation could be found in a sign carried at a street happening in Berkeley: "Jesus was a hippy."[29]

The psychedelic young, unlike their alcohol-drinking parents, were on a spiritual quest. Aldous Huxley had been the first user of psychedelic substances to understand this potential. Ginsberg had concurred, and so had Leary and his assistant, Richard Alpert, as soon as the pair had left Harvard. After undergoing an LSD-prompted spiritual crisis at Leary's Millbrook estate, Alpert had fled to India, embraced a mishmash of Indian religious ideas, and returned to the United States as the spiritual leader Ram Dass. Deemphasizing drugs as the means to spiritual fulfillment, Dass nevertheless believed that psychedelics could, if administered as religious sacraments, aid the user in the search for spiritual fulfillment. Even before leaving Millbrook, Leary had reached a similar conclusion. After a brief stay in India, Leary tried to bring religious ideas, especially concerning the interrelatedness of everybody and everything, into his lectures on psychedelics. By the late 1960s he publicly advocated a personal spiritual search using meditation, chants, yoga, and prayer rather than drugs, but at the same time he continued to take large quantities of LSD. Leary's public emphasis upon nondrug spirituality

[29] Tuli Kupferberg, "The Love of Politics and the Politics of Love," *Berkeley Barb*, April 14, 1967, 8, and Kupferberg interview, *Berkeley Barb*, May 12, 1967, 8; art students in Andrew Wilson essay in Grunenberg and Harris, eds., *Summer of Love*, 91; Sinclair in Alexander Bloom and Wini Breines, eds., *Takin' It to the Streets* (New York, 1995), 301; Simon Frith, *Sound Effects* (New York, 1981), 14; Jesus sign in "Berkeley Hips Warm," *Berkeley Barb*, April 14, 1967, 4.

may have had more to do with his legal problems over a drug bust than his beliefs.[30]

Many young Americans were in spiritual crisis in the mid-Sixties. "American churchmen," concluded one observer, "seemed to have neither the patience nor the fortitude to deal with people who were, well, *unsettled*." Certainly youthful dissatisfaction with bland mainstream Protestantism played a role, and the sudden changes in post–Vatican II Catholicism jarred many Roman Catholics. The civil rights movement, especially as advocated by Martin Luther King Jr., suggested that religion and secular life should be more connected. The Cold War had produced a permanent war fever, the Vietnam War raised troubling questions, and many young people were terrified of nuclear war. Lacking a long-term perspective, young Americans lived lives of great anxiety that bordered on desperation, even though objective evidence did not support extreme fear. Psychic anxiety required religious reassurance, but existing religions failed to heal. "Do your own thing," wrote the hippie journalist Jerry Hopkins. "Be what you are. If you don't know what you are, find out." Youth was ripe for a religious revival, but the inadequacy of existing religious institutions propelled a spiritual longing that brought a search for spirituality from nonorthodox sources, whether psychedelic drugs or Eastern religions.[31]

The spiritual quest was never systematic. Like the Beats and beatniks, hippies knew what they disliked – orthodox, traditional religion. In the Sixties the young had only a vague idea of what they wanted. They took LSD to gain insights that they believed would inform the necessary spiritual search, but in pursuing

[30] On Dass see Colette Dowling, "Confessions of an American Guru," *New York Times Magazine*, December 4, 1977, 41ff; Don Lattin, *The Harvard Psychedelic Club* (New York, 2010), 115–18, 149–58. On Leary see Lattin, *Harvard Psychedelic Club*, 119–26, 131–3; Greenfield, *Leary*, 226–32, 279–90, 297–307, 342–3, 370–3.

[31] Warren Hinckle quoted in his "Hippies," 17; Hopkins in Zimmerman, *Counterculture Kaleidoscope*, 13. In general see Robert S. Ellwood, *The Sixties Spiritual Awakening* (New Brunswick, NJ, 1994); James J. Farrell, *The Spirit of the Sixties* (New York, 1997); Steven M. Tipton, *Getting Saved from the Sixties* (Berkeley, 1982).

spirituality, they mostly rejected existing religious systems. To adopt a system would be to substitute a new orthodoxy for the existing orthodoxy, which would inhibit further explorations and change. Disinterested in theology, philosophy, or other organized thought, hippies borrowed methods to express feelings or handle emotions from various non-Western religions. Individual spirituality came from the quest for authenticity. Gary Snyder advocated Zen Buddhism's meditation; Alan Watts favored "Beat Zen" to throw off repression. Hippies mixed Zen practices with Mahayana Buddhism, which stressed unity of material and spiritual worlds, and Tantric Hinduism, which promoted sex.[32]

Native American shamans were also favored, especially if they used peyote or "magic" mushrooms. Carlos Castaneda, an anthropology graduate student at UCLA, tracked down Don Juan, a native healer in a remote part of Mexico. Castaneda, unlike many hippies, wanted more than to sample the shaman's drugs. Rather, he asked Don Juan, a Yaqui Indian, to teach Castaneda to become a shaman. The elder resisted, which the pupil interpreted as an expression of Don Juan's desire to prevent his secrets from falling into an outsider's hands. Later, after Castaneda had gained the leader's trust, the young American realized that Don Juan's reluctance was rooted in the shaman's fear that the rationally educated Castaneda could not handle the power of the drug-induced challenge to the Western belief system that the healer accepted. In the end, potent drugs and clashing worldviews caused Castaneda to have a shattering, life-altering experience.[33]

Exotic travel allowed escape from an oppressive present and made possible transformation of the self. Favorite destinations included Marrakesh, the Ganges River in India, and the mountains of Nepal. Spiritual seekers went for low costs, cheap drugs, and the presence of religious holy men. Memories were not always fond. About young Americans in Nepal, Kate Coleman recalled, "Almost everyone I met was a seeker and a moron."

[32] Zimmerman, *Counterculture Kaleidoscope*, 133–4.
[33] Carlos Castaneda, *The Teachings of Don Juan* (Berkeley, 1968).

Perhaps it was better to stay home and found a new religious group: Children of God, Hare Krishnas, Brotherhood of the Source, Brotherhood of the Sun, Synanon (which used faith and community to end drug addiction), Unification Church, People's Temple (Jim Jones, who later poisoned his followers), Church of All Worlds (followers of Robert Heinlein's *Strangers in a Strange Land*), or the Love Israel Family. They started as Dionysian hippies in the Haight, became Jesus Freaks, and resettled as primitive Christians in the Pacific Northwest.[34]

The counterculture challenged not only orthodox religion but also orthodox views about society, politics, and individual psychology. Hippies were big fans of the radical Scots psychiatrist R. D. Laing. In the widely read *The Politics of Experience* (1967), he argued that mental illness did not truly exist. Rather, the concept was entirely a political construct of a deeply disturbed society. If a person was maladjusted, it was not due, as Freud had argued, to problems in the womb or with parents in childhood. Rather, the problem was the deep alienation of the self that was natural in present-day society. The self-preservation of the existing order required the political system to incarcerate nonconformists, including drug users, in mental hospitals.

Some in the counterculture preferred science-based therapeutic systems to work out their needs. Abraham Maslow's Human Potential Movement was rooted in Viennese psychiatry, which continued to enjoy prestige in the Sixties. Maslow's emphasis on the need for individual self-transformation resonated with hippies. Frederic Perls's Gestalt Therapy offered a similar promise. Perls said, "Do your own thing." In contrast, Werner Erhardt's seminar training, popularly called EST, stressed the need for self-control. After caffeinating recruits on coffee, EST refused to allow them to go to the restroom. Being able to endure the resultant discomfort was taken as proof of the triumph of self over

---

[34] J. Anthony Lukas, "Beatniks Flock to Nepal," *New York Times*, December 26, 1966, 1, 11; Ralph Blumenthal, "In Tangier," *New York Times*, December 26, 1966, 1, 10; Joshua Eppinger Jr., "Exploring the Road to Marrakesh," *San Francisco Sunday Examiner-Chronicle*, December 7, 1969, T4; Coleman interview in Hayes, ed., *Tripping*, 228; MacFarlane, *Hippie Narrative*, 99–100.

a primitive biological function. Drugs were welcome in many therapeutic systems. The principal place for exploration was the Esalen Institute at Big Sur, California. Joan Baez lived there for a time, and Bob Dylan satirized the setting in "Desolation Row."[35]

Hippies also escaped from mainstream values with the fiction they read. They devoured J. R. R. Tolkein's *Lord of the Rings*, which gained huge sales when published in the United States in 1965. A retreat to Middle Earth meant living a mental life inside a moral world devoid of Western hypocrisy and confusion. Hippies also read Herman Hesse, especially the novel *Siddhartha*. A German writer, Hesse had absorbed the East as an idea signifying a state of soul. This technique plunged the self into an exotic cultural milieu in which counterculture adherents could free themselves from mainstream values. But exoticism could also be guilt-driven, a search for mystic primitivism, or a form of neocolonialism. In the Sixties youthful Americans were looking for salvation by seeking out the "other," for example, by wearing headbands to become white Indians, by embracing Eastern religious practices, or by becoming a Hindu or Zen mystic. India particularly appealed because it represented a "third way" in the Cold War. The adoption of Indian otherness enabled an indirect comment on politics.[36]

The counterculture also used non-Western music to sidestep the mainstream. For example, Jefferson Airplane's "White Rabbit" (1966) opened with an exotic section that resembled Ravel's "Bolero," which was widely played on radio during the Sixties. "Bolero" was exotic because of its flamenco flavor. While the "Bolero" motive in "White Rabbit" was proudly macho, the guitar solo was seductive, intoxicating, and almost uncontrollable. Grace Slick's vocal line mimicked the guitar's thrusts and turns. Lyrics urged being otherworldly by taking drugs and withdrawing from society. Slick's words conquered the "Bolero" line,

[35] Barbara Ehrenreich, *The Hearts of Men* (New York, 1984), 88–94 (quote at 94); Robert V. Daniels, *Year of the Heroic Guerrilla* (New York, 1989), 61. See also Jeffrey J. Kripal, *Esalen* (Chicago, 2007).
[36] Zimmerman, *Counterculture Kaleidoscope*, 61–4, 88–90.

which suddenly switched to European harmony. In other words, Alice's drug world felt most comfortable when Western harmony intruded. The final admonition to hallucinate took place over Western harmony. But the ending provided no resolution and no clarification. Slick signaled individual discovery, but danger, too. The song suggested escalation with no end in sight – precisely where the United States was headed in Vietnam in 1966.[37]

In many respects, 1967 marked the peak of the hippie movement, which was strange in two respects. The idea had barely existed or been noticed in 1966, and hippies continued to be important, even growing in numbers in 1968 and 1969, and then the movement trailed off in the 1970s. Most articles about hippies in major newspapers appeared between 1967 and 1970. But 1967 was important for another reason. San Francisco experienced the "Summer of Love," and thousands of hippies, many of them teenage runaways and bored high school students, crowded into the Haight to listen to music, have sex, and take drugs, especially LSD. An estimated seventy-five thousand young people passed through San Francisco that summer. Most stayed only a week or two. A crash pad for runaways opened, but many hippies chose to live on the street, which became dangerous, as thugs moved into the area, especially late at night. A free hotline was set up, so parents could try to contact children, and so children could reassure parents that they were safe.[38]

---

[37] Zimmerman, *Counterculture Kaleidoscope*, 65–75; Simon Reynolds essay in Grunenberg, ed., *Summer of Love*, 155.

[38] This conclusion is based on an electronic search of articles about hippies in the *New York Times*, *Los Angeles Times*, *Washington Post*, *Chicago Tribune*, and *Seattle Times*. On the Haight see Richard Goldstein, "A Reason for Hippies," *San Francisco Chronicle*, June 5, 1967, 1, 12–13; Jack Viets, "Hippies Begin Their Summer of Love," *San Francisco Chronicle*, June 22, 1967, 1, 14; Carolyn Anspacher, "Hippies in Danger," *San Francisco Chronicle*, June 27, 1967, 1, 12; Jeff Jassen, "Violence Flares on Street of Love," *Berkeley Barb*, June 2, 1967, 1; Hunter S. Thompson, "The Hashbury Is the Capital of the Hippies," *New York Times Magazine*, May 14, 1967, 14ff. See also Nicholas von Hoffman's fifteen-part series in the *Washington Post*, October 15–29, 1967. The seventy-five thousand estimate is in Terry H. Anderson, *The Sixties* (New York, 1999), 98. On the phone hotline see George Gilbert, "Hot Line between Hip and Straight," *San Francisco Chronicle*, July 10, 1967, 1, 11.

Media hype, including reports in *Time* and *Newsweek*, helped inundate the Haight that summer. So did the music industry. When the pop singer Scott McKenzie sang, "San Francisco (Be Sure to Wear Flowers in Your Hair)," a national hit single on radio in May 1967, the lure only grew. After McKenzie's success, other bands tried to get a hit by reprising the idea, including Eric Burdon's "San Francisco Nights." Local bands, such as the Grateful Dead and the Jefferson Airplane, played free concerts in Golden Gate Park, but they took to doing so with little public announcement out of fear of attracting uncontrollable crowds. Jerry Garcia, who sympathized with the idea of free concerts and shared the hippie opposition to capitalist greed, found his band financially strapped and became annoyed at the idea that every performance had to be free.[39]

Despite the hoopla and excitement that pulled young people into the Haight, the reality could be grim indeed, especially for the naïve, unsophisticated, and very young. In addition to marijuana and LSD, there was a great deal of speed on the street during the Summer of Love. Chester Anderson of the Haight hippie bulletin warned: "Pretty little sixteen-year-old middle-class chick comes to the Haight to see what it's all about and gets picked up by a seventeen-year-old street dealer who spends all day shooting her full of speed again and again, then feeds her 3,000 mikes [of LSD] and raffles off her temporarily unemployed body for the biggest Haight Street gang bang since the night before last."[40]

For many hippies, the high point of the summer took place not in the Haight but at the Monterey Pop Festival. Prominent bands, such as the Mamas and the Papas and Jefferson Airplane played, but the event became legendary because of knockout performances by two new superstars, Jimi Hendrix and Janis Joplin. A native of Seattle, Hendrix was a self-taught guitar player who had earned his chops on the black southern "chitlin circuit." Now he broke through to astonish an almost entirely white

---

[39] "The Hippies," *Time*, July 7, 1967, 22ff; "The Hippies Are Coming," *Newsweek*, June 12, 1967, 28–9; Garcia in Troy, *Captain Trips*, 104.

[40] Anderson in Thorne Dreyer, "Love and Haight," Austin *Rag*, June 5, 1967, 1.

audience with a strange, loud, and electrifying style of play that was uniquely his own. While some antics, such as playing a guitar upside down, or behind the back, were standard techniques among top artists in African American clubs, they had not been seen before by most of the audience. Hendrix draped himself in brightly colored clothes and beads like a hippie, but his garb also expressed black pride. Self-indulgent in drugs and sex, he can rightly be seen as the first black hippie, a label he acquired in London, where his superstardom had originated.[41]

Janis Joplin, backed by Big Brother, sang her heart out in some of the top performances of her short career. Largely as a result of the Monterey show, Big Brother signed with Columbia Records and their second album, *Cheap Thrills* (1968), became the first San Francisco album to top the charts. Unlike other San Francisco performers, Joplin had Texas roots, including familiarity with black music in churches and honky-tonks as well as her own prior singing experience in Austin. There was more bluesy pain in her songs than in those of any other white performer. The pain was real. Desperately unhappy with her conventional middle-class family, she fled to San Francisco both to make it musically and to live in a less suffocating environment. However, Joplin failed to find real happiness, because of her addictions and her complicated bisexuality. Alcohol and pills were a witch's brew. Like Hendrix, she overdosed on drugs in 1970.[42]

Los Angeles produced its own music for tripping. While the Beach Boys dropped their earlier surf music to catch the psychedelic wave, the big talent was Jim Morrison, a one-time beach bum in the Los Angeles hippie haven of Venice. Calling his group the Doors in honor of Aldous Huxley's book about psychedelics, Morrison defied convention by including songs that openly promoted drugs. In contrast with San Francisco Acid Rock's riffs,

[41] On the Festival see Zimmerman, *Counterculture Kaleidoscope*, 15–17; Ralph J. Gleason, "Memories of a Pop Festival," *San Francisco Sunday Examiner-Chronicle*, June 25, 1967, Datebook, 29. On Hendrix see Charles R. Cross, *Room Full of Mirrors* (New York, 2005), 190–6; "It's Jimi Hendrix," *Rolling Stone*, March 9, 1968, 12–13.

[42] On Joplin see Alice Echols, *Scars of Sweet Paradise* (New York, 1999), 161–76.

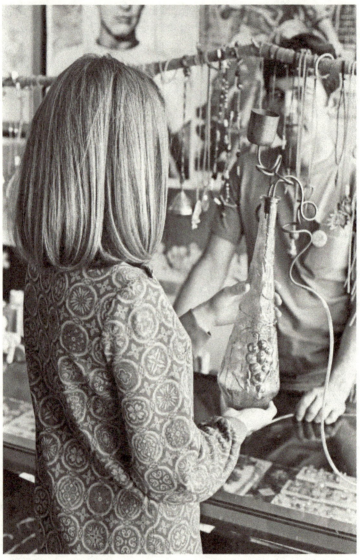

FIGURE 7. In 1967 a woman customer inspected drug paraphernalia at a head shop in Los Angeles.

Los Angeles Times Photographic Archive, Library Special Collections, Charles E. Young Research Library, UCLA.

improvisations, feedback, and weird distortions, the Doors offered polished, calculated, and formulaic songs. "All I sensed," said Garcia, "was sham." The use of a harmonic keyboard gave the music a commercial quality that offended many hippies, but this very trait considerably broadened the appeal to reach those for whom Acid Rock had sounded too strange. Morrison urged listeners to "Break on Through (To the Other Side)." His lyrics consistently glorified psychedelic drug use as the key to life, an idea that seemed less convincing after he died of an overdose in 1971.[43]

The East Coast produced its own hippie music, albeit a different, darker strand. New York's gray skies, gritty streets, and urban tensions, noted by the Mamas and the Papas in "California Dreamin'" (1966), led some observers to doubt that there could be any hippies in Gotham. Ed Sanders, a counter-culture poet in Greenwich Village, founded the Fugs. Unlike the California groups, the Fugs defiantly used obscene lyrics to challenge authority. They also sneered at mainstream politics with the song "Kill for Peace" (1966). Although this provocation did not square with the usual hippie proclamation of universal love, New Yorkers liked edginess. Andy Warhol created the Velvet Underground, but Lou Reed's music was not accessible to the average listener. Warhol's esoteric light shows gave the Velvets a following, and they were filmed in the world's first qua-drophonic rock videos. Songs such as "Heroin," however, were hardly psychedelic.[44]

[43] Garcia in Gans, ed., *Conversations with the Dead*, 63. On Morrison see Jerry Hopkins, "The Rolling Stone Interview: Jim Morrison," *Rolling Stone*, July 26, 1969, 15–18, 22; *The Doors* (1991 film), directed by Oliver Stone.

[44] On the absence of hippies in New York see Paul Morrissey of the Fugs and Ultra Violet in Richard A. Ogar, "Warhol Mind Warp," *Berkeley Barb*, September 1, 1967, 9. On the Fugs see Ed Sanders, *Tales of Beatnik Glory* (2nd ed., New York, 1990); Carlo McCormick essay in Grunenberg and Harris, eds., *Summer of Love*, 223–38; Gair, *American Counterculture*, 172–3. On the Velvets see Victor Bockris, *The Life and Death of Andy Warhol* (New York, 1989), 181–8; Gair, *American Counterculture*, 173, 197; Branden W. Smith essay in Grunenberg and Harris, eds., *Summer of Love*, 237–68.

The most important New York contribution to the new music came from the hit musical *Hair* (1967). Created by Galt MacDermot, Gerome Ragni, and James Rado as an off-Broadway production, this sensational show moved in 1968 to the big stage and played for four years. The musical's hero was Claude, a high school dropout who became a hippie living on the streets of New York. A groovy kid drawn to rock, he embraced counter-culture values of peace, love, and faith in a brighter future. The naïve Claude believed that because he believed in God that he was protected from evil, but he was drafted into the Vietnam War and killed. This grim tale, totally drenched in euphoric music from "The Age of Aquarius," sent the audience a caution-ary message about the dangers that might come from unthink-ingly embracing the hippie life. Like the Fugs, *Hair* introduced politics into the counterculture.[45]

Perhaps the best known musical prophets of psychedel-ics were the Beatles. Their early interest in Indian religion and music affirmed a spiritual quest, which was often associated with drugs. Although the cover of *Rubber Soul* (1965) featured bul-bous psychedelic lettering, it was hard to detect that "Norwegian Wood" might refer to marijuana. "Tomorrow Never Knows" on *Revolver* (1966) used a line from Leary's *Psychedelic Experience*. John Lennon had read the book while high on LSD. For a long time the British superstars sang about drugs in code to avoid being banned from radio. Then came *Sgt. Pepper's Lonely Hearts Club Band* (1967). "Lucy in the Sky with Diamonds" gave a hint, and "A Day in the Life" concluded with a call to turn on. After Leary heard the album, he said, "My work is finished. Now, it's out." Two weeks after the album release, Paul McCartney revealed that he had dropped acid. "It opened my eyes," he said. "We use only one-tenth of our brains." John Lennon and George Harrison then admitted their own use of LSD. Employing a global satellite hook-up to five hundred million people in thirty-one countries,

---

[45] The show transcript is in Galt MacDermot, *Hair* (New York, 1969). Also important are the off-Broadway and Broadway cast recordings. The later film is inauthentic and mediocre.

the Beatles shortly afterward embraced a main counterculture idea by singing, "All You Need Is Love." *Magical Mystery Tour* (1967) suggested that the Beatles were completely devoted to psychedelia.[46]

Ignoring lollipop dreams and marmalade skies, the Rolling Stones responded to the Beatles with their own dark psychedelic album, *Their Satanic Majesties Request* (1967). If psychedelics opened the doors of perception, broke on through to the other side, and challenged everything, then these boundary-obliterating drugs blurred good and evil: ethics were now situational. In a decidedly postpsychedelic song, "Sympathy for the Devil" (1968), Mick Jagger presented the devil's viewpoint in a way that jarred any listener who had been brought up with traditional Judeo-Christian teachings. Was this gray moral conclusion the ultimate contribution of psychedelics and the new music to the new social order? As tripping surged, so did interest in magic, astrology, and the occult. In the Haight, witches and warlocks began to make public appearances.[47]

For Bob Dylan, who had taken LSD in 1964, songwriting in the psychedelic age shifted from the political to the personal. Lyrics on *Bringing It All Back Home* (1965) and *Highway 61 Revisited* (1965) did not offer explanation. Rather, they opened possibilities of meaning for the listener by extinguishing thought and surrendering to despair. This appeal to the senses instead of reason mirrored the blues, which worked through contradictions not intellectually but bodily and with feelings. Bluesy emptiness, when combined with psychedelics, could produce redemption. The final verse of "Mr. Tambourine Man" suggested tripping on the beach close to nature to forget one's sorrows. "Like a Rolling Stone" revealed the power of voodoo, shamans, and psychedelics.

[46] Philip Norman, *Shout!* (rev. ed., New York, 2013), 334 (McCartney quote); Greenfield, *Leary*, 312 (Leary quote).

[47] Robert Christgau, "The Rolling Stones," *The Rolling Stone Illustrated History of Rock and Roll*, ed. Jim Miller (2nd ed., New York, 1980), 190–200. On the occult see Robert Hurwitt, "Love-Quake Solstice Foreseen," *Berkeley Barb*, June 16, 1967, 3; Leo Laurence, "Death of Hip," *Berkeley Barb*, October 13, 1967, 5.

Describing a world that youth despised, Dylan used vivid images rather than the mind. In "Ballad of a Thin Man," the narrator mocked Mister Jones for not understanding that the narrator was high. Other performers swept into the psychedelic craze included Donovan ("Mellow Yellow"), the Byrds ("Eight Miles High"), and Country Joe McDonald ("Colors for Susan").[48]

"Drug song lyrics," argued the journalist Warren Hinckle, "may, in fact, be the entire literary output of the hippie generation." Heads were, to quote the communication theorist Marshall McLuhan, "post-literate." Previous generations, since the eighteenth-century Enlightenment, had approached life by using reasoned words. In mainstream culture, law and social order were preserved by ideas rooted in language and by the use of precise language in agreed-upon fashion. A great deal of traditional culture was based upon faith in the solidity of language. Hippies, however, distrusted both traditional culture and the words that were used to defend it. Accordingly, they disdained traditional writing precisely because they perceived that it chained them to a past that they did not want. Not only was the written word linear, which implied scientific progression, but reading was solitary, depending upon the reader personally to interact with the words. Freaks wanted emotionally charged language that vicariously massaged feelings, and they preferred group activities enhanced by electronic sound.[49]

At the deepest level, the hippie crisis was a crisis of belief. Amid the crumbling of social, cultural, and political verities that they no longer accepted, freaks searched desperately to give their own lives new meaning. During periods of stable beliefs, all but minor challenges to orthodoxy would be considered deviance or heresy, but when a great cultural unfolding is underway, as was true in the Sixties, challenges are acceptable and quickly become rife. The collapse of stability drives those who need structure away

---

[48] On Dylan see Bromell, *Tomorrow Never Knows*, 47, 52, 60, 130–9; Barry Shank, "That Wild Mercury Sound: Bob Dylan and the Illusion of American Culture," *Boundary 2* 29:1 (Spring 2002), 97–123. On psychedelic songs see Keith interview in Hayes, ed., *Tripping*, 236; Pete Johnson, "Pills and Pop Music," *Los Angeles Times*, July 30, 1967, 1, 19.

[49] Hinckle, "Hippies," 19.

from traditional pathways. One possible outcome is to become a hermit, but the other possibility, and it was the path that hippies chose in the Sixties, is the use of emotional language, the adoption of romantic ideas, and the embrace of Dionysian hedonism as a way of life. Rock music encoded all of these countercultural desires. Hippies were no more irrational than the poets Shelley, Byron, and Keats, who took up romanticism in response to the break-up of the Enlightenment worldview in the aftermath of the Napoleonic Wars.[50]

The Human Be-In had been advertised as "The Gathering of the Tribes." By 1967 hippies had begun to express a growing interest in Native Americans, and particularly in the use of the psychedelic cactus peyote as a sacred religious rite. Many people were leery of LSD because it was a strong chemical substance. Fears about long-term damage from its use were widely expressed in the mid-Sixties, and for a time the government claimed that acid caused genetic defects. The same claims could not be made for "magic" mushrooms or peyote, both of which had been used by native inhabitants of the Americas for thousands of years. Both of these psychedelic substances were restricted within tribal cultures to use for religious purposes, and both substances contained impurities that caused nausea or vomiting prior to or during the psychedelic trip. This high price of admission made the drug more solemn; side effects were too serious to imagine mushrooms or peyote as recreational drugs taken for fun. Instead, both substances met spiritual needs.[51]

The U.S. government had recognized the religious significance of peyote by allowing members of certain tribes to use the otherwise banned substance for religious purposes under the protection of the First Amendment to the U.S. Constitution. A number

---

[50] Nathan Adler, "The Antinomian Personality: The Hippie Character Type," *Psychiatry: Journal for the Study of Interpersonal Processes* 31:4 (November 1968), 325–38.

[51] On genetic defects see Richard D. Lyons, "Genetic Damage Linked to LSD," *New York Times*, March 17, 1967, 43, 46; John N. Wilford, "LSD Again Linked to Genetic Harm," *New York Times*, January 4, 1968, 28. On peyote see Hayes, ed., *Tripping*, 49–51, 185–91, 269–72, 397–400; Gaskin, *Haight Ashbury Flashbacks*, 68–74.

of peyote users had then created the Native American Church
to seek a similar protection for users who did not belong to a
tribe recognized to have the right to use peyote. The courts were
ambivalent about the Native American Church's claim to lawful
use of peyote, but members did gradually gain a right to peyote under limited conditions. The government could seize peyote
from church members, if the cactus was destined to be sold to
or used by outsiders. Hippies flocked to New Mexico, in part, to
join the Native American Church, or to learn from its members
how to use peyote for spiritual purposes.[52]

Throughout American history, many whites had despised
American Indians. Hippies expressed a great reversal: they
despised mainstream culture and embraced Native American
culture precisely because it was perceived to be oppositional to
mainstream values. If ordinary Americans approved of dams,
drove on highways, and lived in suburbs, then Indians were
praised, correctly or not, for resisting "improvements," respecting
the land, and being exceptionally close to nature. When Charles
Artman, the son of a Methodist minister, a college dropout, and
a homeless hippie, erected a teepee on public land in Berkeley,
California, he proclaimed his disbelief in government, any form
of land ownership, and white society. Artman saw himself as in a
similar condition to the native inhabitants of the local area who
had been dispossessed by whites in the earliest (Spanish) stage of
white settlement.[53]

Not everyone approved of the hippie infatuation with Native
Americans. Rupert Costo, a member of the Cahuilla Band,
denounced hippies: "It is the way of the Bum." Buffy St. Marie,
the Canadian-born folksinger who was half-Cree, also objected.

---

[52] On the Native American Church see Sigurd Ozols, "Charlie Brown and
the Peyote Raid," *Berkeley Barb*, August 20, 1965, 2; ad, *Berkeley Barb*,
January 20, 1967, 8; Smith, *Hippies, Indians, and the Fight for Red Power*,
47–8, 67–76.

[53] On the reversal see Tom Engelhardt, *The End of Victory Culture* (New York,
1995). On Artman see W. J. Rorabaugh, *Berkeley at War* (New York, 1989),
134–5; Smith, *Hippies, Indians, and the Fight for Red Power*, 78–9; Sydney
Kossen, "LSD Priest Runs for Berkeley City Council," *Washington Post*,
February 19, 1967, M1.

"It doesn't make any sense to me," she explained, "these kids trying to be Indians. They'll never be Indians. The white people never seem to realize they cannot suck the soul out of a race." The hippie borrowing of Indian dress, values, or habits, including the use of peyote or mushrooms, appalled her. Not only could the borrowing never work, because whites, in St. Marie's ethnocentric worldview, lacked the capacity to be anything but white, but the attempt to be Indian threatened the psychic existence of real natives. Whites were "soul suckers." She continued, "It's the weirdest vampire idea. It's very perverted." St. Marie's problem, she finally explained, was "that people are always trying to identify with a race they've conquered." Neocolonialism was the root of her complaint.[54]

By 1967 hippies who lived communally began to talk about themselves as tribes. They thought of themselves as analogous to American Indians because they believed themselves to be *inside* the United States but not truly *of* the United States. But the claim of tribal identity meant more than "acting Indian." Hippies knew that they were not Indians, and that their behavior would not turn them into Indians. Hippies were, in fact, disaffected young middle-class whites. The use of a tribal identity referenced Indians, whom hippies admired for being apart from mainstream culture and for using peyote, but the assertion of a tribal identity also suggested that individual hippies could band together in small-scale units to avoid the anomie that had afflicted the more individualistic and anarchic Beats. To a hippie, a tribe consisted of a small number of people who shared ideas, goods, and space. A tribe was larger than a nuclear family, but it was smaller than a neighborhood. A tribe might be the inhabitants of a communal house, or it might be a loosely affiliated group that lived in several distinct spots. Hippies, like Indians, were not all alike. Hippies disagreed among themselves about many issues, which necessitated many distinct hippie tribes. And hippies believed

[54] Rupert Costo, "Hippies Are NOT American Indians," *San Francisco Sunday Examiner-Chronicle*, June 25, 1967, Datebook, 26; John Bryan, "Buffy on Hippies," *Berkeley Barb*, June 30, 1967, 10.

that nonhippies, including racial minorities, could have tribes, too. Hence, the call for the Be-In urged the "Gathering of the Tribes."[55]

As millions of young Americans embraced the counter-culture, in whole or in part, during the late Sixties, ordinary Americans grew increasingly uncomfortable. The whole culture seemed to be in upheaval. Hippies used this time of anxiety to argue that mainstream Americans should accept the presence of the emerging counterculture. The principal basis of the claim, as with so many other things involving baby boomers, was sheer numbers. One of the most popular buttons at the time read simply "We Are Everywhere." If hippies came together in large numbers at one location at a particular time, the estab-lishment would be forced to make concessions. Furthermore, large-scale mobilization gave hippies heart, because it showed everyone how many counterculture adherents there were. Finally, such a mass assemblage could encourage more young people to become hippies.

The easiest way to bring hippies together in unprecedented numbers was to stage a spectacular rock concert featuring prom-inent musicians. The event would enable individuals to affirm authenticity, express spirituality, and show community, an idea that was gaining importance inside the counterculture. "Rock 'n' roll," said Paul Kantner of the Jefferson Airplane, "is the new form of communication for our generation." Michael Lang was a Brooklyn-born resident of Miami who had already enjoyed success owning an early head shop. After he filled a race track in Miami in 1968 with a concert organized on short notice, he conceived of an even larger outdoor concert in Woodstock, New York in August 1969. Lang had familiarity with Woodstock, which was on the edge of the Jewish entertainment district in the Catskills. It was ninety-eight miles from New York City, which was close enough to attract hordes of youths from the heavily

---

[55] On the tribal concept see Leland Meyerzove, "A Psalm upon the Gathering of All Tribes," *San Francisco Oracle*, #5, January 1967, 7; Steve Levine, "A Gathering of the Tribes," *San Francisco Oracle*, #6, February 1967, 9.

populated suburbs. The site was less than a day's drive from Boston or Washington.[56]

If Lang could rent a large pasture in this cow-grazing area, he could build a huge stage with an unprecedented sound system. Attendance might top two hundred thousand. With that many tickets sold, prices could be low, but performers could be paid well. Jimi Hendrix topped the list at $30,000. Fans could sleep in tents on the ground during warm summer weather. To attract a crowd, he would feature all the major bands. They would come because the event was too important to miss. Food, drink, and drugs would be plentiful. He did not need to organize the supply of acid. In a cleverly designed poster with a dove and a guitar, the festival promised "Three Days of Peace and Music." To signal that the festival was not a rock concert, the band names were printed in small type. "Woodstock was like a big picnic party," said Ravi Shankar, "and the music was incidental." Everyone would have a blast, and no one would ever forget the event.[57]

Woodstock almost did not take place. Lang failed to understand the fear of hippies in small-town America. The town of Woodstock, home to Bob Dylan, flatly refused to issue a permit, and after nearby Wallkill rejected a proposal, Lang found himself in the unenviable position of having signed contracts with bands but without any place to hold the concert. Posters and tickets had already been printed using the Woodstock name, so the festival was destined to keep the name. Woodstock ultimately took place in nearby Bethel, New York, because of Lang's determination, because Max Yasgur, a local farmer willing to rent his land, believed in the festival, and because Elliot Tiber, the countercultural son of a local motel owner, controlled the Chamber of Commerce, which under the town's rules, issued permits for cultural events. When the town council threatened to cancel the

[56] Michael Lang with Holly George-Warren, *The Road to Woodstock* (New York, 2009), 19–27, 44, 49; Mike Evans and Paul Kingsbury, *Woodstock* (New York, 2009), 8, 27 (Kantner quote).

[57] Lang, *Road to Woodstock*, 53–6, 60–1, 86; Evans and Kingsbury, *Woodstock*, 52, 89 (Shankar quote), 251.

festival, Lang used charm, money, and legal threats to keep the ball rolling.[58]

The Woodstock Festival took place on August 15–17, 1969. Although Lang presold 186,000 tickets, more than twice as many people showed up. Unarmed off-duty police provided security. The roads were so clogged that some musicians had to be flown to the stage by helicopter. The crowd quickly tore down the fence to create a "free" concert. Despite the fact that many concertgoers could get no closer than half a mile to the stage, all could see the elevated platform, and everyone could hear the concert. The sound system was the largest one ever constructed to that date. There were two seventy-foot speaker towers, sixteen speakers, and two thousand amps of power. Hugh Romney ("Wavy Gravy") of the Hog Farm was in charge of food, but his rural commune was overwhelmed by sheer numbers. On Saturday he greeted everyone, "Good morning! What we have in mind is breakfast in bed for four hundred thousand." Food ran out, and townspeople supplied homemade sandwiches. Although six hundred portable toilets had been provided, they were inadequate in number. Drugs did not run out, but the brown LSD tablets made many people dizzy. Aid stations for drug overdoses worked long hours.[59]

During much of the concert, it rained. The speaker towers attracted lightning, and the performers had to stop during the storms. Jerry Garcia got a bad shock. The Dead were stoned when they performed. The crowd was muddy but happy. High points of the concert were Country Joe McDonald of Berkeley leading the "Fish" cheer, and Jimi Hendrix playing "The Star-Spangled Banner" in a manner never heard before or since. The festival ended just after sunrise with a third of the fans asleep on the

---

[58] Elliot Tiber with Tom Monte, *Taking Woodstock* (Garden City Park, NY, 2007), 59–61, 84, 88, 91, 101, 134, 178, 180, 182; Lang, *Road to Woodstock*, 50–3, 109–29, 151; Evans and Kingsbury, *Woodstock*, 41, 43; "Woodstock Pop-Rock Fete Hits Snag," *New York Times*, July 17, 1969, 56; Richard F. Shepard, "Woodstock Festival Vows to Carry On," *New York Times*, July 18, 1969, 16.

[59] Evans and Kingsbury, *Woodstock*, 8, 56, 102, 104 (Romney quote), 226; Lang, *Road to Woodstock*, 98, 136, 153, 155, 200.

ground, a third zonked on drugs, and a third wanting more music. "More, more, more," they chanted in futility, in what could be considered to be a baby boomer anthem. Lang filmed the festival, but many bands refused to sign releases, so the first version of *Woodstock* (1970) skipped many major bands. These songs were added to the 1994 film, which contained forty extra minutes of music. Not everyone rose to the occasion. Jefferson Airplane, in particular, gave a limp performance. A young Martin Scorsese shot much of the film and thereby launched a career in which he became a major Hollywood director.[60]

The media paid little attention to Woodstock until the crowds clogged the roads. Then they had trouble getting reporters near the place. Much of the coverage came from freelance writers who were rock fans. While Max Yasgur lost money on his land rental, and Lang only made money in later years from film distribution and memorabilia, both were happy with the result. Yasgur noted that there were no fights, assaults, or homicides. It really was three days of peace and love. He hinted that the younger generation had something to teach their elders, which was not a message popular in town. "We felt as though it were liberated territory," one participant said. "I don't think any of us believed there were that many hippies in the U.S.A.," another noted. Lang believed that he had performed a public service. He had demonstrated that the hippie movement was not just a small number of oddballs, and that mainstream Americans would have to take into account that many of their own children had accepted the counterculture with its unique ideas about drugs, music, and spiritual seeking. One other conclusion could be drawn. Woodstock, more than any single moment in the Sixties, proved that cultural transformation was underway.[61]

---

[60] Evans and Kingsbury, *Woodstock*, 143, 170, 215; Lang, *Road to Woodstock*, 224. On the film see Scorsese foreword to Evans and Kingsbury, *Woodstock*, 6–7; Evans and Kingsbury, *Woodstock*, 244, 250; Lang, *Road to Woodstock*, 164–6.

[61] Lang, *Road to Woodstock*, 246, 251–5. On press coverage see Barnard L. Collier, "200,000 Thronging to Rock Festival," *New York Times*, August 16, 1969, 1, 31; Barnard L. Collier, "300,000 at Folk-Rock Fair," *New York*

Just a few days before the Woodstock Festival, the teenage female followers of Charles Manson, a self-styled hippie, murdered the popular (and pregnant) actress Sharon Tate and four other people at Tate's home in Benedict Canyon in Los Angeles. The mass murders, calculated by Manson to start a race war in which he imagined that he and his sex partners would be the sole survivors destined to repopulate the earth, had occurred after Manson had failed as a singer-songwriter. Listening repeatedly to the Beatles' *White Album* (1968), the dejected Manson heard voices calling him to bring wrath and destruction. At the time he was dropping LSD daily and having sex with his groupies as frequently as possible. Two years earlier, during the Summer of Love, Manson, then recently released from prison, had become a bejeaned and long-haired hippie while living in the Haight, before his relocation to Los Angeles.[62]

On Friday, December 5, 1969 Manson's groupies were disclosed publicly to be responsible for the Tate murders. Fear swept across Los Angeles whenever a long-haired male appeared. Police harassment of hippies soared. Then on the next day, Saturday, December 6, the Rolling Stones showed up to play before three hundred thousand attendees at the Altamont rock concert, about

---

Times, August 17, 1969, 1, 80; Barnard L. Collier, "Tired Rock Fans Begin Exodus," *New York Times*, August 18, 1969, 1, 25; William E. Farrell, "19-Hour Concert Ends Bethel Fair," *New York Times*, August 19, 1969, 1, 34; "Woodstock: Like it Was," *New York Times*, August 25, 1969, 1, 30; Richard Reeves, "Mike Lang Plus John Roberts Equals Woodstock," *New York Times Magazine*, September 7, 1969, 34ff; *Life*, August 1969, Woodstock Edition (Special Issue); Andrew Kopkind, "It Was Like Balling for the First Time," *Rolling Stone*, September 20, 1969, 1, 20, 23–4, 26; Griel Marcus, "The Woodstock Festival," *Rolling Stone*, September 20, 1969, 16–18; Andrew Kopkind, "Coming of Age in Aquarius," *Hard Times* (1969), in Bloom and Breines, eds., *Takin' It to the Streets*, 612–17. Participants quoted in "A Fleeting, Wonderful Moment of Community," *New Yorker* (1969), in Bloom and Breines, eds., *Takin' It to the Streets*, 609; Lang, *Road to Woodstock*, 167.

[62] On Manson see Zimmerman, *Counterculture Kaleidoscope*, 158–61; "Several Suspects and Car Hunted in 5 Coast Killings," *New York Times*, August 11, 1969, 1, 29; John Kendall, "Night of Terror," *Los Angeles Times*, July 29, 1970, 1, 3. See also Vincent Bugliosi with Curt Gentry, *Helter Skelter* (New York, 1974).

a hundred miles southeast of San Francisco. The weather was cold, wet, and windy, and the good vibes at Woodstock were nowhere to be found. Even the acid seemed to be in a bad mood. The festival organizers had hired the Hell's Angels to provide security. Soused on beer as well as who knew what else, the Angels kept pushing the crowd back from the stage. One Angel slugged Marty Balin of the Airplane. Later, while the Stones were playing, the Angels stabbed to death Meredith Hunter, a young African American who stood near the stage listening to the Stones. The Stones eventually stopped performing, and the Grateful Dead, who were the next act, refused to go on. A deeply depressed Jerry Garcia hastily retreated to San Francisco.[63]

Although psychedelic drugs, rock music, and the search for spirituality were very important to the hippie movement, they formed only one aspect of the emerging counterculture. The pursuit of authenticity and individualism included other significant dimensions. Freaks were determined to live freely, openly, and honestly, even if doing so offended the mainstream society that they despised. They hated hypocrisy, and particularly the mainstream's prudish pretensions about sexuality. The rise of

---

[63] On Manson see Charles T. Powers, "Bizarre Tale of Black Magic," *Los Angeles Times*, December 5, 1969, 1, 3; Ron Einstoss and Jerry Cohen, "Manson, Five Others Indicted," *Los Angeles Times*, December 9, 1969, 1, 30; Ron Einstoss, "Talkative Manson Arraigned," *Los Angeles Times*, December 12, 1969, 1, 24–5; Robert Stone, *Prime Green* (New York, 2007), 201–2. On Altamont see Jim Wood, "300,000 Say It with Music," *San Francisco Sunday Examiner-Chronicle*, December 7, 1969, A1, A8–A10; Jackson Runnels, "Cops Probe Four Deaths," *San Francisco Chronicle*, December 8, 1969, 1, 30; Ralph J. Gleason, "On the Town," *San Francisco Chronicle*, December 8, 1969, 49; "What to Call Altamont?" *Berkeley Barb*, December 12, 1969, 2–3; "The Kid They Killed at Altamont," *Berkeley Barb*, December 19, 1969, 1, 5–6, 13, 17; Robert A. Wright, "200,000 Attend Coast Rock Fete," *New York Times*, December 7, 1969, 85; Henry E. Weinstein, "Dodge City to Rock Accompaniment," *Wall Street Journal*, December 17, 1969, 18; Nicholas von Hoffman, "Violence at Altamont," *Washington Post*, January 2, 1970, C1, C5; "Let It Bleed," *Rolling Stone*, January 21, 1970, 18–20, 22–8, 30–2, 34, 36; John Burks, "In the Aftermath of Altamont," *Rolling Stone*, February 7, 1970, 7–8; Troy, *Captain Trips*, 129–30. See also *Gimme Shelter* (1970 film), directed by David Maysles.

the counterculture took place against a backdrop of profound changes in sexual ideas and practices that engulfed the country during the Sixties. Without those changes, the counterculture might not have occurred. As Chapter 3 shows, hippie views about sex were heavily influenced by the introduction of the birth control pill, by looser sexual mores among Americans, both hip and straight, by the emergence of new gender relations, and by the rise of feminism.

3

Bodies, Sex, and Gender

During the Sixties, mainstream sexual attitudes and practices were transformed. Americans continued along a decades-long path of throwing off Victorian prudishness. Divorce gradually increased, as did out-of-wedlock births, and sexual topics, such as abortion, were discussed more openly. At the same time, censorship of books, magazines, plays, poetry readings, and films more or less ended. The biggest changes were the invention of the birth control pill, widespread adoption of the pill by young single women, and the end of the middle-class double standard that had allowed young men much more sexual freedom than had been available to young women. At the same time, many women embraced feminism, which challenged traditional gender roles. Amid these changes, hippies occupied a paradoxical position. Freaks embraced beliefs and behaviors that shocked traditionalists, but old ways were disappearing rapidly, and to some extent hippies merely endorsed society's shift toward sexual looseness. At the same time, they showed a decided ambiguity about feminism.

Hippies worshipped the human body. The *San Francisco Oracle* called for "the freedom of the body" and "the pursuit of joy." This elemental celebration was rooted in the philosophy of the hippie counterculture. The body's existence was a matter of simple fact, and freaks reveled in facing facts openly. To do so was part of the search for authenticity. "Hippies despise phoniness; they want to be open, loving, and free," noted the counterculture journalist Hunter S. Thompson. Glorification of the body beautiful also expressed a preference for simplicity and for honesty. Nothing, including the body, should be hidden from view. To hide the body was proof of impure motives. Mainstream culture's prudish attitude toward the body was proof of its corruption. Nudity expressed purity. Allen Ginsberg declared that his poetry was about "naked personal subjective truth." To purge corruption, one must return to the Garden of Eden to embrace naked Adam and Eve. In "Woodstock," the singer-songwriter Joni Mitchell yearned to return to the garden.[1]

Freaks wanted to strip away society's cultural baggage, and that included the body being covered with conventional clothes. The rock group Moby Grape asked whether it was acceptable to walk in the street "Naked, If I Want To" (1967). The song expressed both authenticity and individual choice. In "Lather" (1968), Grace Slick of the Jefferson Airplane sang about a thirty-year-old male who wanted to be naked at the beach. Admiration of the body also expressed preference for the natural over the man-made, in a society given to material excess. Hunter Thompson added, "They reject the plastic pretense of Twentieth-Century America, preferring to go back to the natural life." The natural was perceived to be the most authentic. This countercultural attitude toward human anatomy contrasted with mainstream squeamishness about showing certain body parts, particularly sexual parts, or public discussion of most bodily functions. "Being sexy," wrote the best-selling author Helen Gurley Brown, "means that you accept all the parts of your body as worthy and loveable."[2]

---

[1] *Oracle* in Sandy Troy, *Captain Trips* (New York, 1994), 95; Hunter S. Thompson, "The Hashbury Is the Capital of the Hippies," *New York Times Magazine*, May 14, 1967, 29; Allen Ginsberg, *Howl: Original Draft Facsimile*, ed. Barry Miles (New York, 1986), 156; Mitchell in Hugh Gardner, *The Children of Prosperity* (New York, 1978), 17.

[2] Thompson, "Hashbury Is the Capital of the Hippies," 29; Brown in David Allyn, *Make Love, Not War* (Boston, 2000), 20.

Hippies were fascinated with nudity, which increased throughout American society in the Sixties. As censorship declined, nonpornographic nude drawings appeared in art books; major museums removed fig leaves from sculptures. In 1964 topless female dancers, some with enhanced breasts, appeared in clubs in North Beach in San Francisco, and avant-garde plays like Michael McClure's *The Beard* (1965) offered nude or faux nude scenes on stage. Foreign language "art" films that included nudity circulated in obscure movie theaters. The Swedish film *I Am Curious (Yellow)* (1967), in which a colored overlay partially obscured nudity and sex, played to packed houses. *Hair* (1967) opened off-Broadway in New York with one nude scene that teased the audience with shadowy lighting, and *Oh! Calcutta* (1969) was the first Broadway play to feature fully-lighted frontal nudity for the entire cast. At one Airplane concert, Grace Slick spontaneously stripped to the waist and sang.[3]

To feel natural, hippies often walked inside their homes naked. "An at-home entertainment," reported Hunter Thompson, "is nude parties at which celebrants paint designs on each other." They liked to sunbathe nude in the backyard or on the apartment rooftop. Depending upon the particular view, neighbors did not always mind, but some objected to their children seeing such sights. Freaks found this puzzling, because children liked going naked. Only adults were uptight about the sight of human flesh. Hippies who lived in communes often went nude. One freak explained, "We were down to rags anyway." Hippies also confronted social norms by stripping in public, for example, at Be-Ins, or by skinny-dipping in a pond. In the documentary film about the Woodstock festival, one can easily spot the real hippies. The authentic, full-time devotees of the counterculture, when stripped, were suntanned all over. The sham hippies at the concert had brown backs and white buttocks.[4]

---

[3] Allyn, *Make Love, Not War*, 25, 27, 54–70, 119–21, 127–9. Slick in Gretchen Lemke-Santangelo, *Daughters of Aquarius* (Lawrence, KS, 2009), 28.

[4] Alastair Gordon, *Spaced Out* (New York, 2008), 66; Thompson, "Hashbury Is the Capital of the Hippies," 120; freak in Lemke-Santangelo, *Daughters of Aquarius*, 71. On nudity at home see Stephen Diamond, *What the Trees Said*

FIGURE 8. In 1970 Michael McCormick was crowned "The Mud King" at the Sound Storm Music Festival in Poynette, Wisconsin. Robert Pulling. Wisconsin Historical Society, WHS-66506.

Not everyone had a backyard or a rooftop suitable for sunbathing, however, and in 1965 California hippies demanded the creation of nude beaches. When government officials, fearing a public backlash, resisted, hippies staged nude "wade-ins." These protests were among the earliest examples of hippie involvement in politics, and they revealed a developing sense of community. Shortly afterward, officially nude public beaches opened in California, including one in San Francisco, and hippies flocked there in record numbers in the mid-Sixties. Considering the cold wind that almost always blew off the Pacific Ocean, the high turnout was surprising. A confused clothed young man who accidentally stumbled onto the nude beach at San Gregorio, south of San Francisco, fled after dozens of naked hippies surrounded him to chant, "Clothes off! Clothes off! Clothes off!"[5]

Nude beaches, of course, were party spots littered with empty beer cans and remnants of marijuana roaches. They also functioned as pick-up spots, where the merchandise, so to speak, could be fully inspected prior to any assignation. This could be seen as another example of the hippie penchant for authenticity and honesty. There were more practical aspects as well. If one went to a nude beach, it helped to bring along both an appropriate attitude and a good-looking bod. The absence of clothes removed social class signifiers. Although nudity made gender differences more pronounced, it did establish a kind of equality, at least among the well-endowed. Some regulars wore designer sunglasses to maintain social prestige. Dark glasses also made it possible to avoid unwanted eye contact.[6]

Muscle Beach at Venice in Los Angeles became famous for surfers and body builders, some of whom used heavy weights set

(New York, 1971), 19, 32, 80; Iris Keltz, *Scrapbook of a Taos Hippie* (El Paso, TX, 2000), 34, 101.

[5] Allyn, *Make Love, Not War*, 41; Terry H. Anderson, *The Movement and the Sixties* (New York, 1995), 261; "Feel Free for Nude Beach Parties, Says SFL," *Berkeley Barb*, May 13, 1966, 1; "Predicts Nude Beaches Will Bloom," *Berkeley Barb*, February 3, 1967, 3; "Crowd Cool as Fifteen Bathe Nude on SF Beach," *Berkeley Barb*, October 13, 1967, 4. The San Gregorio incident happened to an acquaintance.

[6] Lemke-Santangelo, *Daughters of Aquarius*, 72.

up at the beach. Others, including Jim Morrison of the Doors, used the beach to smoke pot. Long a home for painters, poets, and students, Venice became a hippie stronghold by 1965. Hippies were too poor to use a gym that charged fees, although some had jobs working in gyms to get a free place to work out. The running craze of the Seventies, promoted by Jim Fixx, got its start with the desire to look good. For freaks, building a beautiful bod was more a matter of odd jobs. Men gardened, dug wells, erected buildings, and cut a great deal of firewood, while women also gardened, cooked from scratch, and tended children. Physical labor, more than any planned exercise regimen, built and maintained muscles.[7]

The body was celebrated in other ways that emphasized devotion to the natural. Much to the irritation of the mainstream, hippies cared neither about dirt nor body odor, because both were thought to be natural and authentic. In the Haight, wrote one journalist, "There is a permeating odor consisting of urine, marijuana and unwashed clothing." As the first generation who had been raised on television, freaks had watched hundreds if not thousands of deodorant ads. Now they rejected deodorants as a capitalist plot to extract money from the people. Nor did soap hold a high priority among the Great Unwashed. "We equate cleanliness with unreality," one freak said. "So what do you do with the aromatic hippie?" asked the columnist James J. Kilpatrick. However, hippie women enjoyed homemade scented soaps, and both male and female freaks used body oils and lotions, including potions that could be licked. Hippies also cared for the body with massages, yoga, meditation, Tai Chi, Rolfing, hydrotherapy, and acupuncture. The body was a site for sensuality and emotional liberation. Increased body sense made sex more important.[8]

[7] Carolyn See, "Venice: Last Poor Beach," *Los Angeles Times*, November 5, 1967, B20ff. On Morrison see Jerry Hopkins and Danny Sugerman, *No One Here Gets Out Alive* (New York, 2006), 39, 53–9. James F. Fixx, *The Complete Book of Running* (New York, 1977). On physical labor see Lemke-Santangelo, *Daughters of Aquarius*, 61; Roberta Price, *Huerfano* (Amherst, MA, 2006); T. C. Boyle, *Budding Prospects* (New York, 1984).

[8] Paul Coates column, *Los Angeles Times*, September 13, 1967, 3; freak in "The Haight Ashbury Scene," *San Francisco Sunday Examiner-Chronicle*,

Hippies used their bodies to announce their countercultural identity. Men and women handled this issue somewhat differently, because their relationship to mainstream culture was not exactly the same. While Americans expected a certain amount of wildness from young men, these males were supposed to pledge conformity to social norms. Male wildness had to be exercised as "time out," like Carnival in Latin or Caribbean cultures, within an overall respect for society's rules. A passionate, momentary lapse into an inappropriate sexual escapade was forgivable, but wearing a beard or having hair so long that a guy could not get a job were outrageous because those actions were defiant, calculated, and premeditated attacks upon orthodoxy and the social contract. "Through long hair," declared the bushy radical activist Jerry Rubin, "we're engaged in a sexual assault that is going to destroy the political-economic structure of Amerikan society." (Alienated youth used "Amerika" to suggest the country was fascist.) Cultural revolution, said Abbie Hoffman, meant, "Anybody can do anything." Long hair represented this challenge.[9]

Nothing enraged older men so much as male hippies who wore long hair. Wooing older voters in his campaign for governor, Ronald Reagan said hippies "dress like Tarzan, have hair like Jane, and smell like Cheetah." One of the most frequently uttered angry male sneers of the era was: "Get a haircut." This was not friendly advice given out of concern for the well-being of the local barber, although the barber noticed that fewer young

January 1, 1967, California Living, 12; Kilpatrick column, *Seattle Times*, November 19, 1967, 12; Gilbert Zicklin, *Countercultural Communes* (Westport, CT, 1983), 6, 39; Anderson, *Movement and the Sixties*, 262; Jentri Anders, *Beyond Counterculture*, (Pullman, WA, 1990), 202–3.

9 Anderson, *Movement and the Sixties*, 255, 261. On hair see Jerry Rubin, *Do It!* (New York, 1970), 96; Dominick Cavallo, *A Fiction of the Past* (New York, 1999), 89–90 (Hoffman at 90); David Gans, ed., *Conversations with the Dead* (New York, 1991), 108; Bill Graham and Robert Greenfield, *Bill Graham Presents* (New York, 1992), 184; Diamond, *What the Trees Said*, 168; "Shave, Haircut and $200 Square Things with Hippie," *New York Times*, March 25, 1968, 65. On the Haight as a Carnival see Nadya Zimmerman, *Counterculture Kaleidoscope* (Ann Arbor, MI, 2008), 170.

FIGURE 9. In 1966 the "Generation Gap" was visible when Los Angeles police arrested a long-haired youth for drugs on the Sunset Strip.
Los Angeles Times Photographic Archive, Library Special Collections, Charles E. Young Research Library, UCLA.

men were visiting the shop. Longhairs were refused service at stores; one was not allowed to buy gasoline at a gas station. When an arrest was made, police gleefully cut hair, particularly if the victim was about to be released and the charges dropped. Did the passport photo show no beard? Then the beard had to come off before traveling abroad. In *Easy Rider* (1969), rednecks killed the hippies Dennis Hopper and Peter Fonda for being longhairs. School principals routinely measured hair length on the top of the head with a ruler and suspended thousands who failed to meet the local standard. Despite tough sanctions, long hair gradually spread from hippies to mainstream youths.[10]

The male generational fight over hair was not really about hair. "The change," wrote Tuli Kupferberg of the Fugs, "is the message." The main issue was the younger generation's failure to conform to social norms. Even youths who were not hippies were expressing a defiant individualism. It was, noted one observer, "the painful breaking-away of a new culture from an old." Older men's preference for short hair, particularly the very short buzz cut, was a generational style closely associated with military service in World War II. In choosing long hair, hippies were being defiant, choosing to be different, poking fun at their own fathers, some of whom had reached the age where long hair was no longer possible, and commenting indirectly and negatively upon military service in an era when military barbers fleeced privates. To World War II veterans, the mocking of the military was outrageous. To hippies, long hair meant showing guts and taking a stand. "We want to be identified," said one. "Yeah, it's our Boy Scout uniform," joked another. Beards also caused trouble. Robert Stone, a Navy veteran who had grown a beard in California, was harassed and beaten by truckers at a bus stop in rural Pennsylvania.[11]

[10] Beth L. Bailey, *Sex in the Heartland* (Cambridge, MA, 1999), 139 (Reagan quote), 141; Stew Albert, *Who the Hell Is Stew Albert?* (Los Angeles, 2004), 38; Christopher Gair, *The American Counterculture* (Edinburgh, Scotland, 2007), 175; Robert Greenfield, *Timothy Leary* (Orlando, FL, 2006), 320; Anderson, *Movement and the Sixties*, 249, 283. The gas station incident is in "Conoco Kidd Won't Sell Fluid to Hippy Types," Austin *Rag*, October 23, 1967, 16. On police haircuts see Thorne Dreyer, "The High Price of Hip," Austin *Rag*, February 5, 1968, 1, 8–9; "Long-Hairs Harassed," Detroit *Fifth Estate*, September 15, 1967, 4; "Leary Arraigned in Narcotics Case," *New York Times*, December 12, 1967, 40. On school disputes see Gael Graham, "Flaunting the Freak Flag," *Journal of American History* 91:2 (September 2004), 522–43.

[11] Tuli Kupferberg, "The Hip and the Square," *Berkeley Barb*, August 4, 1967, 8; "Roving Rat Fink" column, *Berkeley Barb*, June 23, 1967, 15 (second quote); identified and Boy Scout in Don Duncan, "Pad Tour Ends in Headache, Feeling of Frustration," *Seattle Times*, September 12, 1967, 1; Robert Stone, *Prime Green* (New York, 2007), 110–17.

The irony, which was lost on the elders, was that young women liked long-haired men. In having to choose between the short hair demanded by old men and the long hair required by young women, there was no contest. What youth would prefer paternal approval over that from a girlfriend? Why women – and not just hippie women – were so enamored of long hair in the Sixties is not so clear, although the association of short hair with the military may have played a role, because women were often hostile to the Vietnam War. Or maybe long hair was just a generational marker, a fad started by the Beatles, and young women looked for a sign of a youth who subscribed to the younger generation's values. Male long hair had practical disadvantages, because it often kept men from getting jobs, frequently brought harassment, and even clogged the shower drain. It did, however, save money otherwise spent at a barber shop, which was always a consideration for impoverished hippies.[12]

In the Sixties only a few male hippies wore earrings, pierced noses, or had tattoos. This is not surprising, because freaks were middle class and 97 percent white. One African American leftist asked, "How many black hippies do you see?" Almost none were found in the Haight, even though the neighborhood adjoined the black Fillmore district. To youths brought up in a culture lacking any male body adornment, the adoption of earrings, pierced noses, or tattoos was seen as extreme. Unlike long hair, which could always be cut on short notice to take a "real-world" job, it was not so easy to remove body adornments. Earrings and pierced noses might suggest being an eccentric rather than a hippie. Tattoos were closely associated with the carny underworld, the mob, and criminals. Despite hostility to the establishment, heads had little desire to be identified with any of those outlaw groups, each of which had its own customs that were as offensive to hippies as mainstream practices. Long

---

[12] Leslie Brody, *Red Star Sister* (St. Paul, MN, 1998), 35; Micky Dolenz and Mark Bego, *I'm a Believer* (New York, 1993), 82; Kathleen Kinkade, *A Walden Two Experiment* (New York, 1973), 170; Don Duncan, "Will Hippies Create More Honesty, Less Pretense?" *Seattle Times*, September 14, 1967, 63.

hair meant exercising individual choice and being authentic to the self.[13]

Despite the penchant for nakedness, male hippies cared about clothes, because they announced one's countercultural identity to the world, and freaks loved being noticed. Indeed, never since the first peacock preened has a generation announced its arrival with such ostentatious show. Distinctive dress was also a way to reject the mainstream's rigid use of starched white shirts, ties, formal business suits, and highly polished shoes. Counterculture clothing, accordingly, was bright, colorful, and outrageous. It also displayed the body. Most hippie men were neither muscular nor cool. Long hair, loose shirts, and colorful pants suggested that they were in touch with their emotions and receptive to non-Western traditions. To keep long hair out of the eyes, hair might be tied back in a ponytail, often using a cheap rubber band, or a colorful bandanna printed with an American Indian or a foreign design was wrapped across the forehead. Hippie men often wore handmade necklaces strung with carved beads. A peace symbol or a heart-shaped locket might dangle from the front. A male leather purse might be carried over the shoulder.[14]

In warm climates, hippies often went bare-chested, or colorful printed T-shirts were favored, occasionally with slogans on

[13] Middle class and 97 percent white are in Lemke-Santangelo, *Daughters of Aquarius*, 35. Leftist in "Commies Versus Hippies," *Berkeley Barb*, June 2, 1967, 7. On rejection of earrings, pierced noses, and tattoos see covers of *Berkeley Barb*, May 5 and June 16, 1967. Note photographs in Gene Anthony, *Magic of the Sixties* (Salt Lake City, 2004); Barney Hoskyns, *Beneath the Diamond Sky* (New York, 1997); Mike Evans and Paul Kingsbury, *Woodstock* (New York, 2009).

[14] Grunenberg essay in Christoph Grunenberg, ed., *Summer of Love* (London, 2005), 13, 17, 36; Nannette Aldred essay in Christoph Grunenberg and Jonathan Harris, eds., *Summer of Love* (Liverpool, UK, 2005), 102, 109, 111–12; Carlo McCormick essay in Grunenberg and Harris, eds., *Summer of Love*, 234; Anderson, *Movement and the Sixties*, 255, 261; Guy Strait, "What Is a Hippie?" (1967), in Alexander Bloom and Wini Breines, eds., *Takin' It to the Streets* (New York, 1995), 310–11; Sherri Cavan, *Hippies of the Haight* (St. Louis, 1972), 49–50, 82; Stephen Gaskin, *Haight Ashbury Flashbacks* (2nd ed., Berkeley, 1990), 52–3; Zimmerman, *Counterculture Kaleidoscope*, 148.

the front or back. Political slogans, however, were uncommon. In cool places, homemade tie-dyed shirts were preferred, usually worn with the top several buttons left open to show chest hair. For more formal events, wealthier hippies dressed in tight-fitting mod shirts from London's Carnaby Street, or imitations of that style. Amid the "color nightmare," one shirt had "two shades of green, with a brown stripe," noted the columnist Robert Heilman. These shirts featured paisley designs, swirling psychedelic patterns, colors that glowed in the dark, or Madras plaids from India. The idea was to be as decorated as possible. Sleeves might be ruffled or fringed, often in vividly contrasting colors. Clashing colors might pulsate. Silk frock coats, military overcoats, Mexican blanket vests, or gaudy patchwork or striped jackets, worn unbuttoned, completed the upper portion of the ensemble.[15]

Extrawide belts were made of thick leather, or narrow belts contained colorful strands of rope. Oversized metal buckles were worn, at a time when airports did not yet have metal detectors. Buckles often featured favorite band names, zodiac signs, or sculpted American eagles. Tight-fitting jeans were very common, but hippies often preferred bright-colored or white jeans over the more traditional blue. Jefferson Airplane even did a radio commercial praising white Levis. Jeans were often worn without underwear because that was thought to be more natural. It also saved money. "Outlaw Underwear!" read a sign at Woodstock. In the Seventies bell-bottom jeans appeared. "No one," said the Yale law professor turned hippie sympathizer Charles Reich, "can take himself seriously in bell bottoms." Fancier pants included bright printed fabrics in swirling colors, plaids, or stripes. These trousers might be worn very low on the hips. Sometimes they were exceptionally, even painfully, tight, and at other times they billowed out flamboyantly. Many hippies prided themselves on

---

[15] Cavallo, *Fiction of the Past*, 89; "The Chic Hippie Look," *New York Times*, November 6, 1970, 71; Robert Heilman column, *Seattle Times*, April 17, 1967, 21; "Dropouts with a Mission," *Newsweek*, February 6, 1967, 92. On chest hair see Allyn, *Make Love, Not War*, 132. On pulsating colors see Sally Tomlinson essay in Grunenberg, ed., *Summer of Love*, 126.

bare feet, but others wore either cheap sandals or sneakers or expensive leather boots.[16]

To the older generation, this male garb was unsettling on several levels. The rejection of traditional mainstream dress was almost total. For middle-class parents, the failure of sons to wear starched white shirts and ties, even for such formal events as hippie weddings, meant that sons were rejecting the idea of being middle class. (White shirts were so identified with the middle class that sociologists routinely used "white collar" as short hand.) This was precisely what hippies intended. The wearing of blue jeans upset parents, because jeans were identified with farmers, the working class, and the poor. By insisting on tight jeans, youth were engaging in a sexual display that challenged the middle-class view that respectability required loose-fitting clothes. Hippie dress challenged orthodoxy on every level. "Like father, like son, like hell," read graffiti in San Francisco.[17]

Bright-colored jeans suggested femininity and raised questions, in parental minds, about male hippie masculinity. This anxiety was increased by necklaces, male purses, and fringed shirts. These trends worried parents, who also noticed that daughters were borrowing ideas from male attire. The great androgyny was underway. In Ronald Tavel's play, *Gorilla Queen*, staged at the avant-garde Judson Theatre in New York in 1967, the hero was a great ape who expressed both masculine and feminine traits. The audience had to guess the ape's gender. Tavel observed, "Sexual identity in our society is so confused that nobody knows what is male and female any more." The expression of androgyny was rooted in hippie values. One hippie, Laurie Baxer, explained,

---

[16] Jefferson Airplane ad in Gair, *American Counterculture*, 7, 172; T. P. letter, *Berkeley Barb*, May 12, 1967, 6; Woodstock sign in Elliot Tiber with Tom Monte, *Taking Woodstock* (Garden City Park, NY, 2007), 113–14; Reich in Grunenberg essay in Grunenberg, ed., *Summer of Love*, 38; Town Squire ad, *San Francisco Oracle*, #3, November 1966, 2; "Artist Village Sandals Custom Made," ad, *Berkeley Barb*, July 22, 1966, 7; Tuli Kupferberg, "The Hip and the Square," *Berkeley Barb*, August 4, 1967, 8.

[17] On tight jeans as sexy see Allyn, *Make Love, Not War*, 132. Graffiti in Howard Thompson, "Screen: Flower Children's Manifesto," *New York Times*, December 20, 1967, 52.

"We view it as a kind of blasphemy that a man is masculine because he has short hair and feminine because he has long hair."[18]

Traditionalists were furious. They wanted men to be hard, rational, calculating, and competitive, suitable for fighting wars, digging coal, forging steel, or knifing rivals in the hurly-burly business world. In contrast, women were supposed to be soft, emotional, nurturing, and cooperative, traits associated with families and motherhood. Borrowing from Eastern ideas about the duality of the masculine and feminine, hippies affirmed that both men and women needed to combine the "yin" and the "yang" to make a whole person. In practice, hippie women moved only a little toward the masculine pole, while hippie men readily adopted feminine ideas by being willing to show emotion, to adopt an attitude of nurturing, and to favor the cooperative over the competitive. In reality, the counterculture tended toward the feminine, which gave women greater influence. Male hippie dress was a more radical departure from the traditional male norm than was female hippie garb.[19]

Hippie women wore long hair, a fact that did not upset elders. They also tied hair back in ponytails and used bandannas to keep hair out of the eyes. Beads around the neck accompanied by lockets did not surprise. Low-cut blouses, however, drew disapproval, especially when it was obvious that many female hippies did not wear bras. Many elders believed that unsupported breasts, far from being natural, as hippies claimed, were unhealthy and would lead eventually to sagging breasts. Others, devoted to middle-class respectability, thought that bobbing breasts were sexually alluring. Blouses sometimes left the midriff bare, and the belly button could then be decorated. Hippie women also wore male work shirts, which were less suggestive than

[18] On androgyny see Barbara Ehrenreich, *The Hearts of Men* (New York, 1984), 107, 114; Bailey, *Sex in the Heartland*, 10. Tavel in Elenore Lester, "In the Parish Hall, the Hippies Go Ape," *New York Times*, March 26, 1967, 73; Baxer in "Dropouts with a Mission," *Newsweek*, February 6, 1967, 92.

[19] Lemke-Santangelo, *Daughters of Aquarius*, 61–2. On yin and yang see Diamond, *What the Trees Said*, 85; *Berkeley Barb*, May 5, 1967, cover.

low-cut blouses, but raised questions about a proper devotion to femininity. Women often decorated blouses and shirts with their own colorful hand sewn metallic sequins, glass baubles, spiraled stitchery, swirling symbols, or exotic patches. "What is important," said a psychiatrist, "is that it is their own product." Self-decorated simple clothing expressed individualism and cost little.[20]

Many hippie women followed the beatniks by refusing to use makeup, which was a startling break with social customs. The natural look was a philosophical position that affirmed authenticity, but it also saved money. Makeup, however, was inexpensive, and many women applied it in novel ways. Facial painting in psychedelic swirls or in fluorescent colors that glowed under strobe lights was commonly applied for a rock concert or other celebration. Perhaps only one-half of the face might be painted, which created a most interesting effect. Heavy mascara might suggest cat's eyes. In a tribute to Eastern religions, a third eye might be painted in the middle of the forehead. Fake tattoos that could be washed off might be painted around the neck and shoulders. These markings could be color-coordinated with blouses or dresses, or they could be designed to celebrate special occasions. Flowers, lizards, frogs, butterflies, or other fauna were often favored.[21]

Hippie women's jewelry was often homemade. Native American beads or other exotic pieces from non-Western nations were worn. Love tokens were popular. The folksinger Joan Baez gave cufflinks to Bob Dylan. He later gave her his girlfriend's nightgown. Baez sang about this unequal exchange in one of her most popular songs, "Diamonds and Rust" (1975). Her values,

---

[20] Cally Blackman essay in Grunenberg and Harris, eds., *Summer of Love*, 201–2; Lemke-Santangelo, *Daughters of Aquarius*, 35; Joseph Conlin, *The Troubles* (New York, 1982), 230; psychiatrist in Steven V. Roberts, "The Hippie Mystique," *New York Times*, December 15, 1969, 42. On bras see Lemke-Santangelo, *Daughters of Aquarius*, 72.

[21] On no makeup see Anderson, *Movement and the Sixties*, 261. On facial painting see Conlin, *Troubles*, 231; Richard Goldstein, "A Reason for Hippies," *San Francisco Chronicle*, June 5, 1967, 12.

she suggested, would outlast his, just as her gift had. Mood rings were also popular, because the changing color supposedly revealed emotions. Hippie jewelry often showed flamboyant design with unusual shapes and color combinations. Pierced ears were common, and they were often decorated with homemade earrings. Charm bracelets with astrological signs or items collected in travels were common. Scarabs, borrowed from ancient Egyptian culture, were esteemed. So were snake bracelets. Lockets or other decorative containers sometimes contained drugs or birth control pills.[22]

Women's belts were often more outlandish and decorated then men's. Buckles were large, but less prominent than on male belts. Female freaks often wore men's jeans, especially colored jeans. Jeans were cheap to buy, were durable, and required less care than skirts. Jeans were less popular than later, however, because women's jeans were rare in the late Sixties, and some women could not fit comfortably into men's jeans. Women wore pedal pushers, which were designed to fit women, as well as culottes, which had a separate section for each leg but appeared at first glance to be a skirt. In an expression of nostalgia, hippies dressed in secondhand Victorian or Edwardian clothes or in copies of those clothes. Unusually long patterned dresses became known as granny dresses. Female freaks also wore brightly colored skirts, including mini-skirts, with bold patterns and psychedelic swirls. Mary Quant, inventor of the mini-skirt, said the design suggested sex in the afternoon. Many women also tie-dyed blouses, shirts, and skirts. Colored leggings also were worn. Many hippie women went barefoot, but they also wore sandals, sneakers, and boots.[23]

[22] "Squirrels, Beads, and the Hippie-Bead Fad Give Navajos a Lift," *New York Times*, September 7, 1968, 24; David Hajdu, *Positively Fourth Street* (New York, 2001), 297; Joan Baez, *And a Voice to Sing With* (New York, 1987), 83–98; Blushing Peony ad, *San Francisco Oracle*, #4, December 16, 1966, 20; Stephen ad, *Berkeley Barb*, May 12, 1967, 7; LSD tablet container is in Anthony, *Magic of the Sixties*, 75.

[23] Carlo McCormick essay in Grunenberg and Harris, eds., *Summer of Love*, 231–2; Charles Perry, *The Haight-Ashbury* (New York, 1984), 6; In Gear ad, *San Francisco Oracle*, #3, November 1966, 3; Footlight Shop ad, *San Francisco*

Because female fashion was never truly stable, hippie women's choices about dress did not provoke the same anger as the male rejection of middle-class dress did. Parents did not object to long-haired daughters or granny dresses. Most parental anxiety was about daughters turning on men sexually by foregoing bras, wearing low-cut blouses, showing the midriff and belly button, or swinging hips in very tight jeans. Youth, however, had its own ideas. At the same time, parents were puzzled that young women donned men's clothes, especially work shirts and jeans, because traditional working-class men's clothes might offend men. Everyone noticed the androgynous clothes. If young men and women talked about sex more openly, and expressed desire more readily, hair and clothing no longer needed to mark gender. When hippies chose to dress without reference to gender, they embarked on a course that had lasting implications for gender relations. Meanwhile, elders claimed that they could not tell sons from daughters. Hippies, however, had no trouble making the distinction.[24]

The key to the sexual revolution of the Sixties was the birth control pill, which became available by prescription in 1960. "In its effects," wrote the journalist Ashley Montagu, "I believe that the pill ranks in importance with the discovery of fire." Prior to the pill, the best way for an unmarried woman to avoid an unwanted pregnancy was sexual abstinence. Young middle-class men slept around but wanted to marry virgins, and 75 percent of female college graduates in 1965 were virgins; four years later, only 45 percent were. Young middle-class women disliked the double standard that allowed playboys but forced women to guard their virtue, but men did not get pregnant. The only cures for pregnancy were an early marriage, which was more common

Oracle, #7, April 1967, 43. On granny dresses see Cavan, *Hippies of the Haight*, 50; Byron Fish column, *Seattle Times*, August 8, 1968, 23. On Quant see John D'Emilio and Estelle B. Freedman, *Intimate Matters* (New York, 1988), 306. On tie-dye see "The Psychedelic Tie-Dye Look," *Time*, January 26, 1970, 38.

[24] Anderson, *Movement and the Sixties*, 262; Ehrenreich, *Hearts of Men*, 114–15; Lemke-Santangelo, *Daughters of Aquarius*, 41, 45.

than was normally admitted, a secretive pregnancy followed by adoption with the fear that word of what had happened would leak out and ruin a young woman's reputation, or an illegal and dangerous abortion that could lead to death or the inability to have children. Shrewd women aroused men but proved unwilling to go "all the way," until the engagement ring was produced. In a society where middle-class men were supposed to support wives, women looked for husbands by sizing up earnings potential as well as character and appeal.[25]

Significant change in sexual practices among middle-class singles formed a backdrop to the hippie movement. The pill changed the calculation about sex, although it did not do so immediately. In the early Sixties, when the mainstream media rarely commented on sexual matters, use of the pill spread only slowly, often by word of mouth, and almost always among married women. Most physicians and clinics flatly refused to prescribe the pill to unmarried women. The pill was not designed, in this view, to promote sex, but to allow sexual relations to continue inside marriage when health, finances, or other personal considerations made it undesirable for a married woman, who often had several children, to give birth to more children. In a 1964 survey of University of Kansas women students, 91 percent said sex was wrong when a couple was not engaged. In this still conservative environment, abortion remained illegal and little discussed. Mainstream publications resisted any mention.[26]

By the mid-Sixties, unmarried young women began to use the pill in a different way. With support from parents terrified of a daughter's pregnancy, college students put pressure on college health services to provide the pill to any female student, whether

---

[25] Statistics are in Annie Gottlieb, *Do You Believe in Magic?* (New York, 1987), 239. Allyn, *Make Love, Not War*, 10–22, 30–40 (Montagu at 33), 94–5, 97; Bailey, *Sex in the Heartland*, 75–80; Edwin O. Smigel and Rita Seiden, "The Decline and Fall of the Double Standard," *Annals of the American Academy of Political and Social Science* 376 (March 1968), 6–17.

[26] Statistic is in Bailey, *Sex in the Heartland*, 119. On the pill in the early Sixties see Allyn, *Make Love, Not War*, 33–6; Bailey, *Sex in the Heartland*, 1, 7, 105–6, 108–9.

married or not. And they wanted it: the pill enabled young women to take control of their own sexual lives, end the double standard, experiment, and enjoy sex as much as did young men. According to a *Good Housekeeping* poll, however, public opinion, dominated by older people, still resisted giving the pill to single women. One interviewee said, "I truly pity a generation growing up with the morals of alley cats." Of course, the pill, unlike abstinence, was not foolproof, and increased demands for legal abortion were soon heard. If the pill enabled women to enjoy sex, then abortion was a necessary corollary to take care of unwanted pregnancies.[27]

Why should the pill be restricted to women in college? Why should every women not have an unfettered right to birth control? Hippies, both women and men, certainly thought so. Condoms, diaphragms, the inserted IUD, and the pill all rose in popularity among young singles. Suddenly, much more sex seemed to be going on. This change took place throughout the culture and coincided with the sexual maturation of the older boomers. Why wait? Instant gratification had broad appeal. While the average age of marriage rose, premarital sex became more common. It was no longer necessary for respectable young women to wait until marriage (or engagement) to have sex. Sex became a matter of opportunity, whim, and taste. Everyone knew the Boy Scout slogan: be prepared. For both women and men, it was best to take one's contraceptive kit on any trip, whether across the land or by drugs, because one never knew when an appropriate occasion might arise. Benjamin learned this lesson when the older Mrs. Robinson seduced him in the hit film, *The Graduate* (1968). As sexual hedonism rose throughout the society, it became a main theme of the emerging hippie counterculture.[28]

[27] Allyn, *Make Love, Not War*, 39, 51–2, 97–9; Bailey, *Sex in the Heartland*, 7–9, 80–134 (quote at 118).

[28] Marriage age is in U.S. Bureau of the Census, *Historical Statistics of the United States, Colonial Times to 1970* (Washington, DC, 1975), 19; Simon Frith, *Sound Effects* (New York, 1981), 240–2; Wes Wilson in Leonard Wolf, ed., *Voices from the Love Generation* (Boston, 1968), 211; Albert Ellis, "Sexual Promiscuity in America," *Annals of the American Academy of Political and Social Science* 378 (July 1968), 58–67.

"We would not be normal," wrote the journalist Jacob Brackman, "For normality was now disease." Hippie sexual liberation was rooted in the decline of sexual repression in the larger society. As repression eased, passions rose. "We went crazy," wrote Jerry Rubin. "We couldn't hold it back any more." In the novel *Loose Change* (1977), Sara Davidson featured a Rubin-like character who felt cheated unless he had sex three times a day. Freaks believed that sexual repression had turned men deprived of sex and love into violent warriors. The poet Gary Snyder agreed. "Our capacity for violence," said Jefferson Poland, "is a spill-over, a natural consequence of our repressed sexuality, our caged libidos." Poland's Sexual Freedom League (SFL) coined the slogan "Make Love, Not War." The cure, according to one advocate, was "sheer, undiluted orgy-ism." This was the "first positive step in unrepressing our repressions." If pleasure pursuits increased, wars would cease.[29]

Live for the moment, just to have fun. Hippies advised, "Just say yes." Janis Joplin said "get it while you can." In addition, repression of sex, freaks believed, was behind society's rejection of cooperation and enthusiasm for ruthless competition, and the result had been rapacious dog-eat-dog capitalism. The radical philosopher Herbert Marcuse stressed this point in *Eros and Civilization* (1955), a popular book among the young in the Sixties. Another product of sexual repression was the sublimation of natural desire into materialist consumer culture. Those blocked from screwing were forced to find happiness through buying instead. Thus, free sex promised to emancipate men and women from ego-driven aggression, prevent war, tame capitalism, and promote happiness based on natural means. Expressing

---

[29] Brackman in Anderson, *Movement and the Sixties*, 254; Rubin in Judith C. Albert and Stewart E. Albert, eds., *The Sixties Papers* (New York, 1984), 440; Snyder in Robert V. Daniels, *Year of the Heroic Guerrilla* (New York, 1989), 62; Poland and slogan in Allyn, *Make Love, Not War*, 50; Richard Thorne, "A Step toward Sexual Freedom in Berkeley," *Berkeley Barb*, February 4, 1966, 5 (quote). See also Lemke-Santangelo, *Daughters of Aquarius*, 64, 152–3.

authenticity and individualism, the liberation of desire would produce utopia, and a very sexy utopia at that.[30]

Free love was the answer. Mimi Lobell, coauthor of a book on open marriage, explained, "You may want good French food most of the time, but now and then you want a pizza." Open marriages expressed the new hedonism in which feelings triumphed over fidelity. For years Ken and Faye Kesey had an open marriage. Faye did not seem to mind her husband's affairs, because she knew that the "great man" needed her and always returned to the nest. She was his rock and she loved him. They remained married for forty-five years until his death. But marriage need not preclude passionate affairs. When the Keseys lived in La Honda and the Pranksters were being created, Ken fell for Mountain Girl (Carolyn Adams) and fathered their daughter, Sunshine. By 1966 Mountain Girl had moved to the Haight to run the Grateful Dead's commune. She became Jerry Garcia's lover, and they later married.[31]

The collapse of traditional sexual mores led teenagers to run away from restrictive middle-class homes to join the hippies. The Haight was inundated during the Summer of Love. The number of runaways caught in Berkeley rose from 424 in 1966 to 846 in 1968. In 1968 authorities nationally apprehended one hundred thousand runaways. Unlike earlier epidemics, many of these transients were female. Underage girls who were taken into custody were more likely to be locked up than were their male counterparts. Older hippies harbored runaways, as did rural communes. The number of shelters for runaways soared. Shelters were favorite places for young teens because the operators shared their charges' dislike of middle-class culture. Young hippie women who tried to live on the street were frequently

---

[30] Slogan and Joplin in Anderson, *Movement and the Sixties*, 258, 260. On Marcuse see Allyn, *Make Love, Not War*, 196–9; Zimmerman, *Counterculture Kaleidoscope*, 131.

[31] Lobell in Allyn, *Make Love, Not War*, 215; Lemke-Santangelo, *Daughters of Aquarius*, 48–9; Scott MacFarlane, *The Hippie Narrative* (Jefferson, NC, 2007), 41, 110; Rick Dodgson, *It's All a Kind of Magic* (Madison, WI, 2013), xv, 54–6, 94–7.

sexually assaulted. Some hippie men saw nothing wrong with underage sex; they believed children to be naturally wise and uncontaminated by adult culture's inhibitions.[32]

Hippies carried the Dionysian celebration of sex to the uttermost. "As far as I'm concerned," said one former hippie, "much if not most of the energy driving the counterculture, the protests, the activism was just from kids trying to get laid." The main idea was: "If it feels good, do it." Or as graffiti in Berkeley put it, "Feeling is good for you." About the Beatles, Stephen Diamond wrote, "The music made you feel good." Abbie Hoffman said that *Sgt. Pepper* summed up his "inner feelings." Bob Dylan sang about feelings in "Like a Rolling Stone" (1965). For freaks, many different things felt good. "We emancipated primitives of the coming culture," wrote one hippie journalist, "are free to do what we feel now because we understand that logic and proportion and consistency and often even perspective are part of the old control system and we're done with the old control system." The attack on logic could also be heard in the Jefferson Airplane's "White Rabbit" (1967). Ringo Starr frequently said, "Tomorrow never knows." Not only was this the title of one of John Lennon's most famous psychedelic songs, but the phrase also advocated living for the moment.[33]

The music exploded with feelings. Grace Slick powerfully commanded finding love in the hit single "Somebody to Love" (1967). At the 1967 Monterey Pop Festival, when Janis Joplin and Big Brother and the Holding Company sang "Combination

---

[32] Berkeley statistics are in W. J. Rorabaugh, *Berkeley at War* (New York, 1989), 148. Lemke-Santangelo, *Daughters of Aquarius*, 137–44; MacFarlane, *Hippie Narrative*, 222, 224; Leo E. Laurence, "House Bust Considered a Betrayal," *Berkeley Barb*, October 27, 1967, 4; William Estes, "Increase in Runaway Youth Plagues Police," *Los Angeles Times*, April 13, 1967, SF1; J. Anthony Lukas, "Police Hopeful of Easing Hippie Problem Here," *New York Times*, October 18, 1967, 1, 36.

[33] Former hippie in Allyn, *Make Love, Not War*, 196; slogan in Anderson, *Movement and the Sixties*, 258; graffiti in Rorabaugh, *Berkeley at War*, 134; Diamond, *What the Trees Said*, 72; Hoffman in Jonah Raskin, *For the Hell of It* (Berkeley, 1996), 110; Keith Lampe in *Mobilizer*, September 1, 1967, in Albert and Albert, eds., *Sixties Papers*, 405; Starr in Simon Reynolds essay in Grunenberg, ed., *Summer of Love*, 149.

of the Two," a background singer invited the audience to hear the band in San Francisco by contrasting "Fillmore" with "feel more." Powerful feelings suggested love. Or did they? Relationships in the counterculture were deep, recalled Jentry Anders, but fleeting. In "Love or Confusion" (1967), Jimi Hendrix confronted the fact that love could be fickle. In "Stone Free" (1967), he endorsed being a serial lover. The new songwriters, observed Robbie Robertson of the Band, were exploring the feelings of the people in the street.[34]

Seeing behavior as a moral question, Reverend T. Walter Herbert, a Protestant minister who served the Berkeley campus community, inverted the counterculture formulation to ask, "Does this feel right to me?" Invoking morality in the service of feelings posed risks. The Berkeley activist Michael Rossman recalled, "The whole fabric and most intimate textures of our lives kept changing." Jerry Rubin believed, "Our generation is in rebellion against abstract intellectualism and critical thinking." He noted, "The intellect is but a spark on the ocean of emotion." The entire rational, scientific edifice erected at the time of the Enlightenment was being questioned. Rossman concluded, "We have no precedent for the depth of the cultural transformation we are entering." One Berkeley undergraduate declared, "My generation has learned that what people do is simply what people do. There is no right or wrong." When values collapsed, sex went wild. The Beatles caught the point in their song "Nowhere Man" (1965).[35]

The main change was the sharp increase in casual heterosexual sex, as mating took place among strangers at the beach or after brief meetings in bars. For many hippies, sex was almost

---

[34] Big Brother and the Holding Company, "Combination of the Two" (1967), *Monterey Pop Festival, Vol. 1* (1992); Anders, *Beyond Counterculture*, 213–14; Robertson interview, *The Last Waltz* (1978 film), directed by Martin Scorsese.

[35] Herbert in *Issue*, Spring 1965, 28; Michael Rossman, *On Learning and Social Change* (New York, 1972), 31; Rubin, *Do It!*, 213; Jerry Rubin, *Growing (Up) at Thirty-Seven* (New York, 1976), 36; Rossman and undergraduate in Rorabaugh, *Berkeley at War*, 143, 154.

mandatory. If one did not pursue an opportunity, it was proof of a hang-up and lack of liberation. "Balling" was not so much fun as a duty. The Beatles satirized the situation with "Why Don't We Do It in the Road" on the *White Album* (1968), and later Judith Rossner's novel, *Looking for Mr. Goodbar* (1975), offered a warning. Partner consent in the here and now was all that mattered. Nor was there pretense of romance or love in these encounters. Casual sex was thought to be liberating because it took place without cultural context, moral regulation, and societal approval. Spontaneity was proof of authenticity. When elders expressed dismay, annoyed hippies replied that sex was no big deal.[36]

The breakdown in traditional moral principles, when combined with the inclination to fulfill every sexual desire in the name of liberation produced trouble. Men devoted to self-gratification could easily become sexual exploiters. At the same time, women who liked to meet groovy strangers made themselves vulnerable to unwanted attention. Hippie women, in a break with the past, often hitchhiked alone. They found it easy to get rides, because female freaks, easily recognizable by their dress, were thought to be available. Some of these women were victimized. When drugs were added to the volatile mix, the result was that the number of sexual assaults soared. In Berkeley there were twenty-one rapes in 1965, fifty-two in 1966, and 116 in 1970. Nationally, the number of reported rapes rose from twenty-three thousand in 1965 to thirty-eight thousand in 1970.[37]

Hippie sexual exploration, however, went beyond casual heterosexual encounters in the missionary position. Orgies, declared one freak, allowed individuals to engage in fantasies or fetishes that would not work with a mate. Group sex offered opportunities

---

[36] Conlin, *Troubles*, 227–8; Lemke-Santangelo, *Daughters of Aquarius*, 64–5; MacFarlane, *Hippie Narrative*, 93–5; Barry Miles essay in Grunenberg, ed., *Summer of Love*, 99–110.

[37] Gerard J. DeGroot, *The Sixties Unplugged* (Cambridge, MA, 2008), 215; Bailey, *Sex in the Heartland*, 10; Sylvan Fox, "The Two Worlds of the East Village," *New York Times*, June 5, 1967, 63; Berkeley statistics are in Rorabaugh, *Berkeley at War*, 174; national statistics are in U.S. Bureau of the Census, *Historical Statistics of the United States, Colonial Times to 1970*, 413.

FIGURE 10. Changing sexual mores allowed the Rated-X Bookstore to operate in Madison, Wisconsin, in the early 1970s.
Lance Neckar. Wisconsin Historical Society, WHS-51709.

to seek authenticity, discover spontaneity, and express individualism. Unusual positions were studied with great attention in the ancient Indian text, the *Kama Sutra*. Enhancement of pleasure was a major theme in Tantric Hinduism. Alex Comfort, *The Joy of Sex*

(1972), wrote one of the first widely sold and heavily illustrated sex manuals. Many hippies bought Comfort's book: they liked the explicit drawings that portrayed both partners in the nude and were pleased that the male had a beard. Publication prior to the mid-Sixties would have been banned as pornography. Radical feminists published their own best-selling guide, *Our Bodies, Ourselves* (1973). The teaching of sexual technique was on its way to becoming a major new industry.[38]

Hippie values spread into mainstream society, which moved away from tradition. San Francisco proved a leader in the new attitudes toward sex, in part due to the large size of the local hippie counterculture, and in part due to liberal local judges who accepted publications and performances that were not tolerated in other parts of the country. Lenore Kandel's collection of sexually explicit poetry, *The Love Book* (1965), was, to the establishment, pornography, but Kandel asserted and gained the right to sell and recite its lines in public, although not without harassment from the conservative San Francisco police. She performed at the Human Be-In in January 1967. Meanwhile, Michael McClure, a minor Beat poet, authored the play, *The Beard* (1965), in which two iconic American characters, the outlaw Billy the Kid and the screen actor Jean Harlow simulated cunnilingus on stage. Hippies bought Kandel's poetry and flocked to see McClure's play.[39]

Rebelling against orthodoxy at every turn, hippies experimented with group sex, which took many forms. Multiple partners offered all sorts of possibilities. Three in a bed could be fascinating, as suggested in Joel Grey's song, "Two Ladies," from the 1966 Broadway musical *Cabaret*. Borrowing from the

---

[38] Allyn, *Make Love, Not War*, 166–74,183, 229–30; J. B., "Hooray for Orgies!" *Berkeley Barb*, May 13, 1966, 6.

[39] On Kandel see Lemke-Santangelo, *Daughters of Aquarius*, 48, 59–60; Paul Meilleur, "Hip-View of Haight Love Book Bust," *Berkeley Barb*, November 18, 1966, 1, 3; Lee Meyerzove, "Kandel and McClure," *San Francisco Oracle*, #4, December 16, 1966, 3, 21–2; "Vendors Fined in Love Book Case," *San Francisco Chronicle*, June 24, 1967, 2. On McClure see "Return of the Beard," *Berkeley Barb*, July 22, 1966, 6; John Brownson, "Michael McClure," *San Francisco Oracle*, #1, September 20, 1966, 7; Michael McClure, *The Beard* (New York, 1967; orig. 1965), 6, 94–6.

radical psychological experts R. D. Laing and Wilhelm Reich, *Performance* (1968) featured Mick Jagger as a retired rock star living with two women. Jagger's hedonism startled the violent antagonist. The film argued that sexual liberation would end violence. Then there was *Three in the Attic* (1968), a film in which three co-eds "kept" a male hippie student in the attic. At first the guy felt that he was in heaven, but he found the apparently insatiable appetite of the co-eds beyond his capacity and soon declined into exhausted depression. In sexual games, once the double standard was removed, women discovered that they often more than held their own with men, whose fantasies of endless women clashed with the reality of spent male potency. Women laughed and moved on to the next guy.[40]

In *The Harrad Experiment* (1967), the novelist Robert Rimmer described a liberal arts college where the double standard had been abolished, where sex among students was open, casual, and encouraged, and where study of the *Kama Sutra* was part of the curriculum. Rimmer's book was very popular within the hippie counterculture. The author came to his unorthodox views as a result of personal experience. At the time that he published the book, he had been in a polygamous marriage for twenty years. In Los Angeles the Sandstone Retreat was organized to put Rimmer's ideas into practice. The founders avoided publicity. Recruitment was without advertisement, by word of mouth. This policy was designed to prevent violence from outsiders as well as legal prosecution.[41]

Jefferson Poland, founder of the Sexual Freedom League (SFL) in San Francisco, said that while beatniks had often lived together, they had been quite conservative, because they were monogamous couples who could only love one person at a

---

[40] John Kander and Joe Masteroff, *Cabaret* (New York, 1967), 41–6; Jagger in Nannette Aldred essay in Grunenberg and Harris, eds., *Summer of Love*, 100–10; Allyn, *Make Love, Not War*, 74–84, 225–7; Gordon Ball, *Sixty-Six Frames* (Minneapolis, 1999), 95, 111, 133; Zicklin, *Countercultural Communes*, 49.

[41] Allyn, *Make Love, Not War*, 71–5; Anderson, *Movement and the Sixties*, 253; Kevin interview in Charles Hayes, ed. *Tripping* (New York, 2000), 248. On Sandstone see Allyn, *Make Love, Not War*, 225–7.

time. Poland thought this possessiveness toward another person neurotic. Accordingly, the SFL sponsored orgies. One observer contrasted a swingers' party with an orgy. At a swingers' party strangers drank, undressed, paired off, and had sex. They were uptight. At an orgy, hippies dined on cushions on the floor with music and incense, gradually shed clothes while eating, shared a hookah, and paired off. Then, they re-paired over and over. New combinations developed. In the morning, everyone kissed good-bye. Expanding on this concept, San Francisco astrologer Gavin Arthur hosted group sex parties in his mansion during the Summer of Love. "Plural marriage" was also advocated. Maxine Sanini explained that her "senior lover" was Sergei, age twenty-seven, while her "junior lover" was David, age eighteen. Sanini did not disclose her own age, but she had a nineteen-year-old son by her second husband.[42]

But why should one reject sex with half of humanity? Although few freaks considered themselves to be homosexuals, and some were homophobic, hippies could see no logical or philosophical basis for exclusive heterosexuality. Even if one preferred persons of the opposite sex, there might be times when a person of the same gender would be acceptable as a sexual partner. Availability mattered. Bisexuality and homosexuality were promoted as values consistent with the notion of universal free sex. Was heterosexuality a hang-up, an unnatural inclination programmed by society? Hippies wanted to find out, and the only way to find out was to smash taboos. Freaks had a complicated relationship with homosexuality, because sexual categories in the late Sixties were unfixed and in flux.[43]

At a time when most homosexuals were still in the closet, the hippie homosexual and bisexual minority used the

---

[42] Jefferson Poland letter, *Berkeley Barb*, May 20, 1966, 6; Harpo, "Clap Hands for the Orgy," *Berkeley Barb*, September 8, 1967, 7, 11; Zimmerman, *Counterculture Kaleidoscope*, 129; "Pansensualism No Flash in Pan," *Berkeley Barb*, February 25, 1966, 2.

[43] Allyn, *Make Love, Not War*, 145–65, 218–19; Lemke-Santangelo, *Daughters of Aquarius*, 62; Paul Berman, *A Tale of Two Utopias* (New York, 1996), 138; Frances Fitzgerald, *Cities on a Hill* (New York, 1986), 25–119. See also John D'Emilio, *Sexual Politics, Sexual Communities* (Chicago, 1983).

counterculture as a mask. Hippie openness about sex created both an opportunity and a crisis among homosexuals. While the counterculture's claim that "anything goes" provided cover for gay and lesbian hippies to engage in homosexual practices that mainstream society despised and which most hippies, in fact, rejected as personal choices, the hypocrisy proved a heavy burden inside a counterculture that claimed to be devoted to openness and honesty. The counterculture's commitment to frankness allowed for engaging in conduct without guilt that mainstream society condemned, but at the same time the counterculture's demand for openness put closeted homosexuals in an awkward position. In effect, they were invited to come out of the closet, but they worried about the reception that awaited them.[44]

Hippie casual sex led to an explosion in sexually transmitted diseases (STDs). The Berkeley Health Department reported 150 cases of gonorrhea, the most common disease, in 1960 and 560 in 1965. The pill prevented pregnancy, but it did nothing to block transmission of gonorrhea, genital warts, herpes, or syphilis. AIDS was unknown, while gonorrhea and syphilis were easily treated with moderate doses of penicillin. Drug-resistant strains barely existed. Genital warts and herpes were considered nuisances rather than serious health problems. The tracing of sexual partners by public health officials, however, became almost impossible due to orgies and casual sex with strangers. David Smith, cofounder of the Haight-Ashbury Free Medical Clinic, estimated that three-quarters of the Haight's residents were either exposed to or had gonorrhea, by far the most common STD. Other common health problems seen at the clinic included sunburn, hepatitis from shared needles, drug-induced psychoses, and malnutrition. Diseases unknown in the United States, including scurvy, showed up in the Haight.[45]

---

[44] On stress see Tiber, *Taking Woodstock*, 63–77, 113–24. On hippie homophobia see Gair, *American Counterculture*, 140, 197.

[45] Berkeley statistics are in *Daily Californian*, October 7, 1965, 1. On the Free Clinic see David E. Smith and John Luce, *Love Needs Care* (Boston, 1971), 27, 126, 174–80, 186; David Perlman, "A Medical Mission in the Haight-Ashbury," *San Francisco Chronicle*, June 17, 1967, 1, 7. On STDs see

Many hippies barely knew how to care for themselves, distrusted most physicians as part of the establishment, and practiced less hygiene than in Third World nations. But drugs and sex were the heart of the problem. Nationally, gonorrhea cases nearly doubled from 318,000 in 1965 to 579,000 in 1970. By 1972 there were 340 free clinics across the country. To improve awareness about STDs, as well as the dangers of drug overdoses, Eugene Schoenfeld began to write a syndicated column in 1967 in the underground press called Dr HIPpocrates. The *San Francisco Chronicle* became the only mainstream newspaper to run the weekly column. Schoenfeld recommended condoms to prevent the spread of disease, urged sexually active young people to seek immediate treatment for suspected STDs, and called for abstinence or the pill to prevent pregnancy.[46]

In many ways, the counterculture's devotion to free sex was the projection of an adolescent male fantasy. Desires were not always realized. Patrick Gleeson, a professor and "para-hippie," said, "Not many hippies have managed to achieve sexual freedom." With a ratio of three to five males to each female in the Haight, chances for free love were slender. Then, too, men were indifferent to women's needs. One woman recalled, "They wanted instant gratification – no foreplay." Men wanted "Free Land, Free Dope, Free Women" and "Peace, Pussy, Pot." Hippie men also fulfilled their desires without any breadwinner responsibilities. The SFL tried to obscure these truths with high-minded principles. "The SFL," explained one press release, "is concerned with the question of war, the war that is within ourselves." When desire and conscience worked in harmony, there would be "more peaceable persons." The best way to end both racial violence at home and the war in Vietnam was free sex.[47]

DeGroot, *Sixties Unplugged*, 217; Lemke-Santangelo, *Daughters of Aquarius*, 66; Allyn, *Make Love, Not War*, 216.

[46] Cases computed from U.S. Bureau of the Census, *Historical Statistics of the United States, Colonial Times to 1970*, 8–9, 77; Taylor essay in John Case and Rosemary C. R. Taylor, eds., *Co-ops, Communes, and Collectives* (New York, 1979), 17–48 (number of clinics at 20); "Hip Pocrates," *Berkeley Barb*, March 31, 1967, 1. See also Eugene Schoenfeld, *Dear Doctor Hip Pocrates* (New York, 1968).

[47] Lemke-Santangelo, *Daughters of Aquarius*, 2, 8–34, 73; Bennett M. Berger, *The Survival of a Counterculture* (Berkeley, 1981), 152. Gleeson in Wolf, ed.,

When Jefferson Poland founded the SFL in the early Sixties, he discovered that men were far more interested in orgies than were women. The SFL eventually admitted only couples to the semipublic parties, but even that provision did not fully work. Couples arrived, and the woman who had been enticed by the man with a promise that she did not have to stay quickly left, while the man scouted from the ever-dwindling number of women for a sex partner for the evening. Sex, or at least casual sex without any mention of romance or love, appealed more to men than to women. The SFL got pushback. Barbara Lucas called the group "reactionary, and Dehumanizing as Hell!" because it made women into sex objects. To raise money for the SFL, Poland sold his own sexual services to men and women. He charged men more.[48]

The underground press celebrated the new sexual attitudes with plentiful sex ads, most of which were men seeking women. Max Scherr, publisher of the *Berkeley Barb*, hired many good-looking hippie women, who gained the opportunity to show their devotion to free love by going with the boss. Cartoons in the papers expressed a male fantasy world. Robert Crumb's *Zap Comix* (1968), so called because they were X-rated and had to be sold in wrappers or under the counter at the cash register even in Berkeley, featured the bearded "Mr. Natural" chasing anyone in skirts. "People are hot about sex," said Crumb. In 1967 Paul Krassner's *Realist* published a cartoon of Disney's characters assuming various sexually alluring positions, but Disney's lawyers quickly stopped this satire. Male cartoonists in the *Berkeley Barb* routinely celebrated a kind of raunchy female nudity that no woman would have approved. In one cover a large bearded

Voices from the Love Generation, 70; gender ratio is in Daniels, *Year of the Heroic Guerrilla*, 49; second quote and slogans in Allyn, *Make Love, Not War*, 103; "Sex Freedom League Aims Clarified," *Berkeley Barb*, April 15, 1966, 1.

48 Allyn, *Make Love, Not War*, 41–53; Lemke-Santangelo, *Daughters of Aquarius*, 64; Barbara Lucas letter, *Berkeley Barb*, June 3, 1966, 6. Poland's fees are in Allyn, *Make Love, Not War*, 325, note 49. See also "Roving Ratfink" column, *Berkeley Barb*, September 10, 1965, 2; "Nude Fest for Sexual Freedom League," *Berkeley Barb*, February 18, 1966, 1; "History's Own Version of Nude Party," *Berkeley Barb*, March 4, 1966, 1–2; Jefferson Poland, *Sex Marchers* (Los Angeles, 1968).

hippie held a diminutive naked woman in the palm of his hand. Underground press editors were overwhelmingly male.[49]

For a while hippie women bought the male line on the virtues of sexual freedom, but women gradually began to see that what men called sexual freedom was mostly just new packaging for male exploitation of women. One guy recalled, "I remember once I tried to see how many women I could sleep with in one day." Thus, within a commune, it was men who proposed that everyone sleep with everyone else. (In most communes, this excluded homosexuality.) Sleeping around in this fashion increased sexual experience, and greater experience suggested the capacity to develop better skills in bed. In addition, bed-hopping meant that sexual liberation theory was matched by practice. Some, usually men, argued that theory and action needed to be congruent in order to end hypocrisy, which was a major counterculture concern. Others, often citing their own parents' bad marriages and divorces, felt that middle-class norms were hopelessly mired in outdated cultural practices that tended to loveless sex and materialism as a substitute for passion.[50]

But within the hippie commune it was men who showed up at women's beds, and not the other way around. When a female freak refused to sleep with a guy, she felt guilt at the conflict between her avowed commitment to sexual liberation and her desire to say no to a particular proposition. Men called women who said no a "bad trip." The woman risked being hauled before the entire commune

[49] Rodger Streitmatter, *Voices of Revolution* (New York, 2001), 208–9, 212, 218; Lemke-Santangelo, *Daughters of Aquarius*, 24–6. On the underground press see Robert J. Glessing, *The Underground Press in America* (Bloomington, IN, 1970); Abe Peck, *Uncovering the Sixties* (New York, 1985); Arthur Seeger, *The Berkeley Barb* (New York, 1983). On Crumb see Anderson, *Movement and the Sixties*, 275; *Berkeley Barb*, November 22, 1968, 9 (quote). "The Disneyland Memorial Orgy," *Realist*, #74 (May 1967), 12–13. *Berkeley Barb*, June 16, 1967, cover. For a furious counterattack see Robin Morgan, "Goodbye to All That," New York *Rat*, February 9, 1970, 6–7, in Albert and Albert, eds., *Sixties Papers*, 509–16.

[50] One guy in Allyn, *Make Love, Not War*, 102; Lemke-Santangelo, *Daughters of Aquarius*, 65; Brody, *Red Star Sister*, 90; Kinkade, *Walden Two Experiment*, 169; Kate Millett, "Sexual Politics" (1970), in Albert and Albert, eds., *Sixties Papers*, 475–7.

and accused of having bourgeois sexual hang-ups. She could then only purge herself of the charge by sleeping with some guy she detested. "It was," recalled one woman, "too much trouble to say no." The men, of course, rarely slept with all the women. They excluded those whom they found unappealing. While a woman, in theory, might demand sex from a particular man, this rarely happened, and if it did, he was likely to honor the request as "no big deal." The search for authenticity and individualism was perhaps more difficult than was sometimes admitted.[51]

Hippies argued that romance was old fashioned, a leftover from the older generation's corrupt culture. This attitude turned sex into a mere animal function. Accordingly, freaks often defined having sex as an act of love. "They exaggerate everything," wrote one mainstream journalist, "principally their hedonism and love for 'love.' " The equation of sex with love posed its own problems. "Many of us," recalled Margot Adler, "were simply too young to love well." Hippie women often accepted being "earth mothers." The idea appealed because it sounded natural and authentic. While men expressed masculinity as voyageurs, darting around like fire flies exploring the ether above, women were anchored to the earth, because both women and the soil symbolized fertility. Earth mothers wore flowing clothes and could have sex freely, because it was natural, but they could also transform themselves into nonsexual, nurturing beings who offered comfort (and food) to men in need.[52]

The word *love* was used a great deal, although it often lacked precise meaning, merely refracted pop culture, or became entangled in other agendas. Buttons read "Love" or "God Grooves." Hyped advertising for the dull film *The Trip* (1967), starring Peter Fonda and Dennis Hopper, proclaimed "Listen to the

---

[51] Bad trip is in Allyn, *Make Love, Not War*, 103; one woman in DeGroot, *Sixties Unplugged*, 218; Brody, *Red Star Sister*, 119, 140; Zimmerman, *Counterculture Kaleidoscope*, 138–41.

[52] On no romance see Conlin, *Troubles*, 227–8; DeGroot, *Sixties Unplugged*, 215–16; Eric Britter column, *London Times*, August 8, 1967, 8 (quote); Margot Adler, *Heretic's Heart* (Boston, 1997), 156. On earth mothers see Lemke-Santangelo, *Daughters of Aquarius*, 27–8, 37, 72; Frith, *Sound Effects*, 242.

Sound of Love," adding "Feel Purple" and "Taste Green." Also
playing was *King of Hearts.* "What are you dropping out from,
hippie?" questioned the radical journalist Jeff Jassen. "Love isn't
always all you need," he argued. "Sometimes you need to think."
Tuli Kupferberg of the Fugs rock band said, "Love is the freedom
of the beloved." He warned that hippies risked being contami-
nated by society. Love and joy were positive goods in themselves.
"Man's true life is inside," he claimed. "Only the spirit is real."
He concluded, "Sensory gratification and love are the first desiderata." Society needed "a revolution of love." A letter writer in
the *Berkeley Barb* concluded, "We assert the right to enjoy ourselves, which is the right to love."53

The love generation asserted the belief in love at every opportunity. In the Haight hamburgers were called love burgers, and
a sign in the Blushing Peony's store window read: "There is no
difficulty that enough love will not conquer." Freaks wore sweat-
shirts that proclaimed "LOVE" on the back. Not everyone was
convinced. "We have long observed," wrote the mainstream columnist Dick Nolan, "that the hippies really love nobody, and
aren't too crazy about themselves, for that matter." The journalist Richard Goldstein said that when hippies shouted "love"
at the police, which happened frequently, they were making a
protest. In what he called the Love Cosmology, only those who
were turned on were enlightened. Thus, the devotion to love was
an affirmation of high-mindedness. Love led flower children to
seek community, which negated the self. The gentle soul looked
to Buddhism, and this soft form of communalism was what the
hippies meant by love. They believed that gentleness could not
coexist with capitalism. The most important love symbol was the
flower: it was passive, beautiful, and harmless.54

53 Button ad, *Berkeley Barb,* June 16, 1967, 6; film ads, *Berkeley Barb,* September
   29, 1967, 11, 15; Jeff Jassen, "X-Hip Editor Free at Last," *Berkeley Barb,*
   October 6, 1967, 2; Tuli Kupferberg, "The Love of Politics and the Politics
   of Love," *Berkeley Barb,* April 14, 1967, 8–9; Jerry Rosenfield letter, *Berkeley
   Barb,* March 17, 1967, 6.
54 Sign in Horace Sutton, "A Hippie Place to Blow the Mind," *San Francisco
   Sunday Examiner-Chronicle,* July 2, 1967, Travel, 3; Dick Nolan column, *San*

Journalists puzzled over the hippie obsession with love. The advice columnist Ann Landers shrewdly argued, "What they call love is often a temporary feeling of euphoria produced by drugs." A teen advice columnist wrote, "Their dress and manner is just a make-believe mask they hide behind." June Bingham, a freelance writer, believed that hippies had "black despair" under the drug-crazed surface. Hippies, she noted, did not realize that the state could not be based on love, because only the individual could sacrifice for a higher purpose through love. "The four-letter word LOVE," wrote the mainstream columnist Jeff Berner, "is just what kids around the country haven't been brought up with." Hippies rejected their parents' materialism for sex. "If a man makes love to every beautiful woman he can," went Berner's version of the hippie philosophy, "he's not an obsessive-compulsive; he's a lover trying to make the world manifest." The Be-In taught that inspiration generated love. Hippies believed, "Every living being has the birthright to be loved." To Berner, the sentiment was naïve, but the "Now Generation" lived only in the present.[55]

Psychologists and psychiatrists looked for deeper meanings underneath the proclamation of love. According to one psychologist, hippies were not so much rebelling against parents as ignoring them. Counterculture youths nostalgically idealized their grandparents, who seemed less materialistic than the parents, but this identification with grandparents could also be seen as regressive. A San Francisco psychiatrist wrote that hippies were from affluent families but lacked emotional security within those families. They flocked to the Haight and talked about "love" to find security. "What's wrong," said Dr. Benjamin Wolman, a New York psychiatrist, "is that the parents are leading hollow,

Francisco Sunday Examiner-Chronicle, July 2, 1967, B3; Richard Goldstein, "A Reason for Hippies," *San Francisco Chronicle*, June 5, 1967, 12.

55 Ann Landers column, *Washington Post*, October 17, 1968, K5; Marty Loken, "Teen-Gauge," *Seattle Times*, April 22, 1967, 13; June Bingham, "The Intelligent Square's Guide to Hippieland," *New York Times Magazine*, September 24, 1967, 25ff; Jeff Berner column, *San Francisco Sunday Examiner-Chronicle*, July 9, 1967, Datebook, 28.

empty, shallow lives and not giving their children anything to hold onto." Young people were attracted to the counterculture because of its "vitality" and "moral stance." Children were raised neither with discipline nor with self-restraint. Freedom ought not to mean indulging impulses, warned the doctor.[56]

Controversy over love increased gender conflict, because women felt that love was too important to be abandoned in the name of sexual freedom, but hippie men often thought of love and sexual freedom as distinct concepts. In this view, the exercise of sexual freedom was what one did while waiting for love to strike. Sex was like eating, a perfectly natural function that should not be denied. Hippie women were much less comfortable with the idea of loveless sex, although they sometimes indulged in such sex as an expedient. "If you feel any affection or attraction for someone," recalled Roberta Price, "it's downright rude and quite awkward not to make love if the opportunity comes along." Both women and men practiced serial monogamy, but men rarely advocated it. Hippies referred to "my old man" and "my old lady." These words evoked the nostalgic past and sounded suspiciously like affectionate phrases used by a married couple.[57]

Despite talk about sexual freedom, which often meant living together for some time in monogamy prior to marriage, hippies married surprisingly often. The prevalence of marriage and the use of elaborate hippie ceremonies suggested that marriage was very important to countercultural couples. Far from rejecting middle-class values, hippies often embraced their own quirky version. Of course, hippie weddings were different. Abbie

---

[56] John Leo, "Dominant Mothers Are Called the Key to Hippies," *New York Times*, August 6, 1967, 78; "Scratch a Hippie and Find Affluence, Says Doctor," *Seattle Times*, September 17, 1967, 2; Wolman in John Leo, "Hippie Scene Laid to Empty Lives," *New York Times*, October 19, 1967, 53.

[57] On love see Allyn, *Make Love, Not War*, 101–2; DeGroot, *Sixties Unplugged*, 215; Price, *Huerfano*, 255 (quote); Kinkade, *Walden Two Experiment*, 171. On serial monogamy see Lemke-Santangelo, *Daughters of Aquarius*, 73; Diamond, *What the Trees Said*, 134; Price, *Huerfano*, 179–80, 188, 255, 291; Ross V. Speck, et al., *The New Families* (New York, 1972), 48–9; Zicklin, *Countercultural Communes*, 85.

and Anita Hoffman married in New York's Central Park. An Episcopal priest who married a couple in San Francisco noted, "It was the first time I ever married a bride with bare feet." Services were often not religious, and sybaritic celebrations followed the formal ceremony, which was frequently held outdoors in a natural setting in a back yard. Many hippie unions crossed traditional religious or ethnic lines, and sometimes two religious officials presided. Kahlil Gibran's *The Prophet* often served as a guide. Handwritten do-it-yourself vows might be read. Alcoholic punch might be accompanied by magic brownies. Rock music might be played. Rather than a honeymoon, poor hippies might retire to the bedroom that they had been sleeping in for several years while guests partied all night.[58]

Few male freaks accepted women's liberation, which had started as a small movement with the publication of Betty Friedan, *The Feminine Mystique* (1963). The movement gained momentum in the late Sixties, with the creation of the National Organization for Women in 1966 and many local feminist groups. So long as hippie women were willing to pair off with hippie men, these organizations seeking female equality had little impact upon the counterculture. Indeed, freaks argued that insofar as they had done away with the double standard that countercultural men and women had become sexual equals. Among the love generation, both men and women believed that men and women were different: Women were nurturing, cooperative, emotional; men were hunters and protectors. Hippie women, however, could not ignore the many questions that feminism raised about the status of women. Women's liberation, recalled Leslie Brody, gave men "vertigo."[59]

[58] Hoffman in Raskin, *For the Hell of It*, 93–4; priest in Dave Felton, "Haight-Ashbury Revisited," *Los Angeles Times*, October 30, 1967, 6; Michael Rossman, *The Wedding within the War* (Garden City, NY, 1971), 370–91; Michael Smith, "2 Hippies Wed," *Chicago Tribune*, January 13, 1968, 6; Lemke-Santangelo, *Daughters of Aquarius*, 76, 80.

[59] Lemke-Santangelo, *Daughters of Aquarius*, 59–60; Brody, *Red Star Sister*, 65 (quote). On women's liberation see Susan M. Hartmann, *From Margin to Mainstream* (New York, 1989); Ethel Klein, *Gender Politics* (Cambridge, MA, 1984).

Some hippie women simply ignored feminism. They nostalgically wanted the counterculture to return to a simpler past. For these women, granny dresses were the appropriate attire, and they settled into serial monogamy that led to living with one man for a long period of time, and often to marriage. Despite the fact that such women came from middle-class families, these women were usually unsophisticated and often not very well educated. They frequently ended up in a traditional relationship in which men supported them. In many ways, they sought to replicate the lives of their grandmothers by baking bread from scratch, keeping a garden, sewing clothes, and bearing and tending children. Hippie women often had children. Associating mostly with other like-minded women, they bonded in sisterhood. They showed little interest in holding a job outside the home, and they often sought out men whose career ambitions kept them near home and precluded a regular job. The men were musicians, writers, artists, freelance editors, as well as farmers or crafts workers. Taking care of men was a theme in the Grateful Dead's "Sugar Magnolia" and in the Band's "Up on Cripple Creek."[60]

For other hippie women, the counterculture proved to be a way station on the feminist highway. Eagerly embracing sexual freedom as a way to tear down the double standard, these women soon tired of bed hopping. They also noticed that hippie men seemed withdrawn and unambitious. Hippie women were often from a higher social status than the men. For a middle-class white male, being a freak meant rejecting the economic, social, and political opportunities that naturally came to such men at that time. This sort of sacrifice only came among the very principled, who declared society so corrupt that they could not contaminate themselves by participating in it, or among the very lazy, who preferred endless music listening or pot smoking to other activities. The desire for authenticity could prove to be unproductive. Living among and observing these men over a

---

[60] Lemke-Santangelo, *Daughters of Aquarius*, 57, 59; Ball, *Sixty-Six Frames*, 50; Zimmerman, *Counterculture Kaleidoscope*, 112. See also Speck, *New Families*, 46, 66–113.

considerable period of time led many hippie women to conclude that the counterculture could not survive without women's work, and that the women did not need the men to thrive. It was a short step from that conclusion to becoming a full-fledged feminist.[61]

The greater interest in and open discussion of human sexuality in the Sixties led to a discussion of orgasms. Hippies considered sex to be a strictly physical act that was fulfilling in and of itself, but women noticed that this idea expressed a male presumption in which the physical act, as defined by the male, was the predominant element in sex. In other words, hippies defined the sexual act as male penetration of the vagina followed by male orgasm. For men, this idea expressed male biology with an impeccable logic, but women perceived that the male orgasm satisfied men more than it did women. From the male viewpoint, women were supposed to gain satisfaction from male penetration and the subsequent explosion of sperm. Jimi Hendrix conveyed male sexual power, including orgasms, in his improvisations. Hendrix, Mick Jagger, and Eric Clapton were so macho that they could possess anything, including femininity. On stage, they exuded countercultural androgyny. Women, however, knew that male sexual success often left women feeling unsatisfied. They wanted something that was not being provided.[62]

The psychiatrist Sigmund Freud had declared that the female equivalent to the male orgasm was vaginal orgasm, but women found such an orgasm illusory. Deciding that Freud was wrong, and with scientific support from the sex researchers William Masters and Virginia Johnson, feminists said that Freud had argued for the vaginal orgasm primarily because vaginal friction was necessary for a male to reach climax. What women needed

---

[61] Adler, *Heretic's Heart*, 202–3, 212, 219, 225, 230, 233; Lemke-Santangelo, *Daughters of Aquarius*, 37, 87, 90, 93–4, 158–65; Price, *Huerfano*, 189. The theme of hard-working women is also in T. C. Boyle, *Drop City* (New York, 2003).

[62] Zimmerman, *Counterculture Kaleidoscope*, 142, 147; "Expert Exposes Failure of US Males as Lovers," *Berkeley Barb*, March 4, 1966, 1–2. See also Valerie Solanis, "The S.C.U.M. Manifesto," *Berkeley Barb*, June 7, 1968, 4, in Albert and Albert, eds., *Sixties Papers*, 462–3.

was foreplay and particularly clitoral stimulation, which men were reluctant to provide, because this activity did not necessarily lead to male vaginal penetration. To men, additional time spent elongating the sexual act was frustrating. To women, rapid male climax was the problem. The counterculture divided over this issue. On the one hand, the male orgasm, at least to many men, formed a natural point of conclusion. Women should be satisfied with this outcome. On the other hand, hippies believed that the main goal in sex was personal satisfaction. Men needed to help women achieve satisfaction. If a woman needed clitoral stimulation to reach a female orgasm, then she ought to be accommodated.[63]

Male and female differences in physiology, temperament, and desire, the importance of romance and love to women, and the issue of the female orgasm complicated and often contradicted the original (male) hippie idea that sex was simply good in and of itself. Hippie men freely abandoned lovers without regret or remorse, but the spurned women, friends noticed, often plunged into depression. Hippie women did not totally reject the original counterculture view, but they came to understand, better than hippie men, that sex was more complicated than they had originally believed when they had started on their sybaritic quest. This greater complexity led many hippie women to reconsider whether the counterculture was nothing more than the creation of a male fantasy world at the expense of women. Down that road was feminism, either with or without the counterculture.[64]

Greater frankness and openness about sex in the Sixties, when combined with the hippie counterculture's insistence upon sexual liberation, ultimately brought gay men and lesbians out of the closet. The declining belief that homosexuality was a psychiatric disorder, as well as the rise of civil rights ideas and

[63] Allyn, *Make Love, Not War*, 169; Bailey, *Sex in the Heartland*, 10; Anne Koedt, "The Myth of the Vaginal Orgasm" (1968), in Bloom and Breines, eds., *Takin' It to the Streets*, 504–12; Kate Millett, "Sexual Politics," in Albert and Albert, eds., *Sixties Papers*, 475–7.
[64] D'Emilio and Freedman, *Intimate Matters*, 313; Ehrenreich, *Hearts of Men*, 107, 111; Frith, *Sound Effects*, 241–3.

groups along with the new countercultural sensibility among the young led homosexuals to a new path by the end of the Sixties. In 1969, when New York police raided the Stonewall Tavern, a well-known gay bar, the tavern-goers astonished both the police and themselves by fighting back. The Stonewall riot marked the beginning of the gay liberation movement in the United States. This outcome was ironic for the predominantly heterosexual counterculture, but gays and lesbians had abundant reasons to be as hostile to mainstream society as did hippies.[65]

Had mainstream society not undergone a transformation in sexual attitudes and practices during the Sixties, the hippie counterculture might well have been suppressed before it got off the ground. At the same time, the counterculture played a significant role in helping to accelerate the changing sexual mores of the larger society, even though those changes were already underway before the counterculture emerged. The hippie celebration of the body, including nudity, expressed both authenticity and individualism. So did sexually alluring clothes. Freaks particularly disliked mainstream culture's hypocrisy about sex. To hippies, easy sex was both no big deal and proof of their own devotion to authenticity and individualism. Changes in gender relations, including feminism, were harder for the counterculture to handle, but openness made acceptance of all changes easier over the long run. Only when politics entered the picture, as seen in Chapter 4, did hippies find that their desire for a society based on authenticity and individualism clashed with certain hard truths about politics in the Sixties.

[65] Allyn, *Make Love, Not War*, 145–6; Tiber, *Taking Woodstock*, 69–79; Howard Smith, "Full Moon over the Stonewall," *Village Voice*, July 3, 1969, 1, 25, 29. See also Martin B. Duberman, *Stonewall* (New York, 1993).

4

Diggers, Yippies, and People's Park

The hippie relationship to politics in the Sixties was complicated and ambiguous. Self-styled dropouts despised politics, but dropping out made a statement: no politics was a form of politics. "It was," noted John Hopkins of London's *IT* underground newspaper, "alternative politics." While hippies believed that the current "system" was rotten, they agreed on little else. Many were simple hedonists, most had no coherent ideology, others rejected politics as hopeless, and some had burned out after participating in protests. Both hippies and radicals disliked the status quo, but the counterculture's relationship with the New Left was strained. Hard to classify as left or right, freaks often disliked both the left's ideological rigidity and its agenda. Radicals advocated increased state power, but hippies were skeptical about all government. Thus, the two groups lacked much common ground. From 1966 to 1968, however, the Diggers and the Yippies challenged this conclusion, and a radical-hippie political alliance did emerge over People's Park in Berkeley in 1969.[1]

[1] Gerard J. DeGroot, *The Sixties Unplugged* (Cambridge, MA, 2008), 248 (quote). For different views on the hippie-radical relationship see David Farber, *The Age of Great Dreams* (New York, 1994), 170, 220–3; Todd Gitlin, *The Sixties* (New York, 1987), 168–9; Allen J. Matusow, *The Unraveling of America* (New York, 1984), 275–307; Hunter S. Thompson, "The Hashbury Is the Capital of the Hippies," *New York Times Magazine*, May 14, 1967, 29,

In the Sixties some young people who opposed the existing order called themselves the New Left, radicals, or even revolutionaries. Some of these "politicos," as they styled themselves, were Marxists, although they were seldom orthodox communists. They ranged from left-liberal advocates of an expanded welfare state to democratic socialists or Trotskyist, Maoist, and Castro-loving revolutionaries. Like hippies, leftists believed that American politics was corrupt and outdated. They especially criticized their elders for racism and for the Cold War, including the American war in Vietnam, which they saw as imperialist. At the same time, radicals believed in reason, science, and technology, whereas few freaks did. Leftists found hippies to be an embarrassment. Todd Gitlin, one of the founders of the New Left, disliked the counterculture's "frivolity." Loathing young people who dropped out and ignored politics, radicals were often disgusted by self-indulgent drugs and sex. Young Communist Party members, in particular, wore short hair, avoided drugs, and were prudish about sex. No wonder communism was in decline.[2]

Freaks held the politicos in contempt. When radicals marched through the Haight in 1966, longhairs sneered, "Go back to school where you belong!" In response to the plethora of New Left lapel buttons, one hippie button sardonically read, "Free the Indianapolis 500." Some hippies had been involved in earlier civil rights or antiwar protests, and by 1966 they had burned out and given up. Participation in any political protest movement was an emotionally intense experience that rarely lasted longer than two years. For most participants, fatigue either led to voluntary withdrawal or to a breakdown. Particular causes often failed, which produced despair. To idealistic young whites who had struggled

120–4; Rebecca E. Klatch, "The Counterculture, the New Left, and the New Right," *Qualitative Sociology* 17:3 (September 1994), 199–214.

[2] On radicals despising hippies see David Farber, "The Intoxicated State/Illegal Nation," in Peter Braunstein and Michael W. Doyle, eds., *Imagine Nation* (New York, 2002), 17–18; David Farber, "The Counterculture and the Antiwar Movement," in Melvin Small and William D. Hoover, eds., *Give Peace a Chance* (Syracuse, NY, 1992), 12 (quote). The best account of the New Left remains James Miller, *Democracy Is in the Streets* (New York, 1987). See also Gitlin, *Sixties*; Tom Hayden, *Reunion* (New York, 1988).

inside interracial groups for civil rights, black power had been traumatic. African American militants had told the whites to get out. The antiwar movement also had been frustrating. Early peace marches had little influence, the Vietnam War expanded dramatically from 1965 to 1967, and the government increasingly harassed protesters. What was the point of protest politics, hippies asked, if no one listened?[3]

The question of the Vietnam War loomed large among the young. Calling the counterculture a "nirvana army," Ken Kesey had suggested to Acid Test participants that they could choose either the U.S. Army or the counterculture. Country Joe McDonald saw the Haight as "this little dreamland" that enabled youth to escape the war, at least for a time. An anonymous letter writer in the *Berkeley Barb* mused, "There probably would be no Haight-Ashbury without the war." This may have been true, but hippie neighborhoods sprang up in London, Berlin, Toronto, and Tokyo, all cities in countries not engaged in Vietnam. Nevertheless, residents of the Haight could not escape the war. If the Haight was primarily a refuge from the war, how should its residents relate to the organized antiwar movement? Freaks knew that too passionate an embrace of protest risked losing a hippie sensibility. Timothy Leary warned, "Don't get too involved in the antiwar movement; it will tie you up fruitlessly when you want to be exploring inner space."[4]

Although radicals and hippies shared disillusionment with the government, and often had a similar loathing for the Vietnam War and racism, their worldviews were fundamentally different. Politicos believed in science, technology, expertise, and

---

[3] Longhairs in Emmett Grogan, *Ringolevio* (New York, 1990; orig. 1972), 242; button in Terry H. Anderson, *The Movement and the Sixties* (New York, 1995), 264; Gretchen Lemke-Santangelo, *Daughters of Aquarius* (Lawrence, KS, 2009), 9–10. On burnout see Farber, "Counterculture and the Antiwar Movement," 7; Sara Evans, *Personal Politics* (New York, 1979); Mary King, *Freedom Song* (New York, 1987).

[4] Michael J. Kramer, *The Republic of Rock* (New York, 2013), 4, 57–8 (first quote at 57, third quote at 4); Barney Hoskyns, *Beneath the Diamond Sky* (New York, 1997), 221 (second quote); Gordon Ball, *Sixty-Six Frames* (Minneapolis, 1999), 213 (fourth quote).

FIGURE 11. Throughout the Sixties, Timothy Leary was a public advocate for LSD. He wrote books, gave lectures, and held frequent press conferences. In 1969 Leary, accompanied by his wife Rosemary Woodruff, addressed the media in Southern California.
Los Angeles Times Photographic Archive, Library Special Collections, Charles E. Young Research Library, UCLA.

powerful government; freaks supported magic, nature, personal experience, and Eastern religious spirituality. Hippies detected a contradiction at the heart of the New Left. Radicals attacked the existing welfare state and its bureaucracies, but they favored expanding this very state that they condemned. When challenged, leftists answered that a New Left state would work wonderfully. Hippies were skeptical. They felt a heavy-handed government constantly imposing its will on the young, both with the draft and with harassment about hair, music, sex, and drugs. Why would a New Left government be any less oppressive than the present liberal regime? How, the love generation wondered, did radicalism advance the need for authenticity?[5]

---

[5] On hippie skepticism see Loudon Wainwright, "The Strange New Love of the Hippies," *Life*, March 31, 1967, 15; Farber, "Counterculture and the Antiwar Movement," 8, 12–14.

Many hippies showed an affinity for libertarianism. Dog-eared copies of Ayn Rand's novels, *The Fountainhead* (1943) and *Atlas Shrugged* (1957), were available, but freaks were perhaps less libertarian than simply hostile to authority. To the songwriter Bob Dylan, the best way to confront authority was to be an individualist. He said, "People have to learn for themselves." Then, too, hippie culture was, at its root, an outlaw culture. The rock star Jim Morrison declared, "All Americans are outlaws." The outlaw theme frequently appeared in San Francisco rock music. Quicksilver Messenger Service embraced the outlaw image, even before lead singer Dino Valenti went to prison on a drug charge. Outlaw culture had a special appeal to Chet Helms, the organizer of the Avalon Ballroom, and the Charlatans, who had gotten their start in Virginia City, Nevada. The Wild West romance formed a part of the hippie trope, which could be seen in the love of cowboy hats, fringed shirts, jeans, and boots.[6]

Hippies knew what they hated. They rejected oppressive bureaucracies, drug laws, and police harassment, but they were vague about what they believed a good society required in the way of government. The Haight-Ashbury, more than elsewhere, became a place to experiment. Spurned by elected officials, the police, and straight residents, freaks in the Haight had to find their own way to build a viable community. In 1966 hippie-owned businesses opened, tourists flocked to the area to shop, and increasing numbers of street kids zonked on still legal lysergic acid diethylamide (LSD) sat on the sidewalk in front of stores. In addition, shoplifting soared, and break-ins became more common. Recognizing that it was necessary to speak with a common voice to solve these issues, Ron and Jay Thelin, owners of the Psychedelic Shop, applied to join the Haight Street Merchants' Association, but the straight merchants turned

---

[6] Dominick Cavallo, *A Fiction of the Past* (New York, 1999), 149, 172, 181–2 (quotes at 182, 172). On outlaw culture see Peter Coyote, *Sleeping Where I Fall* (Berkeley, 2009; orig. 1998), 109; Quicksilver Messenger Service, *Happy Trails* (1969), back album cover; Charles Perry, *The Haight-Ashbury* (New York, 1984), 7–11, 36–7, 59–65; Nadya Zimmerman, *Counterculture Kaleidoscope* (Ann Arbor, MI, 2008), 22–5.

the Thelins down, and Ron then organized the rival Haight Independent Proprietors (HIP).[7]

Attitudes toward police were behind this split. As far as the straight merchants were concerned, and the police tended to agree, most of the Haight's problems were caused by the presence of the drug-using longhairs. Accordingly, police made routine sweeps of the street, used undercover cops to bust kids for marijuana, and invaded private residences without warrants. They picked up anyone who lacked identification proving that they were not underage. Juveniles were taken to the city detention center until parents arranged for travel home. The police also checked for draft cards. Any young male without a draft card was taken in and presumed to be either a draft evader or an AWOL soldier. Often they were deserters. The arrests appalled both hippies and hip merchants, but they responded differently. Freaks refused to deal with authorities, which made them vulnerable to serious crimes such as rape or murder. Hip merchants, by contrast, had property to protect, and HIP tried to cultivate the police with a campaign: "Take a Cop to Dinner."[8]

Into the middle of this strained and awkward situation suddenly stormed the Diggers. Led by Emmett Grogan (1942–78), Billy Murcott, a boyhood friend of Grogan's from Brooklyn, Peter Berg, and Peter Coyote (nee, Cohon) (1941–), the Diggers had broken away from Ronnie Davis's San Francisco Mime Troupe, after that group's poor finances had forced layoffs. Grogan was the principal author of the early Diggers' handbills passed out along Haight Street and posted on neighborhood telephone poles. He preferred anonymity. A working-class Irish street tough and intermittent heroin user, he once told a crowd

---

[7] Michael W. Doyle, "Staging the Revolution," in Braunstein and Doyle, eds., *Imagine Nation*, 80–1; Wainwright, "Strange New Love of the Hippies," 16; Perry, *Haight-Ashbury*, 76–8, 108; Coyote, *Sleeping Where I Fall*, 133–4; Bradford D. Martin, *The Theater Is in the Street* (Amherst, MA, 2004), 94–5.

[8] Coyote, *Sleeping Where I Fall*, 80; Martin, *Theater Is in the Street*, 95–6; Earl Shorris, "Love Is Dead," *New York Times Magazine*, October 29, 1967, 115; Paul Meilleur, "Hip-View of Haight Love Bust," *Berkeley Barb*, November 18, 1966, 1, 3. "Take a Cop to Dinner" is in Perry, *Haight-Ashbury*, 91.

of hippies in New York, "You're still the children of the ruling classes, whether you like it or not." Diggers, particularly Grogan, felt that hippies did not truly repudiate middle-class values. Despite outward rejection of the mainstream, freaks wanted personal success and material pleasure. As both Grogan and the hippies knew, the longhairs could trade in their voluntary poverty for suburban family comforts at any time with just one phone call home.[9]

The Diggers drew inspiration from a variety of sources. The name honored a radical Puritan group founded by Gerrard Winstanley in England in 1649 that had protested private land rights by digging, planting, and harvesting crops on unused land. The group was also influenced by Antonin Artaud, the French drama theorist and avant-garde playwright, who argued that one needed to find the truth and then proceed to act. "Do it" was a Diggers' motto. Peter Coyote believed that ideological analysis stalled personal action, and that previous ideologies slighted the individual. He saw a need for "wild turf." The main inspiration for the Diggers came from Amsterdam, where the anarchistic Provos (short for Provisionals) currently practiced street theater, staged actions that embarrassed authorities, and educated the hippie masses in a philosophy that was congruent with counter-culture practices. Rather than shaping behavior to fit values, the Diggers provided values that underpinned the druggy, musical, sexy hippie counterculture.[10]

Diggers accepted drug use but only for personal fulfillment and not as a way to find spirituality. Grogan denounced Timothy Leary and Richard Alpert as "LSD shamans" and "charlatan fools." Noting that hippie thrill-seeking offered only temporary

[9] Coyote, *Sleeping Where I Fall*, 57; Grogan, *Ringolevio*, 237, 301; Perry, *Haight-Ashbury*, 90; Scott MacFarlane, *The Hippie Narrative* (Jefferson, NC, 2007), 17 (quote); Martin, *Theater Is in the Street*, 96.

[10] Coyote, *Sleeping Where I Fall*, 68; Doyle, "Staging the Revolution," 78–9; Bill Graham and Robert Greenfield, *Bill Graham Presents* (New York, 1992), 184 (first quote); Cavallo, *Fiction of the Past*, 119–20, 139 (second quote); John Brownson, "Anarchy 66 Provo," *San Francisco Oracle*, #1, September 20, 1966, 3; Anthony Howe, "Provos: The Dutch Anarchists," *Berkeley Barb*, November 4, 1966, 5.

escape, the Diggers warned that a counterculture lifestyle did not in and of itself lead to meaningful social change. Grogan called the New Left "puritanical." Radicalism distracted from the Diggers' attempt to build community in the Haight. Grogan proposed to replace radical politics with a "love ethic." In a world devoted to love, the middle-class competitive rat race for money would cease to exist. Money, the Diggers believed, blocked "the free flow of energy." The Diggers' goal was to mobilize hippies for an anarchist approach to political and social change. Grogan believed that youths ought to exercise the freedom that American culture promised. The Diggers taught a need for personal responsibility for everything. They floated with events. "There must not be a Plan," they declared in one broadside, "We have always been defeated by our Plan."[11]

About the Diggers, Coyote later mused, "It was a radical anarchist group that was really about authenticity and autonomy." The Diggers also defined gender roles in ways that privileged males. The heart of the Diggers' ideology was hatred of private property, which put them diametrically in opposition to the hippie merchants, whom they accused of selling out and of being co-opted by mainstream society. "Take a Cop to Dinner" as a concept precisely made the point, and the Diggers mercilessly ridiculed the idea in a strident one-page broadside of the same title that began to be handed out along Haight Street. This anonymous diatribe, along with others, created great anxiety among the hip merchants, who were eager to learn who was writing the messages. The Diggers, however, refused to reveal their identities. Emmett Grogan, the principal author of the early handbills, especially kept a low profile. At one point, the Diggers even denied that such a person as Emmett Grogan existed, suggesting that the name was a *nom de plume* used by numerous people.[12]

---

[11] Quotes from MacFarlane, *Hippie Narrative*, 18 (first two quotes); Cavallo, *Fiction of the Past*, 102 (third quote), 98 (sixth quote); Ball, *Sixty-Six Frames*, 257; Martin, *Theater Is in the Street*, 92.

[12] Graham and Greenfield, *Bill Graham Presents*, 184 (quote); Grogan, *Ringolevio*, 316; Perry, *Haight-Ashbury*, 90–2; Martin, *Theatre Is in the Street*, 95–6, 107–8; "Take a Cop to Dinner," broadside, September 1966, in *The Digger Papers* (August 1968), 14. Available at diggers.org.

Diggers believed that modern capitalism had created endless bounty and was capable of creating even more wealth, but capitalists and corrupt politicians had kept that bounty from the masses and instead allowed the wealth to be hoarded by the few or squandered by the state on worthless wars. Finding the New Left far too tame, the Diggers argued that society could only be changed when public opinion changed dramatically. A radical change in human psychology had to precede any revolution. There was a need, Peter Coyote believed, for "personal authenticity." The key to changing psychology was to focus the counterculture's own psychology in a coherent way, to set up alternative institutions within counterculture communities, and then to watch those ideas and practices spread to the rest of society. Diggers called themselves "life-actors": they acted out their ideas in real life. "We will become the political dynamic of the new society," predicted Peter Berg of the Diggers, "because we are *living* a new civilization."[13]

Diggers thought that performance and improvisation were the keys to gain control over one's life. The heart of American individualism was self-reliance, which required the creation of the self. Being American and making up the rules of life as one went along were one and the same. History and scripts were unimportant. To create an identity, an individual invented the self (the role), directed one's own life (the play), and performed one's own life in public (the audience). The process of self-making was a performance. A person could change scripts, roles, and identities as one wished. This concept of being self-made or "born again" (to use evangelical terms) presumed the malleability and mutability of the individual. In American mythology, personal identity was willed. It was neither fixed nor determined by family or personal history. American culture offered a stage without props or scripts upon which life could be performed in a series of

---

[13] Coyote, *Sleeping Where I Fall*, 64–6 (first quote at 64); Grogan, *Ringolevio*, 300–3 (second quote at 300); Perry, *Haight-Ashbury*, 286 (third quote). See also "Trip without a Ticket," broadside, Winter 1966/1967, in *Digger Papers*, 3–7.

improvisations. The only permanent feature was the individual right to self-create as an act of freedom.[14]

In "The Ideology of Failure" the Diggers explained the philosophy that undergirded their actions. Living the hip life meant rejecting middle-class values, consciousness, and dress, but rock music, psychedelic drugs, and easy sex only narrowly separated hippies and straights. Diggers believed that both hippies and straights, despite differences in cultural practices, strived for success. Although liberated from bourgeois conformity, counterculture devotees still indulged in materialism. But a truly hip person ought to resist this temptation. To be hip, it was not enough to give away proceeds from one's worldly success. "We won't, simply won't play the game any longer," vowed the Diggers. "We return to the prosperous consumer society and refuse to consume. And we do our thing for nothing. In truth, we live our protest. Everything we do is free because we are failures. We've got nothing, so we've got nothing to lose." The Diggers ridiculed the "Copsuckers" (i.e., HIP) and the "Gladly Dead" (Grateful Dead). They concluded, "To Show Love is to fail. To love to fail is the Ideology of Failure. Show Love. Do your thing. Do it for FREE. Do it for love. We can't fail."[15]

The Diggers tapped into popular American ideas by advocating that practically everything be free or freely given. This idea built upon the hippie concept of free sex. By emphasizing "free," the Diggers prevented commercial co-optation. They insisted that the rock bands that lived in the Haight should give frequent free concerts for the people in nearby Golden Gate Park. During 1966–7 the Grateful Dead, Jefferson Airplane, Big Brother, and less well-known bands did so, although they had done so even before the Diggers demanded those free parties. At many of these events, Owsley Stanley also passed out free acid, which was legal until October 1966. These impromptu concerts were not advertised in advance because city officials usually refused to grant

---

[14] Cavallo, *Fiction of the Past*, 102–3.
[15] George Metesky [pseud.], "The Ideology of Failure," *Berkeley Barb*, November 18, 1966, 6.

permits to play music in parks and because the bands wanted smaller crowds. Bands usually played from the back of a truck that could leave in a hurry if the police arrived. Word of a concert was spread quickly through the Haight by word of mouth, aided by the Diggers' handbills passed out on the street.[16]

In October 1966 the Diggers, through their broadsides, announced free daily meals at 4 p.m. in the nearby Golden Gate Park panhandle. The project was driven both by the increasing number of homeless hippies and by the Diggers' ideology, which held that action was the best witness to belief: rather than advocate that food should be free, demonstrate that food could be free. "It's free because it's yours," read the handout. Grogan scrounged day-old bread from two bakeries. Stew was cooked in a big pot. Vendors at the city wholesale market provided wilted vegetables, and grocers donated meat trimmings, but Grogan also stole meat. The first day almost one hundred Haight residents brought bowls and spoons to eat the stew, and the feedings attracted one hundred to two hundred people all winter long. After continuing sporadically in the spring of 1967, dinners were abandoned when Grogan returned to New York during the Summer of Love. Later, a group of Diggers provided free meals in New York.[17]

The free food came with a message. As one approached the big pot of stew, the recipient of the Diggers' bounty was required to step through the Frame of Reference. The frame was a thirteen-foot square made of two-by-fours and painted bright yellow. The purpose of the frame was to enable the person to reframe the world, to perceive reality in a new way, just as the free food was a new concept. Walking through the Frame of Reference did change the psychology surrounding the Diggers' food. The food was not a handout given as alms by wealthy capitalists. Indeed, the Diggers refused to accept donations of money

---

[16] On free goods see Zapata [pseud.], "In Search of a Frame," *Berkeley Barb*, November 25, 1966, 6. On free concerts see Coyote, *Sleeping Where I Fall*, 35, 95, 97; Perry, *Haight-Ashbury*, 96–7, 117, 126.

[17] Grogan, *Ringolevio*, 246–7 (slogan at 247); Perry, *Haight-Ashbury*, 97–8, 167, 212; Martin, *Theater Is in the Street*, 98–9.

to buy food. When cash was offered, they burned it publicly. Donations of food were accepted only from farmers or suppliers in the food chain. One was eating not from a charity food line but from the freely given bounty produced by the people, for the people, and of the people. Several hippies reported that understanding the frame improved the taste of the food.[18]

Shortly after starting the daily free food program, the Diggers announced the establishment of the Free Frame of Reference store. The store, located in a converted garage, offered goods to anyone without cost. Ostensibly, merchandise was donated, and a few such items were kept in sight, but careful observers noticed that much of what was available appeared to be new. These goods had been stolen, which was consistent with the Diggers' view that private property should be liberated for those who could make the best use of it. If a person came into the store and asked who was in charge, the attendant on duty replied, "You are." The purpose of this reply was to prevent arrest by an undercover cop, because no control was ever acknowledged. When Paul Krassner, editor of the *Realist*, visited the store, he called it a charity. The Diggers asked him for ten dollars. He handed over the bill, which Grogan burned. The purpose of the free store was not to provide charity but to change people's perceptions about using money to value things.[19]

After the health department closed the Free Frame of Reference, the Diggers rented another space and opened the Trip without a Ticket, another free store, which was promoted in a handout. The new store was better located and drew more people, including curious tourists. Two African American women from the Fillmore district hung out at the store, waiting for delivery of new merchandise, which they then picked up for free, took back to the Fillmore, and sold at a profit. The Diggers pointed out to the women that they were defeating the purpose of the store, but the women only shrugged. The women, however, did help

---

[18] Grogan, *Ringolevio*, 248, 250; Coyote, *Sleeping Where I Fall*, 70–1.
[19] Grogan, *Ringolevio*, 249, 301; Perry, *Haight-Ashbury*, 108–9 (quote at 109); Martin, *Theater Is in the Street*, 100, 102–3.

hippie women with children navigate the difficult requirements
to receive welfare checks. The store had another purpose. AWOL
soldiers traded in uniforms for secondhand clothes, which, when
combined with a bandanna wrapped around a shaved head,
enabled the soldier to pass for a hippie. Diggers also put out
word on the street that the store could provide a forged draft
card from blanks that the Diggers had stolen.[20]

The Diggers' frequent one-page broadsides were the Haight's
main source for news. Unlike the sporadic and spiritually oriented *San Francisco Oracle*, the Communication Company, or
com/co, as it called itself, neither romanticized the hippie movement nor celebrated psychedelics. Indeed, the Diggers, thinking
of themselves as cutting-edge artists with a political message,
were not satisfied with marijuana and acid. They regularly used
hashish, speed, and heroin. Com/co handouts announced rallies,
concerts, or other items of interest to the community. They also
warned residents about bad drugs, which became a big problem
after LSD was outlawed. Much of the acid that was sold was
cut with speed, and the standard treatment for a bad acid trip
could be fatal if the acid contained speed. Whenever a drug in
the neighborhood produced a bad trip, the Free Clinic had the
drug analyzed, and com/co quickly published the result. Com/
co also published poetry and essays embracing community and
denouncing both capitalism and the existing political order.[21]

The group's leaders preferred to stay in the shadows. As former Mime Troupe actors, they understood the danger that came
from getting noticed publicly by the mainstream media. After an
arrest charge that was dropped, Emmett Grogan was shocked to
find his picture and name on the front page of the *San Francisco
Chronicle* the next morning. The photograph caused people in
the Haight to greet Grogan by name. Not only did becoming

---

[20] Grogan, *Ringolevio*, 297–9; Coyote, *Sleeping Where I Fall*, 89–91, 95; Perry,
Haight-Ashbury, 118, 136.
[21] Coyote, *Sleeping Where I Fall*, 86, 89; Grogan, *Ringolevio*, 265; David E.
Smith and John Luce, *Love Needs Care* (Boston, 1971), 170–6. On Diggers'
drug use see Coyote, *Sleeping Where I Fall*, 72–3; Farber, "Intoxicated State/
Illegal Nation," 30.

a celebrity inflate the ego, but it made it impossible to retain respect from other Diggers or from the hippie community, which despised the media. The leadership, to be effective, had to be kept obscure. Except for Claude Hayward and Chester Anderson, publishers of com/co, most other Diggers simply called themselves Diggers, refused to admit individual identity, and acted only in the name of the group. Despite these efforts to keep a low profile, Grogan was too flamboyant to be unknown. Eventually, he returned to New York, organized a branch of the Diggers there, wrote a wild memoir, fell into obscurity, and died of a heroin overdose.[22]

On December 16, 1966 the Diggers used com/co to call for a mass gathering and the Death of Money parade on Haight Street. Participants held signs marked "Now!" A thousand hippies showed up, traffic stalled, and the police arrived in time to see the Hell's Angels motorcycle gang lead the parade. A leading Angel had a girl draped in a cape standing on the back seat of his Harley. She wore a "Now!" sign on her back. As the parade got underway, a police officer pulled over the Angel with the illegal standing passenger. Because he turned out to be on parole, the police took him in. Another Angel was arrested for protesting the arrest. The Diggers then led about three hundred protesters to the police station. They took up bail from the hippie crowd for the Angels. The Angels were touched. They were notoriously antisocial, and no one had ever done them a favor. The Angels reciprocated by hosting a rock party with free beer in the park on New Year's Day. Angels danced with freaks as the Grateful Dead played.[23]

The hippie fascination with outlaw culture explained why middle-class kids romantically embraced the thuggish Hell's Angels. After the party in the park, the Angels played a major role in providing security for the Haight. Already close to Jerry

[22] "In the Clear," *San Francisco Chronicle*, November 30, 1966, 1; Grogan, *Ringolevio*, iii–vi, 257, 400, 466; Coyote, *Sleeping Where I Fall*, 67–8, 72.

[23] Grogan, *Ringolevio*, 259–63; Coyote, *Sleeping Where I Fall*, 96–8; Perry, *Haight-Ashbury*, 114–17; "New Haight to Sound of Angels," *Berkeley Barb*, December 23, 1966, 1, 2.

Garcia and the Dead, they guarded sound equipment at rock concerts, including the Human Be-In in January 1967. Because the city police were both distrusted and disliked, this result is not entirely surprising. The new role for the Angels also fitted with the Diggers' idea that the community ought to control itself. However, the Angels did not provide security without cost, because they were thought to be a major distributor of Owsley Stanley's acid. They did keep the mob out of the neighborhood, but a number of Haight killings were rumored to be retribution for dealers who refused to pay protection to the Angels.[24]

In June 1967, while the Haight was unraveling under the impact of runaways, drugs, crime, and police harassment, four Diggers, including Emmett Grogan and Peter Berg, drove to Denton, Michigan to crash a national meeting of the increasingly radicalized Students for a Democratic Society, the main New Left organization. They arrived in the middle of a session being run by the radical activist Tom Hayden, barged into the room, and proceeded to speak. "Don't organize students, teachers, Negroes," said Berg, "Organize your head." Expressing their anarchistic leanings, they ridiculed the Old Left's obsession with organizational structure, top-down leadership, ideological purity, and issues orthodoxy. Some in the audience were furious, but others, more attuned to the New Left's attempt to break with the ineffective radical past, nodded in assent. Grogan then explained the concept of the life-actor, who acts out convictions in ordinary life in ways that jar other people's perceptions. Listening attentively at the back of the room was Abbie Hoffman, who soon created the Yippies.[25]

Throughout 1967 the Diggers became less important in the Haight. As the neighborhood descended into pathology during the Summer of Love, the original counterculture residents,

---

[24] Coyote, *Sleeping Where I Fall*, 96–8, 109, 112, 118–27; Zimmerman, *Counterculture Kaleidoscope*, 30, 34.

[25] Martin, *Theater Is in the Street*, 117 (quote); Grogan, *Ringolevio*, 395–400; Perry, *Haight-Ashbury*, 213; Doyle, "Staging the Revolution," 85–6; Nicholas von Hoffman, "Hippiedom Meets the New Left," *Washington Post*, June 19, 1967, A3.

including the Grateful Dead and the Jefferson Airplane, moved out. In October the Psychedelic Shop went bankrupt and gave away the remaining merchandise. The few Diggers still in the Haight hosted the Death of Hippie ceremony on October 6, one year to the day after California outlawed LSD. The main purpose of the event was to persuade the media to go away. Many Diggers also left. Some moved to communes north of San Francisco, while others went to Big Sur. A contingent ended up living on Lou Gottlieb's land, Morning Star Ranch, which was known as the Diggers Farm. A court order, however, eventually forced Gottlieb to evict everyone from the property. Peter Coyote migrated out of the Haight to a commune near Point Reyes.[26]

Decades later Coyote reflected upon the meaning of the Diggers for himself. First, he noted that unlike Grogan, a working-class man who resented middle-class hippies as soft, Coyote was of the middle class. The son of a wealthy New York stockbroker, Coyote had fled to the San Francisco Mime Troupe to avoid the middle-class rat race. Second, Coyote joined the Diggers to find authenticity, which was a common theme among both hippies and the New Left in the Sixties. Authenticity, however, posed a problem, he concluded. Being authentic privileged whim and self-indulgence over moral principle or deep philosophical roots. One did whatever one wanted to do at any particular moment. "Do your thing," the Diggers said in a handout. No organization could survive such an incoherent concept. Furthermore, collaboration with others was difficult because one's "authenticity" got in the way. Coyote concluded that authenticity had been one of the counterculture's main weaknesses in the Sixties.[27]

[26] On Death of Hippie see Perry, *Haight-Ashbury*, 243–4, 271–2; Farber, *Age of Great Dreams*, 187; Coyote, *Sleeping Where I Fall*, 135. On Diggers leaving see Perry, *Haight-Ashbury*, 167, 292; Farber, "Intoxicated State/Illegal Nation," 36; Coyote, *Sleeping Where I Fall*, 83.

[27] Coyote, *Sleeping Where I Fall*, xiii, 64, 69, 97–9, 348–50; quote is from com/co, "Don't Drop Half Out," broadside, January 28, 1967, Digger Archives at diggers.org. See also Doug Rossinow, *The Politics of Authenticity* (New York, 1998).

Another attempt to bring politics into the counterculture came from the San Francisco Be-In held in January 1967. The organizers, and especially Allen Cohen, the *San Francisco Oracle* editor, and the poet Allen Ginsberg, wanted Berkeley's frustrated politicos to meet the Haight's hippies. If young leftists loosened up, maybe they could push the freaks into politics. A key Berkeley radical invited to the Be-In was Jerry Rubin (1938–94), a main organizer of the Vietnam Day Committee's (VDC's) antiwar protests in 1965. The son of a Cincinnati Teamsters union organizer, star sports reporter, and former Israeli resident, Rubin had moved to Berkeley to enter graduate school in sociology, but he had quickly dropped out. The VDC demonstrators, Rubin said, were "psychic terrorists." The goal was to shock people into changing their views. Young people, he thought, could "join the revolution and have fun." The impact could be enormous. "We sat in Chinese restaurants and coffee shops," he recalled, "and we knew that we had the power to set off waves of thought across the country."[28]

While grooving with hippies from the Haight, smoking pot, and dropping acid, Rubin concluded, "Ideology is a brain disease." Leftist friends considered him insane when he said, "Karl Marx is outmoded because he never watched television." Rubin's new friends from the counterculture led to innovative political insights. In 1966 the House Un-American Activities Committee (HUAC) issued a subpoena to Rubin. After consulting Ronnie Davis of the Mime Troupe, Rubin decided to confront HUAC with a theatrical performance. "People don't like to read," he noted, "We are an ear and eye culture." So Rubin appeared at the hearing dressed as a Revolutionary War soldier. He was stoned, too. "With that one zap," he later boasted, "I inspired rebellious people everywhere to be outrageous." Rubin's costume so upset the committee that he was escorted out of the room. As the

---

[28] Jerry Rubin, *Do It!* (New York, 1970), 12–13, 38 (first quote); Jerry Rubin, *Growing (Up) at Thirty-Seven* (New York, 1976), 77 (last two quotes); W. J. Rorabaugh, *Berkeley at War* (New York, 1989), 90–1.

marshals carried him out, he screamed to the cameras, "I want to testify."[29]

In early 1967 Rubin decided to run for mayor of Berkeley. "What better way to make fun of the political system," he wrote, "than to run for public office?" Stew Albert, a drug-taking former Maoist, was Rubin's manager. According to Albert, Rubin dreamed of "high, hip and happy, soulful socialism." Rubin's goal was to organize radicals, hippies, and students. Copying the style used by the San Francisco rock posters, his campaign poster set forth his platform. He wanted to bring peace to Vietnam, end poverty, stop police harassment of longhairs, reduce the voting age to eighteen, legalize marijuana, impose rent control, embrace Black Power and Student Power, fight racism, tax the rich, and plant trees and flowers. These issues would dominate the hippie-radical political agenda for decades. Rubin won 21 percent of the vote, losing the middle class in the hills and African Americans in the flatlands, but he carried four precincts near the university populated by students, hippies, and radicals.[30]

After the election Rubin moved to the East and quickly linked up with Abbie Hoffman (1936–89), a Brandeis University dropout. Hoffman's wit balanced Rubin's anger. A one-time mental patient who had studied psychology and worked in sales, Hoffman understood human motivation. Deploying Hoffman's penchant for showmanship, the duo borrowed from the Diggers to stage a series of theatrical protests. However, whereas the Diggers cultivated the community, Rubin and Hoffman targeted the media. The best remembered episode took place when the pair along with Stew Albert and a few accomplices infiltrated the New York Stock Exchange, made their way to the balcony

[29] Stew Albert, *Who the Hell Is Stew Albert?* (Los Angeles, 2004), 71 (first quote); DeGroot, *Sixties Unplugged*, 264 (second quote); Rubin, *Do It!*, 57–65; Rubin in Fred Halstead, *Out Now!* (New York, 1978), 165 (third quote); Rubin, *Growing (Up) at Thirty-Seven*, 78 (fourth and fifth quotes).

[30] Rubin, *Do It!*, 47–51 (first quote at 47); Albert, *Who the Hell Is Stew Albert?*, 57 (second quote); Rorabaugh, *Berkeley at War*, 112. The poster is in Lincoln Cushing, *All of Us or None* (Berkeley, 2012), 15.

overlooking the exchange, and hurled onto the floor a flurry of dollar bills. The brokers grabbed the money as cameras rolled and thereby brilliantly confirmed the image of being greedy, money-grubbing capitalists. Afterward, Hoffman burned a five dollar bill in front of the stock exchange and then melted into the subway as the police arrived. What was one to make of this new style of protest, which made no coherent demands, negotiable or otherwise?[31]

Rubin and Hoffman helped plan the antiwar protest in Washington in October 1967. More than one hundred thousand people showed up, a motley amalgam of short-haired communists, Quaker pacifists, middle-class housewives, families with babes in arms, militant student radicals, curious journalists, and long-haired hippies. While some participants lobbied on Capitol Hill, the main event was a march from Washington to the Pentagon parking lot, where the protesters were greeted by troops that surrounded the building. Some demonstrators sang civil rights songs, Quakers put flowers in the rifle barrels of the troops, and a few hardcore marchers, including the novelist Norman Mailer, charged the hated Pentagon. They were arrested. Rubin and Hoffman's long-haired contingent attracted the media by trying (and failing) to levitate the Pentagon. The hippie Charles Artman originated the idea while stoned, and Allen Cohen of the *San Francisco Oracle* had passed it on to Rubin.[32]

On New Year's Eve, 1967, Rubin, Hoffman, Ed Sanders of the Fugs, Paul Krassner, editor of the *Realist*, and a few others met in Krassner's New York apartment, got high, and laid plans. Forced to drop the name New York Diggers after Emmett Grogan objected, the group created the Youth International Party. It was, Hoffman later said, a "put-on" for the media.

---

[31] Abbie Hoffman, *Revolution for the Hell of It* (New York, 1968), 32–3; Rubin, *Do It!*, 117–18; Jonah Raskin, *For the Hell of It* (Berkeley, 1996), 112–17.

[32] Rubin, *Do It!*, 66–80; Hoffman, *Revolution for the Hell of It*, 38–47; Raskin, *For the Hell of It*, 117–25. On the levitation see Rorabaugh, *Berkeley at War*, 135; Allen Cohen, *The San Francisco Oracle* (Berkeley, 1991), xxxii, xlviii. See also Norman Mailer, *The Armies of the Night* (New York, 1968).

Although the media might choose to see a political party, the idea was to promote the young, who were expressing dissatisfaction all over the world, and to create opportunities to "party," that is, have fun. Neither a political party nor a movement, Yippies were primarily a propaganda tool devised to gain publicity for Rubin and Hoffman. At the end of the meeting, Krassner spontaneously yelled, "YIP-pie! We're Yippies!" The name resonated with hippies. Yippies, Rubin later wrote, were Jewish hippies. Politically radical, especially concerning the Vietnam War, Yippies wore long hair, dressed in counterculture clothes, embraced hippie drugs, music, and sex, and created a hippie-looking component at radical protests.[33]

Given Rubin and Hoffman's exhibitionism, the Yippies were bound to be noticed. They were, said Hoffman, "a potlitical [*sic*] grass leaves movement," a reference both to Walt Whitman's uninhibited freedom and to marijuana. Yippie meetings were filled with pot smoke. Heavily influenced by drugs, Yippies favored the "politics of ecstasy." This idea expressed confidence in a future society based on personal liberation. While hippies followed Timothy Leary's advice to drop out, noted Hoffman, Yippies refused to do so. They embraced life, but they did so on their own terms. "I don't consider myself a leftist," he added. "I'm a revolutionary artist. Our concept of revolution is that it's fun. The left has the concept that you have to sacrifice. Who the hell is going to buy that product? A lot of the left is into masochistic theater, if you ask me." Finding the left dated, Rubin said, "The left would rather hand a soldier a leaflet than a joint." Calling Rubin the "Lysergic Lenin," Timothy Leary advised, "You don't blow up the czar's palace. You blow minds."[34]

[33] J. Anthony Lukas, "Yippies' Leader Tells the Judge Just What His Party Believes," *New York Times*, December 30, 1969, 14 (first quote); Rubin, *Do It!*, 81–6, 176 (second quote at 81); Tom Buckley, "The Battle of Chicago," *New York Times Magazine*, September 15, 1968, 31.

[34] Quotes from Hoffman, *Revolution for the Hell of It*, 102; Buckley, "Battle of Chicago," 30–1; Rubin, *Do It!*, 113; DeGroot, *Sixties Unplugged*, 262; Robert Greenfield, *Timothy Leary* (Orlando, FL, 2006), 333.

The Yippies had a slogan: "Rise up and abandon the creeping meatball!" Rubin explained, "The 'meatball' is whatever bugs you." Paying homage to libertarianism, he declared, "Each man his own yippie." Individualism was affirmed. Yippies had no followers; each Yippie was his own leader. Hoffman said, "We're not leaders, we're cheerleaders." Rubin explained, "Yippies do whatever we want to do whenever we want to do it." In keeping with the counterculture's disdain for work, they demanded "full unemployment for all." For Rubin, the older generation had nothing to teach the children, who had grown up with color TV, guerrilla wars, psychedelics, rock 'n' roll, and moon walks. Television, in particular, had reshaped the young with visual impressions. "Television," wrote Hoffman, "is more like swimming than reading books." According to Rubin, young people concluded, "We can do *anything*." Yippie demands could never be satisfied. The goal was to use demands to create confrontations, turn spectators into actors, and build community.[35]

Rubin, Hoffman, and the Yippies decided to protest at the 1968 Democratic National Convention. "Over 500,000 free spirits," announced the Yippies, "will come to Chicago during Aug. 25–30. They will come to celebrate a free Festival of Life as a living alternative to the death of the National Democratic Party. Over one hundred music groups, celebrities, and theater groups have already agreed to participate." Among those announced were Allen Ginsberg, Timothy Leary, Judy Collins, Phil Ochs, the Fugs, and Country Joe and the Fish. The purpose of this "morality play," Rubin wrote, was to "freak out the Democrats" and show "revolutionary youth culture" as an alternative to the mainstream. To lure the young, Yippies planned a free rock music festival. Ed Sanders promised "poetry readings, mass meditation, flycasting, exhibitions, demagogic Yippie political arousal speeches, rock music, and song concerts ...

---

[35] Rubin, *Do It!*, all quotes at 84, except the sixth quote at 86; Raskin, *For the Hell of It*, 129 (fourth quote); Hoffman, *Revolution for the Hell of It*, 79 (seventh quote).

psychedelic long-haired ... peace leftists will consort with known dope fiends...."[36]

Yippies disagreed about the purpose of the event. Paul Krassner told a press conference, "This is a cultural revolution." He added, "We have no ideology." Seeking a confrontation, the militant Rubin predicted that rock music would "give birth to orgasm and revolution." Publicly, the gentle Hoffman disagreed with Rubin and called for a love fest. Privately, he wrote, "We plan to bring 250,000 people to the Democratic Convention. We expect about 100,000 of them to be committed to disruption or sabotage." Liberals and the underground press attacked the plan, Lyndon Johnson deflated the festival by quitting the presidential contest, and Mayor Richard Daley's government proved inhospitable. Fearful of violence from both Daley's police and demonstrators, California radicals stayed away, and so did many members of Students for a Democratic Society. Performers dropped out, including Country Joe McDonald. Among the few musicians present were the folksinger Phil Ochs and the radical rock band MC5.[37]

Barred from the vicinity of the Democratic National Convention, the Yippies decided to nominate their own presidential candidate: Pigasus, an Illinois-raised two-hundred pound hog that Rubin had bought for $25. Rubin and Stew Albert had rejected a pig supplied by Hoffman as neither large enough nor ugly enough. The campaign slogan was: "Why take half a hog when you can have the whole hog?" They planned a convention with pot smoke filling caucus rooms. When the Yippies held a press conference in Chicago on Friday, August 23, 1968, just days before the convention opened, to introduce Pigasus in the plaza in front of City Hall, police immediately seized the pig, declaring that the Yippies were holding livestock inside the city without a permit. Rubin, Albert, and five other Yippies were

---

[36] "Yippie!," Detroit *Fifth Estate*, April 1, 1968, 8; Rubin, *Do It!*, 161–8 (quotes at 161); Sanders in Buckley, "Battle of Chicago," 31.

[37] Krassner in Carol Kramer, "Eastern Yippies Plan for Chicago," *Chicago Tribune*, March 20, 1968, 32; Rubin, *Do It!*, 161–8 (quote at 162); Raskin, *For the Hell of It*, 127–34 (quote at 127).

arrested. During the fall campaign, Yippies showed off numerous real pigs, buttons of pigs, and images of piglike politicians. "It was shades of *Animal Farm*," said Hoffman.[38]

Among the thousands of pacifists, civil rights activists, anti-war liberals, new leftists, and hardcore revolutionaries who came to Chicago to protest, about two thousand to three thousand freaks gathered in Lincoln Park on the Sunday before the convention opened. Some, but not all, of these longhairs were Yippies. "We were," recalled Rubin, "dirty, smelly, grimy, foul, loud, dope-crazed, hell-bent, and leather-jacketed." Reveling in individualism and authenticity, the hippies smoked pot and made love. That night the police used tear gas and clubs to clear the park. After the Yippies and their hippie allies protested in the streets, breaking windows and setting garbage cans ablaze, they took over Grant Park in downtown Chicago. The longhairs infuriated the police by shouting obscenities, calling the cops pigs, climbing on park statues, sleeping in the park (illegally), and smoking so much marijuana that clouds of it drifted across Michigan Avenue to the front of the hotels, where reporters interviewed party delegates. Neither Mayor Richard Daley nor the police were amused. On Tuesday night tear gas fired into the park drifted back across the street and into the Hilton Hotel ventilation system.[39]

The main legacy of the Chicago convention, however, was the police riot on Wednesday night, August 28, when Daley's cops waded with military precision and nightsticks into the motley crowd of radicals, freaks, and Yippies in Grant Park. Bloodied kids, many having been tear gassed, ran screaming from the park toward the television reporters set up to do interviews with delegates along Michigan Avenue. Then the police attacked the reporters, too, and even invaded the hotels to drag out and beat

[38] "7 Yippies Arrested with Pig Candidate at Chicago Center," *New York Times*, August 24, 1968, 19; "7 Yippies, Their Pig Seized at a Rally," *Chicago Tribune*, August 24, 1968, 6; Rubin, *Do It!*, 176–9 (first quote at 176); Hoffman, *Revolution for the Hell of It*, 93–4 (second quote at 94).

[39] Rubin, *Do It!*, 168–72 (quote at 169); Hoffman, *Revolution for the Hell of It*, 123–31; Raskin, *For the Hell of It*, 158–64.

anyone with long hair. Protesters chanted, "The whole world is watching." And they were. To America's longhairs, the effect was exactly as Rubin and Hoffman had calculated. Hippies disliked the police, and after the Chicago police riot, longhairs all over the United States empathized with the Yippies, even if they did not personally become politically active. The looks, behavior, and arrogance of the longhairs, however, horrified the middle class, who concluded that both hippies and radicals were no good.[40]

Rubin and Hoffman were among eight activists indicted for the Chicago protests in a famous show trial that kept them off the streets during 1969. Other counterculture radicals also landed in serious trouble. John Sinclair, manager of the radical rock band MC5, founded the White Panthers to make alliance with the Black Panthers. Sinclair was sentenced to ten years for selling a small quantity of marijuana to an undercover cop. The most radical group in the counterculture was Ben Moraya's Up against the Wall Motherfuckers, a Puerto Rican gang in New York. In 1968 they proclaimed, "We must take up the gun as well as the joint." A mixture of anarchists, community organizers, and guerrilla soldiers, they put a gun to Bill Graham's head in New York to demand one free weekly show at Fillmore East with edgy bands such as MC5 or Sly and the Family Stone. Graham yielded. Years later, Moraya said they had been Dada artists in despair over what they saw as the coming social collapse.[41]

Bay Area activists decided that the time was ripe to bring radicals and hippies together in the city of Berkeley. By 1969, with the Haight overrun with heroin and crime, many hippies had moved to the south side of Berkeley, where they blended in with long-haired students and radicals. The South Campus area was

---

[40] Rubin, *Do It!*, 173; chant in Buckley, "Battle of Chicago," 136; Raskin, *For the Hell of It*, 142, 165–70. See also Todd Gitlin, *The Whole World Is Watching* (Berkeley, 1980); David Farber, *Chicago '68* (Chicago, 1988); Frank Kusch, *Battleground Chicago* (Westport, CT, 2004).

[41] On White Panthers see Farber, "Counterculture and the Antiwar Movement," 19; Leslie Brody, *Red Star Sister* (St. Paul, MN, 1998), 63. On Moraya's group see Carlo McCormick essay in Christoph Grunenberg and Jonathan Harris, eds., *Summer of Love* (Liverpool, UK, 2005), 237–8; Farber, "Counterculture and the Antiwar Movement," 19 (quote).

ideal for hippies. The shopping district along Telegraph Avenue made a good place to panhandle, and students often bought drugs from freaks. The most important reason for the counterculture inundation, however, was cheap housing. White families had fled the neighborhood's older homes to avoid school desegregation. By 1970 Berkeley contained about twenty thousand white nonstudents in their twenties; in five South Campus census tracts they formed a majority.[42]

In 1967 the University of California evicted hundreds of residents, both hippies and students, from old houses on a block that it owned near the campus. Acting under pressure from Don Mulford, a conservative legislator, the university planned to tear down the housing and build high-rise dorms. Calling the neighborhood a "human cesspool," Mulford argued, "We must get rid of the rat's nest that is acting as a magnet for the hippie set and the criminal element." The low-rent houses were demolished, but the block remained a muddy vacant lot that enraged the neighborhood. Plans for new housing stalled when the rising cost of the Vietnam War forced cancellation of the federal program that the university needed to finance construction. Throughout 1968 the block remained empty, except for an informal unpaved parking lot where commuting students parked free.[43]

Bill Miller, a longtime radical activist and owner of a head shop, The Store, disliked looking at the empty, ugly block. Constantly harassed by police due to the nature of his business, he sought revenge on the establishment. Miller was also a leader of the Provos, a Berkeley group modeled on the Haight Diggers that took its name from the Dutch Provos. The Provos served free hot meals to thirty to fifty people a day in Civic Center Park downtown, which they quickly renamed Provo Park. On weekends free rock concerts were also held there. It was later disclosed that the city had financed the food and concerts in order to lure hippies away from Telegraph. The Provos also operated the Free

---

[42] Statistics are in Rorabaugh, *Berkeley at War*, 145. See also James T. Carey, *The College Drug Scene* (Englewood Cliffs, NJ, 1968).

[43] Mulford in *Berkeley Gazette*, April 6, 1967, 1.

Store, where donated clothes, toys, and kitchen equipment could be obtained. For a time, the Provos provided free bus service between Berkeley and the Haight.[44]

Michael Delacour, owner of a counterculture dress shop called the Red Square on Dwight near Telegraph, also brooded upon the university's muddy parking lot. On April 13, 1969 Delacour, Miller, Stew Albert, and other activists met. Delacour suggested that the eyesore could be used to rally both hippies and radicals to build a park on the land. Constructing the park would be an act of authenticity that also would create community. For hippies, the park would be a green oasis that symbolized a commitment to nature and an affirmation of life. It would also become a site for rock concerts and other community gatherings. Green consciousness was rising, and a year later the first Earth Day would be celebrated. For radicals, the park offered an opportunity to forge a hippie-radical alliance, confront authority, provoke repression, and thereby gain recruits. Abbie Hoffman, visiting from the East, stood on the site with Frank Bardacke and Stew Albert, who explained that the issue would "suck Reagan into a fight."[45]

The campaign for the park began on April 18, when Albert, writing in the *Berkeley Barb* under the name "Robin Hood's Park Commissioner," proposed that the counterculture community seize the idle land from the university by bringing picks and shovels to start construction on a park on Sunday, April 20. This call was important, because at the time the *Barb* enjoyed a circulation of about ninety-five thousand. Expressing an anarchist sensibility, Albert declared, "Nobody supervises, and the trip

[44] On Miller see "Hi, Bill. Hi, Pig," *Berkeley Barb*, January 17, 1969, 7; "No More the Store," *Berkeley Barb*, April 25, 1969, 11. On the Provos see "For Love Not Lucre," *Berkeley Barb*, November 25, 1966, 3; Bill Miller, "Provo Bus Set to Ramble," *Berkeley Barb*, July 14, 1967, 4.

[45] On Delacour see Stanley I. Glick, "The People's Park" (PhD diss., SUNY Stony Brook, 1984), 35–7. The meeting is in California, Governor, *The People's Park: A Report on a Confrontation at Berkeley, California Submitted to Governor Ronald Reagan* (Sacramento, 1969), 3–5; Robert Scheer, "Dialectics of Confrontation," *Ramparts*, August 1969, 48; Glick, "People's Park," 37–9. Albert in Abbie Hoffman, *Woodstock Nation* (New York, 1969), 57.

belongs to whoever dreams." Much to the surprise of Delacour
and the originators, on the appointed day hundreds of hippies,
students, straight-looking professors, curious neighborhood residents, and grandmothers showed up with picks and shovels to
work. They came as individuals rather than as members of any
organization, they wanted to express authenticity, and they were
committed to building community. "For the first time in my life,"
wrote Albert, "I enjoyed working."[46]

The site was soon christened People's Park, a name that had
significance. Not only did it recall People's Songs and other people's institutions created by communists during the 1940s, but
it also posited the right of the younger generation by physical
presence to assert that they were the people – or at least the
people in Berkeley – in contradistinction to the legal claim to the
land by the absentee, wealthy regents of the university. The word
park was also significant. A park was a piece of land in public
ownership for public purposes. It was also devoted to nature,
but a park was not strictly natural. Rather, it was a natural setting that was improved for public purposes by human effort.
Hippies and radicals could neither stop the war nor end racism.
While drugs, music, and easy sex did not express a larger purpose, building a park did. If freaks, radicals, and straights came
together voluntarily through their own efforts without any government involvement to turn a muddy parking lot into a public
park, they were creating a valuable social good through their
own labor. They also gave meaning and significance to their own
lives through this act of community building.[47]

Within a few days, the park began to flourish. Trees, shrubs,
and flowers were planted. Sod was brought in and laid. Gardens
were designed for growing vegetables. These efforts could be
seen as the beginning of urban pea patches as well as the back-to-
the-land movement. Rock bands came and played, and the park

[46] Stew Albert, "Hear Ye, Hear Ye," *Berkeley Barb*, April 18, 1969, 2; Stew
Albert, "Free for All," *Berkeley Barb*, April 25, 1969, 5.
[47] On People's Songs and People's Artists see Robbie Lieberman, *My Song Is My
Weapon* (Urbana, 1989), esp. 67–74, 140–4. On community see Stew Albert,
"Free for All," *Berkeley Barb*, April 25, 1969, 5.

builders took breaks from their work to dance. Marijuana was smoked, and LSD was taken. Couples sometimes coupled on the new lawn. Without governmental support, Delacour's group quickly lost control. One man tried to dig a barbecue pit, while another tried to fill it in. The problem with anarchism was that it produced anarchy. Meanwhile, the university bureaucracy was paralyzed. The city sent a mediator to try to get the park builders to negotiate what would be built, but success was limited. Some people began to sleep in the park to protect it. Attempts to remove these residents brought protests.[48]

As People's Park gained attention, Bobby Seale of the Black Panthers paid a visit. "You mean you just took that land without asking anyone?" inquired Seale, who lacked the ability of the white middle class to assert ownership of everything. Not long after this observation, Delacour met Frank Bardacke, who noted the problem with Delacour's original scheme: it lacked any moral anchor. A former graduate student in political science, Bardacke introduced Delacour to the concept of users' rights. Under this doctrine, all land should be used productively. If land was idle or being poorly utilized, it could be lawfully seized for a new, higher purpose. Accordingly, European explorers had invoked users' rights to take North America from the Indians. Bardacke suggested that the park builders could invoke the same doctrine to gain land from the university. A manifesto expressing this idea, reproduced over a shadowy figure of an American Indian, was published in the *Barb* and widely distributed as a poster throughout Berkeley.[49]

By the second week, neighbors complained about noisy rallies, bongo drums, and bonfires in the park, and University of California officials fretted. The regents were furious at the takeover. Chancellor Roger Heyns, however, wanted to avoid a confrontation. The administration calculated that the next winter's

---

[48] Steve Haines, "Park in Danger," *Berkeley Barb*, May 2, 1969, 3; Steve Haines, "Wolves on Prowl," *Berkeley Barb*, May 9, 1969, 3; Glick, "People's Park," 52–53; Rubin, *Do It!*, 224–8.

[49] Seale in Rorabaugh, *Berkeley at War*, 157; Scheer, "Dialectics of Confrontation," 49; Frank Bardacke, "Who Owns the Park?" *Berkeley Barb*, May 9, 1969, 2.

rains would wipe out the ill-drained park, and the university could then quietly reclaim the site. The university announced that it had obtained funds to build an unwanted soccer field, but the park builders knew that this was merely a ruse to assert control. "They could just as well have said," park supporters sarcastically observed, "they needed it to stage debutante balls for the children of the regents." Conservatives also attacked the chancellor. "Commie illegal takeover of the property is the first step in planned confrontation," warned the *BCU Bulletin*. As if to validate this claim, the militants enthused, "We need the Park to live and grow, and eventually we need all of Berkeley."[50]

Both Heyns and the militants knew that park supporters in Berkeley easily outnumbered the local police and that if police or sheriff's deputies from outside the city were called, Heyns and city officials would lose control. During the Third World Liberation Front strike in early 1969, outside law enforcement had proved to be so inept that Governor Reagan had been forced to call in the California National Guard. The city showed no interest in the park, the regents refused to lease the site to any hippies, and the park originators, sticking to anarchist principles, vowed that they could bind no one. Negotiations collapsed. Governor Ronald Reagan demanded the park be fenced. The chancellor resisted. The fence was provocative, and student opinion, which was ambivalent about the park, would turn against the administration. Heyns was told that he had twenty-four hours to announce that the fence would be built, or he would be removed. The regents sided with Reagan, who held the university's budget hostage. The chain-link fence went up on Thursday, May 15, 1969 at 4:30 a.m.[51]

Reaction was immediate and negative. Inflammatory leaflets were distributed on Telegraph. One read, "Let's tell the University that we want the South Campus area to remain a beautiful place

[50] Debutante balls from a leaflet in Rorabaugh, *Berkeley at War*, 158; *BCU Bulletin*, May 1969, 1; militants in "Proclamation," *Berkeley Barb*, May 9, 1969, 3.

[51] Rorabaugh, *Berkeley at War*, 158–60.

of homes and parks, and not become a place of ugly dormitories and parking lots." At a large noontime rally in front of Sproul Hall, where the Free Speech Movement had been launched in 1964, and where many antiwar rallies had been held from 1965 on, Dan Siegel, a law student, draft resister, and the student body president-elect, spoke. He told the crowd, which included students, radicals, and hippies, how the university had evicted students and hippies from low-rent housing, had demolished the housing, had created a muddy wasteland similar to Vietnam, and then had destroyed the park. The fence disgusted him. Swelling with indignation, he yelled, "Let's go down and take over the park." Listeners chanted, "Take the park! We want the park!" Thousands surged toward the park.[52]

The crowd of two thousand to six thousand radicals, hippies, and students never reached the park, which was heavily guarded. Blocked in the middle of Telegraph Avenue, the protesters split into small groups, broke windows, and set trashcans on fire. Someone opened a fire hydrant. Demonstrators hurled rocks, and police fired tear gas. The Alameda County deputy sheriffs, called the Blue Meanies in Berkeley because they wore blue, were nasty, and resembled the evil characters in the Beatles film *Yellow Submarine*, stopped firing tear gas. One squad loaded and fired birdshot into clumps of people. As demonstrators fled, shots ricocheted in all directions. Pellets struck innocent passersby blocks away. In the center of campus, a bullet fired by the San Francisco Tactical Squad bounced through an open window into a classroom.[53]

In the middle of the riot, radio station KPFA talked on the telephone with John Lennon in Montreal. Lennon, who had been banned by the Nixon administration from the United States, was in the middle of an antiwar protest. He and Yoko Ono were staging a "bed-in," that is, they refused to get out of bed to protest the

---

[52] Leaflet in Gar Smith, "A People's Park Chronology" (Berkeley, n.d.), 12; Siegel and crowd in California, Governor, *People's Park*, 16.

[53] California, Governor, *People's Park*, 17–21; Glick, "People's Park," 91–5; Lawrence E. Davies, "Shotguns and Tear Gas Disperse Rioters near the Berkeley Campus," *New York Times*, May 16, 1969, 1, 50.

Vietnam War. Lennon told KPFA he supported People's Park but deplored violent confrontation. "I don't believe there's any park worth getting shot for," he said. The famous Beatle advised the protesters to hold a festival and sing "Hare Krishna." He added, "The students are being conned! It's like the school bully: He aggravates you and aggravates you until you hit him. And then they kill you, like in Berkeley.... The monster doesn't care – the Blue Meanie is insane. We really care about life. Destruction is good enough for the Establishment. The only thing they can't control is the mind, and we have to fight for sanity and peace on that level. But the students have gotten conned into thinking they can change it with violence and they can't, you know, they can only make it uglier and worse."[54]

All afternoon the battle raged. On Telegraph a city car was overturned and burned. The officer inside had to pull a pistol to escape the angry crowd. The *San Francisco Chronicle* published a photograph of a demonstrator being shot in the back while fleeing down a street. A highway patrol car chased demonstrators down Telegraph, and youths broke the car's windows with rocks. One squad of Blue Meanies fired all the shots along Telegraph. Bricks and chunks of concrete were hurled from rooftops along Telegraph at officers below. Alan Blanchard, assistant manager of the Telegraph Repertory Theater, stood on the roof watching the mayhem below. Suddenly, birdshot was fired at the roof, and Blanchard was blinded. Nearby, another rooftop observer, James Rector, a community college dropout who lived in Oakland, was shot with buckshot in the heart. He died in the hospital four days later. Altogether, 110 people were shot. No one fired at the police.[55]

That night, Governor Reagan called out the National Guard. The guard, along with police, sheriff's deputies, and the highway

---

[54] Lennon in Jon Wiener, *Come Together* (New York, 1984), 92–3.
[55] Glick, "People's Park," 97–107, 114, 116; Scheer, "Dialectics of Confrontation," 42–3; Smith, "People's Park Chronology," 15–17; "Photo Stirs New Furor," *San Francisco Chronicle*, May 19, 1969, 26; "Buckshot Blamed in Berkeley Death," *San Francisco Chronicle*, May 21, 1969, 1, 28.

patrol, occupied Berkeley for seventeen days. Guardsmen often harassed students making their way from their south campus apartments to campus to attend classes or go to labs. On Tuesday, May 20, the guard sealed the edge of the campus around the Student Union, leaving thousands of students, shoppers, onlookers, and university employees trapped inside of a box with no effective exit. Without warning a National Guard helicopter then sprayed the crowd with tear gas. "There is nothing like standing under a helicopter as it swoops down to begin its gassing run to inspire one with new vision," observed the local activist Michael Rossman. A few managed to escape, but most stayed and vomited. The cloud of gas blew up the hill to the university's health center, where it tortured the lungs of polio patients hooked to iron lungs, and it burned the skin on swimmers at the Strawberry Canyon pool, a half mile from the drop zone.[56]

The citizens of Berkeley decided to take back their city from the outsiders. On May 30, which was Memorial Day, twenty thousand to thirty thousand people, including students, radicals, hippies, middle-class families, and grandparents, marched peacefully through Berkeley. Among the participants was a contingent from the San Francisco Mime Troupe. A sorority house banner read, "Power to the People's Park." The Quakers distributed thirty thousand daisies. Young women wore flowers in their hair, and some followed the Yippie practice at the Pentagon protest in 1967 by putting flowers down the rifle barrels of the guardsmen. Many guardsmen sympathized with the desire of the locals to control their own city. Rejecting revolutionary red and black, marchers carried green banners and flags made from old Girl Scout uniforms. "The green flag," predicted Philip MacDougal, represented "new indelible connections in the mind" that would "re-color popular protest in every country in the world, from

---

[56] Glick, "People's Park," 97, 124–6, 130–3, 138–42; Smith, "People's Park Chronology," 26–8; "Helicopter Sprays Students Hemmed in by Guardsmen," *San Francisco Chronicle*, May 21, 1969, 1, 28; "Copter Breaks Up Berkeley Crowd," *New York Times*, May 21, 1969, 1, 30; Michael Rossman, *On Learning and Social Change* (New York, 1972), 227 (quote).

FIGURE 12. During the People's Park protests in Berkeley in 1969, flowers were a symbol of peace. Young women sometimes placed flowers in the barrels of rifles held by members of the National Guard. The soldiers did not seem to mind.

H95.18.1011. Howard Erker, untitled (Woman in a Floral Sun Dress Carrying a Bouquet of Daisies), 1969. Gelatin silver, 14 × 10 in. The Oakland Tribune Collection, the Oakland Museum of California, gift of ANG Newspapers.

this time on." The crowd approached People's Park, but no one tried to enter. The site remained guarded and fenced.[57]

As the local leftists had calculated, the battle over People's Park had a radicalizing effect on both students and hippies within Berkeley. Conservatives who had advocated bringing the guard into the city were discredited, and many moved away. The guard was withdrawn, but the park remained a fenced wasteland. In an exceptionally high turnout, students in 1969 voted 12,719 to 2,175 that People's Park should remain a park. The truth was that the increasingly dense city did have a shortage of parks. Hippies who remained in Berkeley took tutelage from the radicals who had organized the park in the first place. In 1972 a crowd tore down the hated fence. For decades the university tried and failed to build anything on the park site. The city refused to take it over as a public park. The hippie residents, now elderly, remain in place. The park is infested with crime and drugs. It is dangerous to go there.[58]

For many hippies, the lesson learned both in the Haight and in People's Park was that a new anarchistic social order could not be built in any existing American city. There were too many freeloaders and criminals ready to take advantage of the hippie penchant for chaos and distrust of government. The search for community required relocation. Jentri Anders was a Berkeley student who had been drawn into the Free Speech Movement in 1964, the antiwar movement in 1965, and other protests in the late 1960s. After the helicopter unloaded its tear gas on the peaceable crowd sitting outside the Student Union in May 1969, she decided to leave Berkeley. Not long afterward she decamped for a commune in the wet woods of Northern California. For

---

[57] Glick, "People's Park," 74–5; "A Big Park Parade," *San Francisco Chronicle*, May 31, 1969, 1, 12; "Nobody Hates a Parade," *San Francisco Chronicle*, May 31, 1969, 2; Wallace Turner, "Troops Keep Demonstrators from Park in Berkeley," *New York Times*, May 31, 1969, 24; sorority sign in Kenneth Lamott, *Anti-California* (Boston, 1971), 169; *Despite Everything*, June 1969, 1–8, 11 (MacDougal at 1).

[58] Rorabaugh, *Berkeley at War*, 165–6; "UC Students Vote to Keep the Park," *San Francisco Chronicle*, May 23, 1969, 1. See also Terri Compost, ed., *People's Park* (Berkeley, 2009).

many participants in the counterculture, the solution was to leave the city, move to the country, get close to nature, and seek solace from like-minded folk in a rural setting. In such a setting it might be possible to build community. By 1969 the hippie back-to-the-land movement was well underway. Rural communes, not urban ones, would prove far more enduring and produce much of what became the counterculture's legacy.[59]

---

[59] Anders discussed her decision to leave Berkeley in *Berkeley in the Sixties* (1990 film), directed by Mark Kitchell. See also Jentri Anders, *Beyond Counterculture* (Pullman, WA, 1990).

5

Communes

Hippies commonly expressed a yearning for community. In part this was a desire among longhairs to live among the like-minded, distance the self from the mainstream, and avoid harassment by those who disapproved of the counterculture lifestyle with its emphasis upon drugs, easy sex, and rock music. But the search for community also expressed a more generalized youthful longing for togetherness as well as a correct perception that there was little sense of community among the suburban middle-class families from which the hippies emerged. After World War II the parental generation had embraced the nuclear family with a vengeance, abandoned older ethnic relatives, and fled familiar neighborhoods for the sterile suburbs dominated by the anonymity of shopping malls and rooftop television antennas. While the crime-free suburbs offered broad lawns and fresh air for young children, they bored most teens. "Middle-class living rooms are funeral parlors," said one freak. Fleeing to the Haight, the East Village, or other such locales was about escaping the suburbs as much as anything else.[1]

[1] Peter Berg in "Year of the Commune," *Newsweek*, August 18, 1969, 89 (quote). On boring suburbs see Albert Solnit, "Wear and Tear in the Communes," *Nation*, April 26, 1971, 524; Gretchen Lemke-Santangelo, *Daughters of Aquarius* (Lawrence, KS, 2009), 40–1; Hettie Jones, *How I Became Hettie Jones* (New York, 1990), 8–10.

By the mid-1960s large numbers of hippies were finding community in shared housing in the neighborhoods where they lived. At a time when the prosperous white working class was leaving cities in record numbers, hippies shared the rent for houses or large apartments in marginal neighborhoods that were often close to African American ghettoes. In today's terms, rents were incredibly low for inner-city neighborhoods. Gentrification was nonexistent, utilities were cheap, and food cost little. Communal housing allowed for sexual experimentation, although group marriages were less common than was rumored in mainstream society. Landlords who might not have rented to an unmarried couple, however, could be persuaded to rent to a group of young people. Who slept with whom was hard to tell from the outside. Even without orgies, this lifestyle promoted psychedelic trips and philosophical discussions. "We learned skills of intimacy," recalled Allen Cohen of the *San Francisco Oracle*, "and we got used to sharing and being concerned about each other."[2]

Hippie urban communes, however, were not just a group of young people choosing to share space. Many college students also split the rent, and so did young singles trying to reduce costs. As a concept, a commune meant something more. At the heart was a search for community, even though this desire might be expressed without ideological intensity. Finding community, however, could be treacherous. A few hippie communes welcomed into residence anyone who walked in the door, but this idea, which expressed devotion to openness and equality, frequently produced a nightmare. There is, for example, excellent documentation about Rochdale College, a communelike co-op dorm at the University of Toronto that was open to all. It quickly morphed into a crash pad infested with criminals, prostitutes, and heroin addicts. To survive, communards learned to limit visitors' stays to a short time, after which the person had to move on or be invited to join, often by paying part of the rent or food bill.[3]

---

[2] On cheap shared housing in the Sixties see Timothy Miller, *The 60s Communes* (Syracuse, NY, 1999), 14–15, 45 (quote).

[3] On sharing a house versus communal living see Miller, *60s Communes*, xxii–xxiv; Benjamin D. Zablocki, *Alienation and Charisma* (New York,

Although communes varied enormously, just as the counter-culture did, there were some common traits. "We would all like to be able to live an uncluttered life," said Jerry Garcia, "a simple life, a good life and think about moving the whole human race ahead a step, or a few steps, or half a step." Hippie communards were searching for a new social ethos. "We intended to be social reformers and pioneers, not escapists," recalled Bruce Taub of the Earthworks community. This widely shared goal, moreover, involved certain assumptions. Patch Adams of Gesundheit, a residence for health care workers, declared, "Greed is one of society's worst malignancies." Opposed to large-scale capitalism, communards favored cooperation over competition. Agreeing with E. F. Schumacher, *Small Is Beautiful* (1973), hippie communards promoted local solutions. There was, however, much internal disagreement about details. "We called ourselves anarchists," noted Joyce Gardner, "because it was the only name that seemed to fit us all."[4]

Hippies often found the hedonistic lifestyle chaotic and self-destructive. One reason to join a commune, or at least a commune that had rules, was to impose order on the self at a time of cultural upheaval and personal turmoil. By living communally, a person depended upon others to enforce norms and prevent one from going off the deep end. Successful households had rules, even though they often denied having formal leaders. Residents held long and often agonizing meetings. Differences were discussed frankly, which could be brutal, if the entire membership accused one participant of being lazy or wrong-headed. For the commune to function, everyone needed to be on the same page. A hippie named Aaron explained, "It was my dream to belong to a tribe, where the energies flow among everyone, where people care for one another...." Aaron thought of a commune as "a refuge." Residents were trying to be a community.

1980), 7–8; Grace Lichtenstein, "Communal Living Here Lures the Untied but Lonely," *New York Times*, December 7, 1970, 47, 89. On Rochdale see *Dream Tower* (1994 film), directed by Ron Mann.
4 Quotes from Miller, *60s Communes*, 150, 151, 151, 61.

"The premise of all these places," he concluded, "is that we love one another."[5]

Freaks joined with others to find meaning in life. In a communal setting deep friendships blossomed, and group discussions among those who shared values, experiences, and aspirations helped ease loneliness at a time when mainstream culture seemed outdated, frayed, misshapen, or grotesque. Many resisted adapting the self to the existing society. Rather, the goal was to nurture the self in order to find a new way of life, but this idea led many hippies to conclude that a new way of life was necessary to nurture the self. Residents discussed common readings, such as the novels of Herman Hesse or J. R. R. Tolkein, and undertook meditation, yoga, breathing exercises, or encounter sessions. The sense of purpose was strong, but progress in these communes toward remaking the self was painfully slow. "Cities," said one hippie, "have too many sharp edges." Many eventually concluded that only by leaving the city could the self be remade. "The whole scene," predicted an East Village hippie, "is going to fold into tribes that live out in the country and grow their own food, and become independent."[6]

Political radicals often lived in communes, too, but they insisted on calling these houses *collectives* rather than *communes*. In a collective, everyone was duty-bound to a particular political agenda. While radicals and hippies often looked alike and shared many traits in the way they lived communally, politicos usually had more rules and fixed schedules. Residency was often restricted to organization members, and visitors might be screened for political acceptability. In some radical houses drugs were banned. Afraid of police harassment about political activity, collectives often kept a low profile at home. Leftists

---

[5] Larry Eskridge, *God's Forever Family* (New York, 2013), 87–8; Keith Melville, *Communes in the Counter Culture* (New York, 1972), 12–13 (quotes), 22.

[6] Quotes from Lewis Yablonsky, *The Hippie Trip* (New York, 1968), 163, 105. Ross V. Speck, et al., *The New Families* (New York, 1972), 34–52, 57–8, 110–12, 130–2, 145–62; Zablocki, *Alienation and Charisma*, 12–14, 116, 287; Elaine Sundancer, *Celery Wine* (Yellow Springs, OH, 1973), 17–19, 24, 91, 110, 155–8.

had frequent meetings to discuss philosophy, develop the proper political line, and debate tactics. Declaring "smash monogamy," the Weatherman faction of Students for a Democratic Society expected every member to sleep with every other member (including the same sex) in order to break down egos and gender barriers.[7]

Hippie communes were sometimes organized around work. The Grateful Dead, the Jefferson Airplane, and other bands rented large Victorian houses in the Haight where band members lived and practiced. The Dead attracted many visitors, some of whom moved into the house to provide services for the band. Carolyn Adams, who had been Ken Kesey's Mountain Girl, managed the Grateful Dead house very effectively and later married Jerry Garcia. Like many other hippie communes, police harassed the Dead house about drugs. In one raid, two band members were taken into custody, but Garcia, who may have smoked more weed than anyone, escaped arrest by being away. In San Francisco as many as 650 artists lived and worked communally at the Project One warehouse. In Washington, D.C., Ray Mungo, Marshall Bloom, and other staffers at the Liberation News Service, a national organization that supplied stories to most of the country's underground newspapers, shared a large townhouse.[8]

Hippie spiritual seekers also established communes. Some houses were overtly religious, such as those established by the Hare Krishna followers. The leader, A. C. Bhaktivedanta, opposed drugs. "You don't have to take anything for your spiritual life," he advised. Each member had a shaved head, wore a saffron

[7] On collectives see Speck, *New Families*, 114–28; Gilbert Zicklin, *Countercultural Communes* (Westport, CT, 1983), 53–4; Bill Kovach, "Communes Spread as the Young Reject Old Values," *New York Times*, December 17, 1970, 1, 84; J. R. Kennedy, "Communes," Detroit *Fifth Estate*, August 6, 1970, 10. On Weatherman see David Allyn, *Make Love, Not War* (Boston, 2000), 219–21 (quote at 220); Bill Ayers, *Fugitive Days* (Boston, 2001), 142–3.

[8] On the Dead house see Miller, *60s Communes*, 142, 167; Sandy Troy, *Captain Trips* (New York, 1994), xii, 85–7, 97, 107, 114–15. On Project One see Miller, *60s Communes*, 143–4. On Liberation News Service see Raymond Mungo, *Famous Long Ago* (Boston, 1970), 16–18, 25–34.

robe, performed chants frequently, and sold literature or begged for alms on nearby sidewalks. More than fifty young people, mostly males, crammed into the Hare Krishna house in Berkeley. They lived on a vegetarian diet that ran heavily to brown rice. It was suspected that some of them were either draft dodgers or runaway soldiers. They took Krishna names and denied to police having prior identities. As monks, they were not eligible for the draft. Other spiritual seekers lived in houses devoted to the Indian Vedanta Society, to Zen Buddhism, or to Tibetan Buddhism. Jews also established houses to practice Orthodox Judaism, including strict adherence to dietary laws.[9]

The Jesus People communes greatly exceeded all the others. The movement began in 1967, when evangelicals converted street kids in the Haight and established the first hippie Christian commune, the House of Acts in Novato, a suburb north of San Francisco. One convert was Lonnie Frisbee, who returned to Southern California to preach. He stressed Bible study, spoke in tongues, and looked for divine signs. Jesus Freaks often adopted Pentecostal beliefs. Churches opened coffee houses and sponsored communes. Many residents were former hippies, but others came from traditional backgrounds. By 1969 there were more than a hundred Jesus People programs in Southern California. Christian rock stimulated the movement. Andrew Lloyd Webber's rock opera, *Jesus Christ Superstar*, scored big when released as a record in 1970. By the early Seventies the nation had thousands of Jesus communes. The Oregon-based Shiloh group alone ran more than 175 residences. Also influential was the Children of God, which was later accused of being a cult. In 1971 Billy Graham endorsed the Jesus movement.[10]

Most hippie communes were just young people who had a counterculture sensibility finding camaraderie by living with the

[9] On spiritual communes see Miller, *60s Communes*, 92–127. On the Hare Krishnas see Robert Houriet, *Getting Back Together* (London, 1973; orig. 1971), 309–19 (quote at 311); Miller, *60s Communes*, 103–5. On the Farm see Stephen Gaskin, *Haight Ashbury Flashbacks* (2nd ed., Berkeley, 1990). See also Charles P. LeWarne, *The Love Israel Family* (Seattle, 2009).

[10] Eskridge, *God's Forever Family*, 17–38, 53–78, 87–9, 98–104, 126, 134–8; Robert S. Ellwood, *One Way* (Englewood Cliffs, NJ, 1973), ix–x, 17–18, 22, 101–11.

FIGURE 13. In 1970 Arnold Dietrich, leader of the Children of God, posed in front of his downtown Los Angeles mission for hippie youth with his wife, Faith Berg. Charismatic Protestantism surged among the young in Southern California. Some were former hippies, and some were not.

Los Angeles Times Photographic Archive, Library Special Collections, Charles E. Young Research Library, UCLA.

like-minded. Finding the money to keep a commune going in the city was always a challenge. This was especially true when most inhabitants were either unemployed or worked only sporadically at odd jobs. Drug dealing became a source of income for some residents, but this activity could bring unwanted police attention upon the group. Many communards, especially college graduates, worked at regular jobs, often in the arts, in social services, or for low-paying nonprofits. In some households, each member turned over a fixed amount from outside wages as a monthly payment. In other cases, members were expected to turn over entire paychecks. A few urban communes had single mothers with children, and welfare checks were another source of funds. Parental gifts were also welcome. Some parents donated money because they felt sorry for their children. Others did so because they did not want the longhairs to come home and embarrass them in the eyes of relatives or neighbors.[11]

Rent, utilities, and food bills were usually split, but hippies embraced a concept of sharing that went beyond that found in a typical student apartment. "What's so special about sharing?" asked one communard. "It's just being a good neighbor." In some communes clothes were shared. Dirty clothes were piled in a central place, and anyone who wanted a clean shirt or jeans could wash the item to lay claim to it. A few urban communes required that everyone contribute all possessions to the common stock. Books were almost always considered common property, but record albums, which were highly prized, frequently produced controversy. Residents who moved out normally took their records with them. Because it was not practical to register an automobile in the name of the commune, ownership was usually left with the individual. The car key, however, was kept on a hook so that any member of the household could use the car at any time.[12]

---

[11] On urban communes see Miller, *60s Communes*, xxv, 160–5; Speck, *New Families*, v–ix; Steven V. Roberts, "Halfway between Dropping Out and Dropping In," *New York Times Magazine*, September 12, 1971, 44–70; Mark Perlgut, "Communal Living," *New York Times*, November 28, 1971, A7.

[12] On shared property including clothes see Miller, *60s Communes*, 35, 73, 82, 193; Kathleen Kinkade, *A Walden Two Experiment* (New York, 1973), 199;

Food could be a bonding experience, or it could lead to dissolution of the commune. Many hippies were vegetarians. Anyone could wear jeans and listen to rock music, but giving up hamburgers showed sacrifice and commitment. In religious communes, the diet was often prescribed as part of the search for spirituality. Meat, traditionally the product of warrior-like hunting, was considered a hindrance to achieving inner peace in many Asian religious traditions. Meat was also expensive. The cheapest diet in an urban setting was probably brown rice and beans. Rice could be bought for a very low price in a fifty-pound bag at an Asian market. Certain grocery stores gave away wilted vegetables that could be cooked in stews. Urban communes often obtained honey, fresh fruit, or other items from rural communes. Day-old bread came from bakery thrift stores, but many hippie women also baked whole wheat bread at low cost from flour purchased in bulk. Another source of protein was tofu, made from soybeans.[13]

As the number of urban communes grew, the residents became interested in organizing food-buying cooperatives. If several communal households joined together to buy particular items in large volumes, they could get a low price directly from a wholesaler. Giant wheels of cheese, for example, might be purchased and sliced into sections that supplied several different communes with fresh cheese. It was also possible to organize a larger-scale food co-op, such as the Puget Consumers Co-op in Seattle. This hippie co-op became a full-fledged grocery store that served both members and outsiders. Because the co-op ordered food only from organic farmers, shoppers knew that every item in the store was organic, and most of it came from local producers. Members could reduce cash payments for food

---

Carl Bernstein, "Communes, a New Way of Life in District," *Washington Post*, July 6, 1969, C1, C2; "Year of the Commune," *Newsweek*, August 18, 1969, 90 (quote).

[13] On diet see Warren J. Belasco, *Appetite for Change* (New York, 1989), 3–99; Miller, *60s Communes*, 120, 199–200; Speck, *New Families*, 43, 67, 74; Raymond A. Sokolov, "The Food at the Heart of Commune Life," *New York Times*, December 2, 1971, 60. See also Lemke-Santangelo, *Daughters of Aquarius*, 91–2.

by getting credits for working at the co-op. For hippies who worked only sporadically, this system enabled them to cut food bills considerably.[14]

A few communes practiced group marriages. John Presmont changed his name to Brother Jud and established Kerista in the early 1960s. Members embraced hedonism by smoking marijuana and indulging in free love. Later, Kerista maintained a group marriage system in which each communard slept with every one of the opposite gender in rotation. All the males got vasectomies. At the Harrad West commune in Berkeley, followers of Robert Rimmer announced, "All adult members of Harrad West are considered married to all other adult members of the opposite sex." A group called the Family had formed in Berkeley and moved to Taos, New Mexico, where about fifty members crowded into a small adobe house. Calling each other "Lord" and "Lady," they slept in multiples in oversized beds or placed mattresses on the floor and paired off in numerous, varying combinations.[15]

In most urban hippie communes orgies and partner swapping were not the norm. Residents were sometimes married couples, and other residents were unmarried couples. In the latter case a pattern of serial monogamy was common. Relationships, however, often were fleeting, which contributed to the short life of many communes. Unmarried couples who moved into a commune seldom stayed together, but they did not necessarily take up with another member of the group. When a woman or man switched partners, either the new couple or the remaining member of the former couple almost always left. Single women with children were likely to stay because they could count on help with child care from other residents. Young singles in communes were often celibate, and they looked for partners from outside the household. There was a great deal of family feeling

[14] On food co-ops see Craig Cox, *Storefront Revolution* (New Brunswick, NJ, 1994). On Puget Consumers Co-Op see Miller, *60s Communes*, 238.

[15] Miller, *60s Communes*, 134–8 (quote at 136); Lemke-Santangelo, *Daughters of Aquarius*, 67–9; Iris Keltz, *Scrapbook of a Taos Hippie* (El Paso, TX, 2000), 155.

inside a commune, and taking a partner from inside felt too much like incest. There was little homosexuality in hippie communes, although lesbian and gay communes were founded in the 1970s.[16]

Most freaks smoked marijuana, which was usually a communal activity with a joint being passed around. The mild high from the weak pot available in the Sixties built camaraderie but produced little impairment. It was common for one resident to be the major supplier to other members of the group. Hippie communes were also a good source of drugs for college students. Many households were located in low-rent neighborhoods where students also lived. Commune residents often shared psychedelic trips. The communal setting improved the odds of having a nonusing guide for the trip, and the familiar homelike surroundings filled with comfortable furniture made a bad trip less likely. However, lysergic acid diethylamide (LSD) trips lasted a long time, and the inconvenience that this posed for other residents sometimes led the group to encourage trippers to drop acid elsewhere.[17]

Hippies were not necessarily good neighbors. Crammed into overcrowded houses, they blasted loud rock music and parked many beat-up cars and trucks, sometimes painted psychedelic colors, in front of neighbors' houses. There were myriad complaints to police. About one longhair a neighbor said, "Every time I look at him I want to vomit." While some irritation was nothing more than disgust with appearances, other objections were more substantial. Communes attracted visitors, and while freak residents might have wanted peace with straight neighbors, visitors could be obnoxious. When longhairs moved into the neighborhood,

---

[16] Serial monogamy is in Miller, *60s Communes*, 134, 202–4; Lemke-Santangelo, *Daughters of Aquarius*, 66–8, 73; Speck, *New Families*, 48–51, 67–8, 74, 82–3, 90, 107, 110–12; Zablocki, *Alienation and Charisma*, 339, 342, 349. On homosexual communes see Lemke-Santangelo, *Daughters of Aquarius*, 69–71, 163; Miller, *60s Communes*, xxv, 138–9, 205, 213.

[17] On drugs in communes see Miller, *60s Communes*, 6, 24, 118, 120, 162, 205–8, 216, 231; Speck, *New Families*, 1–19, 26–8, 56–7, 78–9, 84, 86, 89, 109, 160–2; Herbert A. Otto, "Communes: The Alternative Life-Style," *Saturday Review*, April 24, 1971, 20.

the crime rate spiked. To some in the counterculture, the doctrine of shared property meant that it was proper to "borrow" items from a neighbor's yard. Burglaries and break-ins soared. While much of the crime came from interlopers, thrill-seekers, rip-off artists, and drug addicts, hippie communards bore the brunt of the blame.[18]

When the media identified a neighborhood as a hippie strong-hold, as happened with both the Haight and the East Village during 1966, tourists and criminals quickly descended. Police and drug busts were not far behind. "If you've got long hair, you're bothered," complained one Massachusetts visitor to the Haight. Health departments made rigorous inspections and ordered evictions from overcrowded premises. Crash pads were closed, which put more youths out on the street, where they were targets for criminals as well as arrests. Amid the chaos, many communards felt responsibility for taking in strays. But the street kids brought lice, crabs, sexually transmitted diseases (STDs), hard drugs, and thefts. The commune ran the risk of being raided and padlocked, causing residents to lose all of their possessions. If a commune was to survive, it had to turn the kids away. Yet turning people away did not fit the hippie philosophy.[19]

Amid this rising tension, the love generation began to flee. They abandoned the Haight and the East Village for more tranquil rural places. Both Allen Cohen, former *San Francisco Oracle* editor, and Ron Thelin, former owner of a Haight head shop, moved to rural communes north of the city. Like many others devoted to individualism, Thelin concluded, "I can change the

---

[18] Miller, *60s Communes*, 27 (quote), 218–22; Robert Greenfield, *Timothy Leary* (Orlando, FL, 2006), 190–1.

[19] On crash pads see Miller, *60s Communes*, 45–6. On hippies as "bait" see Martin Arnold, "The East Village Today," *New York Times*, October 15, 1967, 77. On rising problems circa 1966 see Sherri Cavan, *Hippies of the Haight* (St. Louis, 1972), 47–54; Charles Perry, *The Haight-Ashbury* (New York, 1984), 76–81, 87, 154, 157, 163–6, 184. On police raids see Jack Viets, "Party Pad Raid-24 Hauled Off," *San Francisco Chronicle*, March 15, 1966, 1, 6; Maitland Zane, "Trouble in the City's New Bohemia," *San Francisco Chronicle*, March 15, 1966, 1, 6 (quote); Michael Mahoney, "A Hippie Plan to Foil the Fuzz," *San Francisco Chronicle*, January 17, 1967, 3.

world by changing myself. I can't change others." He found political activism infantile. There were many reasons to leave. In addition to police drug busts and soaring crime, increased city rents played a role, as large numbers of boomers began to enter their twenties and look for independent housing for the first time. In 1967, just as the Summer of Love came to an end, the Grateful Dead gave up the Haight commune. Garcia and most of the band moved to individual homes in rural Marin County, north of San Francisco, where the Dead constructed a recording studio. Only people on the invite list were welcome.[20]

In New York the jarring moment of truth came in October 1967 with the murders of James "Groovy" Hutchinson and his girlfriend, Linda Fitzpatrick. It was a classic hippie tragedy, the media milked the story for all it was worth, and it was worth a great deal. Groovy, an illiterate long-haired drifter from Rhode Island, had only recently arrived in the East Village, where he quickly became popular due to his warm, outgoing personality. Because he showed compassion, hippies found him groovy – hence, his nickname. As was typical of the counterculture, few in the East Village knew his full name. Groovy made his living by selling drugs on the street. It was a dubious and dangerous livelihood in a neighborhood where the mob had long controlled the drug trade. To reduce visibility, he sold only small quantities of marijuana, LSD, and speed to street kids.[21]

Linda, the daughter of a wealthy spice importer, had grown up in a thirty-room mansion in Greenwich, Connecticut. She rode horses, skied, and painted. An elite boarding school dropout, she called herself an artist and hung out in the East Village because it offered excitement. She was seen around the neighborhood with a series of hippie men, the last of whom turned out to be Groovy. Linda, eighteen, was attracted to Groovy, twenty-one, the savvy

[20] "Where Have All the Flower Children Gone? To Communes," *Washington Post*, November 14, 1971, K11 (quote). On the Dead's move see Troy, *Captain Trips*, 119.

[21] Emanuel Perlmutter, "2 Held in Slaying of Hippie and Girl," *New York Times*, October 10, 1967, 1, 36; LeRoy Aarons, "N.Y. Hippie Summer Yields to Ugly Reality," *Washington Post*, October 15, 1967, A7.

street dealer. She was the innocent suburban girl; he was the worldly man. Or so it seemed at first glance. Certainly her toney upbringing was a long way from his grimy world. In reality, both were speed freaks. Groovy squired Linda around the East Village. For Groovy, just meeting a girl that came from Linda's privileged background was a thrill. Linda's parents were clueless, but Linda and Groovy could not be stopped from meeting or doing drugs together. On their last night on earth the couple was high on speed standing on an East Village sidewalk.[22]

It all went terribly wrong when the pair were lured into a dark basement beneath a seedy East Village tenement for an interracial LSD orgy. As a known dealer, Groovy always carried cash. Linda was just a side dish. Both Groovy and Linda had their heads smashed in with a brick, and Linda was raped, although it was not clear whether the rape occurred before or after she died. Groovy's money was stolen, which was the main motive for the robbery-murder. This sordid tale of a dead drug dealer in the East Village would have barely made the news if Linda had not been from the elite. Her family turned up the pressure on the police. The man who had urged the pair into the basement confessed his role in return for evidence against the murderer, who was an unemployed African American known for his surliness. Reporters found that many blacks hated hippies for renouncing the middle-class lifestyle that they could not achieve.[23]

By the late 1960s, many hippies concluded that it was time to find sanctuary in rural America, where crime was low and where one might live on one's own land. Food could be grown organically, which would provide excellent nutrition at low cost. Except

[22] Albin Krebs, "Friends Call Linda Fitzpatrick the Girl Who Had Everything," *New York Times*, October 10, 1967, 36; J. Anthony Lukas, "The Two Worlds of Linda Fitzpatrick," *New York Times*, October 16, 1967, 1, 58.

[23] "Nab 2 in N.Y. Hippie Murders," *Chicago Tribune*, October 10, 1967, A6; John Kifner, "The East Village," *New York Times*, October 11, 1967, 32; Emanuel Perlmutter, "4th Man Sought in Double Slaying," *New York Times*, October 11, 1967, 32; J. Anthony Lukas, "Full Story Is Sought," *New York Times*, October 17, 1967, 1, 40; "2 Men Are Indicted in Hippie Murders in the East Village," *New York Times*, November 2, 1967, 62.

for a few earlier outliers, the hippie back-to-the-land movement began in 1967, accelerated in 1968 and 1969, and continued well into the 1970s. By the early Seventies there were three thousand communes. Although rural communes could be found in all parts of the country, most were located in areas accessible to San Francisco and New York, where hippies had originally congregated. West Coast hippies fled to northern coastal California and further north into Oregon and Washington. These three states accounted for more than one-third of the communes. A second stream moved to the area around Taos, New Mexico and to southeastern Colorado, where land was unusually cheap. About one-quarter of communes were in the Northeast. New York hippies favored upstate New York and rural New England, particularly Vermont.[24]

In 1968, Ray Mungo and Marshall Bloom moved Liberation News Service to a Vermont farm. "It is for us to launch the New Age," Mungo declared. Officially Packer Corner, this literary commune became known as Total Loss Farm. The dozen or so burned-out residents abandoned both radicalism and the news service to embrace the counterculture. This was not unusual among communards. In a sociological study of 120 communes, 57 percent of residents were former antiwar protesters, 22 percent had rioted, and 30 percent had been arrested. Once a person moved into a commune, participation in protests and arrests plummeted nearly to zero. Life at Total Loss Farm was harsh and primitive. Although residents chopped firewood, raised vegetables, and kept a cow, the farm was never self-sufficient. They survived by pooling finances, which meant living off royalties from Mungo's two books, *Famous Long Ago* (1970) and *Total Loss Farm* (1970). Another writer, Alicia Bay Laurel, joined the group. While at Wheeler's Ranch in California, she had written

[24] "The Commune Comes to America," *Life*, July 18, 1969, 16B-23; "Year of the Commune," *Newsweek*, August 18, 1969, 89. Statistic is in Hugh Gardner, *The Children of Prosperity* (New York, 1978), 9. The geographical patterns are visible in the list in Miller, *60s Communes*, 249–85. See also Zablocki, *Alienation and Charisma*, 69–72.

and published *Living on the Earth* (1970), which became a bestseller after Mungo touted it in the *New York Times*.[25]

Escaping from a large-scale, competitive, industrial, capitalist, and polluting society to a rural commune was intended to cleanse the self. Like the author Henry Thoreau, hippies yearned to return to the land, live close to nature, and depend only upon nature and the self, which required banding together in small groups. Gordon Yaswen of Sunrise Hill commune proclaimed "a new Primitive Age." Jake Guest of Wooden Shoe said, "We've got to get back to small subsistence villages and tribes. Instead of huge sewage plants, we need thousands more outhouses and compost piles." While milking a goat, one male communard said, "But here we're learning what really is and what isn't. And now, by God, we're gonna run things *our* way." Distrusting all technology, many communes used cider presses, flour grinders, hand looms, wood stoves, and wash boards. Residents debated whether to use chain saws, which required fuel, or electricity. To buy power from a commercial company supported capitalism and pollution. One compromise was to limit electricity to freezers, pumps, and sometimes record players.[26]

A number of rural hippie colonies had a strong religious or spiritual motif. Communes devoted to spirituality had common core values (even when nasty disputes developed over details), were generally conformist, tended to demand a great deal from members, and had strong leadership, which at times was authoritarian. No single religious commune in the Sixties could be called typical, because the era's spiritual upsurge involved a variety of beliefs. While many residents had been raised as mainstream Protestants, the communes, to the extent that they were Christian, were emotionally expressive. Most communalists felt uncomfortable with any traditional label. Among the few groups to have a formal denominational affiliation was Reverend Jim Jones's

[25] Miller, *60s Communes*, xvii, 16, 86–8, 152 (quote), 160, 162, 165, 196, 199. Statistics are in Zablocki, *Alienation and Charisma*, 115.

[26] Miller, *60s Communes*, 60 (first quote); Houriet, *Getting Back Together*, 10–12, 16, 34 (second quote), 91–2, 206, 210, 213; William Hedgepeth, *The Alternative* (New York, 1970), 4, 18–24, 26 (third quote), 73–6.

People's Temple, which developed the commune at Jonestown, Guyana, where Jones orchestrated the mass murder-suicide of more than nine hundred of his followers in 1978. While half of Jones's followers were black, his San Francisco church had also appealed to young whites caught up in and exhausted by the counterculture.[27]

In the late Sixties, young mainstream Protestants were in a spiritual crisis, but they were underrepresented in communes. So were Catholics. Among those who lived in spiritual communes who had been raised as Christians, residents were split between groups that were in the Christian tradition versus the ones that adopted Asian religious practices. While communards from a Protestant heritage were more likely to be in Christian settings, Catholics tended toward Asian-oriented groups. Persons from the Jewish tradition were overrepresented in spiritual communes that adopted Asian practices, and almost no Jews lived in Christian communes. A few religious communes were devoted to Judaism. Jews, who were only 3 percent of the national population, were heavily overrepresented in secular communes, where they were about one-quarter of the members. Jews were even more heavily represented in urban politically radical collectives. Communes had little appeal to nonwhites, and 99 percent of commune residents were white.[28]

Many communes looked to Asia for spiritual inspiration, and they often combined elements of Buddhism and Hinduism, as well as borrowings from Sufis, Sikhs, Christians, or Native American religious customs, especially pertaining to the use of peyote in religious rites. Many hippies settled in northern New Mexico because of widespread use of peyote by Indians living in that area. Native shamans taught that peyote had to be respected as a powerful conveyor of spiritual truth, and the recipient had to take the drug for the correct reason with proper

---

[27] On Jones see Miller, *60s Communes*, 101–2; Tim Reiterman with John Jacobs, *Raven* (New York, 1982).

[28] Statistics are in Angela A. Aidala and Benjamin Zablocki, "The Communes of the 1970s," *Marriage and Family Review* 17:1–2 (1991), 92–3.

guidance. Furthermore, peyote visions could only be interpreted with immersion in Indian beliefs, folkways, and life practices. The significance of the peyote vision to the native way of life led hippies in New Mexico to put peyote at the center of their own spiritual practices. Unlike Native Americans, however, hippies had no legal dispensation to use peyote for religious purposes.[29]

One of the most interesting rural religious communes was founded by Michael Metelica (later, Michael Rapunzel) (1950–2003) in western Massachusetts. The son of a success-ful real estate broker who had been brought up Episcopalian, Michael dropped out of high school in 1967 at age sixteen and, attracted by media hype, traveled to San Francisco during the Summer of Love. He apparently experimented with drugs and sex enough to realize that they offered no permanent solution to his spiritual yearnings. He was, however, moved by Timothy Leary's call for a spiritual quest. Metelica returned to Leyden, Massachusetts and built a large tree house on vacant property next to his parents' rural home. Soon a number of youthful followers began to move in. One later became Michael's wife. A self-declared spiritual visionary, Michael continued to attract followers. By the time he was twenty perhaps seventy young people were devoted to his personal peaceful spiritual vision of universal brotherhood. The group had a number of names before becoming known as the Renaissance Community.[30]

In 1972 the Renaissance Community bought a portion of Turners Falls, an abandoned mill town. The organization suc-ceeded because Michael insisted that followers turn over all of their assets to the group, which Michael legally owned. All monies were shared, and Michael, along with a few other leaders, made

[29] Keltz, *Scrapbook of a Taos Hippie*, 40, 49, 63, 94, 96, 105, 137; Charles Hayes, ed., *Tripping* (New York, 2000), 185–91, 397–400.

[30] On Metelica's early life see Miller, *60s Communes*, 84–5; Karol Borowski, *Attempting an Alternative Society* (Norwood, PA, 1984), 17–20, 27. See also "Many Religious Communes of Young People Are under the Sway of Compelling Leaders," *New York Times*, December 14, 1969, 82; Howard Blum, "Spirit in Flesh," *Village Voice*, August 12, 1971, 25; Barry Newman, "What's This?" *Wall Street Journal*, December 22, 1971, 1, 18.

all financial decisions. Early followers were from small-town New England middle-class families. Most were high school or college dropouts. Many were women with children who had been abandoned by their menfolk. Everyone worked within the commune, took outside jobs, or set up a business, often with Michael's backing. One early vision probably saved the community from destruction: "No Drugs, No Alcohol, No Promiscuity." Drug users stayed away, and Michael knew that alcohol led to fights. While the sexual limitation did not specifically prohibit unorthodox consensual group sex, it encouraged serial monogamy and marriage. Michael married more than forty couples.[31]

A favorable story in *Mademoiselle* magazine in 1971 included a photograph that explained Michael's appeal. In the picture, he had very long flowing blond hair, parted in the middle, which was the way Christ was commonly portrayed in Victorian America. Michael also wore a splendidly long blond beard. He was dressed for the photo in his normal garb, wearing a tank top that revealed his exceptionally brawny biceps, built up from chopping firewood, he once said, along with skintight jeans. Michael did not so much look like a religious prophet as a sex symbol – the rock star that he wanted to be. On each wrist Michael wore a special handmade leather wrist band. He had broken one wrist in an accident, and he wore the band partly to prevent his bad wrist from painfully snapping backward. The bands, however, also conveyed male power, and he was known to carry and receive private messages that were tucked into each band.[32]

At its peak in 1972, the community, spread across a number of buildings in several separate settlements, contained about 260 followers. The Renaissance Community believed in reincarnation. In one vision, Michael declared that he was the reincarnation of both Saint Peter and Robert E. Lee. Why a rural Yankee would claim a relationship to Lee remains to be explained.

---

[31] Borowski, *Attempting an Alternative Society*, 21, 29 (quote), 42–4, 52–7, 60–7, 103, 108, 153–5.
[32] Mary Cantwell, "Open the Shutters and Let the God Force Through," *Mademoiselle*, December 1971, 142.

When word about being the reincarnation of Saint Peter reached Mel Lyman, founder of the Lyman Family spiritual commune in Boston, Lyman summoned Michael to his urban abode. Far better educated and more sophisticated than Michael, Lyman had attracted middle-class followers with money as well as a few heirs that enabled the Lyman Family to maintain a life-style beyond anything that Metelica could imagine. The meeting between the two did not go well when Lyman informed Metelica that Lyman was the reincarnation of Jesus Christ. Apparently, "Christ" expected "Saint Peter" to pay homage, but Metelica only beat a hasty retreat home.[33]

One of Metelica's methods to recruit followers came from his decision to form a rock band, which had various names. For a time it was called Metelica. Michael, who could barely play a guitar, insisted on being the lead singer. In 1971, Michael booked Metelica into Carnegie Hall, in a concert that was reviewed in the *New York Times*. The newspaper's rock critic praised the ambience in the hall, the décor (which the Renaissance Community had spent considerable effort preparing), and the effective light show, but the critic denounced Michael as a rhythmically poor musician who could not sing. Metelica gave few public performances after this scathing review. In later years Michael no longer had spiritual visions. He also grew tired of giving uplifting sermons to his dwindling number of followers. In the 1980s Michael and his wife lost interest in the Renaissance Community, and in 1987 he was excommunicated from the group that he had founded.[34]

---

[33] Borowski, *Attempting an Alternative Society*, 94 (statistic), 171; Miller, *60s Communes*, 85; Cantwell, "Open the Shutters," 171–2; "Commune Thrives on Million-Dollar Income," *New York Times*, May 18, 1977, 16. On the Lyman Family see Miller, *60s Communes*, 65–6; David Felton, "The Lyman Family's Holy Siege of America," *Rolling Stone*, December 23, 1971 and January 6, 1972; David Johnston, "Once-Notorious '60s Commune Evolves into Respectability," *Los Angeles Times*, August 4, 1985, F1, F10–F14.

[34] Borowski, *Attempting an Alternative Society*, 26, 36–8; Miller, *60s Communes*, 86. The review is Don Heckman, "For Spirit in Flesh, Voices of Commune, the Trip Is Visual," *New York Times*, September 24, 1971, 34.

Rural secular communes were seldom as well run as Metelica's Renaissance Community, but one exception was Twin Oaks in Louisa County, Virginia. This commune began when a number of young people committed to a counterculture way of life read B. F. Skinner's novel, *Walden Two* (1948). Skinner proposed a rural self-sufficient form of life using moneyless labor exchanges. Several young people who met at a Skinner-inspired conference decided to put the plan into practice. At first, Kat Kinkade (1930–2008) and a few others lived in a townhouse in Washington, D.C., but Kinkade knew from the beginning that any reasonable definition of self-sufficiency meant growing a great deal of food in a rural area. By chance, the early founders met a young man who had inherited a little money, and he agreed to buy the land that was needed. In 1967 the group settled on one hundred acres in rural Virginia close to Richmond.[35]

Locals were deeply suspicious of the outsiders, who did not form traditional nuclear families. After bearded men in the group were refused service at local businesses, they shaved their beards. Twin Oaks avoided both confrontation with straights and politics. Kinkade and a few others attended the nearby Methodist Church to make friends. The sheriff still raided Twin Oaks in a search for drugs. Leaders of the community had made it clear to members that drugs were not to be kept on the premises. Farmers were more hospitable in helping the new residents raise crops and expressed surprise that educated young people – most Twin Oaks residents were recent college graduates – might want to try agriculture with all its frustrations. Twin Oaks had trouble from marauding bands of white and black youths who, in a misapprehension about the nature of the commune, showed up either to buy drugs, steal movables, or have sex with the easy hippie chicks that were supposed to be in residence.[36]

[35] Kinkade, *Walden Two Experiment*, 3–12; Miller, *60s Communes*, 56–8. See also Patrick W. Conover, "An Analysis of Communes and Intentional Communities with Particular Attention to Sexual and Gender Relations," *Family Coordinator* 24:4 (October 1975), 460–2.

[36] Kinkade, *Walden Two Experiment*, 7, 19, 106, 183–4, 189, 206. See also Houriet, *Getting Back Together*, 264–305.

Twin Oaks barely survived the early years. Money was scarce, crops failed, and the resulting food bills were so high that several residents temporarily had to take paying jobs in Richmond. At first, residents too readily accepted quarrelsome or lazy newcomers, but after Kinkade recognized that such people threatened the commune, strict rules about admission were put in place. The founders knew that raising food would not enable true self-sufficiency, because some items had to be purchased and property taxes had to be paid. Skinner had suggested producing handicrafts that could be sold by mail. Twin Oaks manufactured hammocks, which became well-known within the larger counterculture community. Hammocks were made during inclement weather, when outdoor farm work was impractical. By making hammocks, Twin Oaks was able to avoid having residents work outside the commune. When residents worked outside, they were less committed to the community and more likely to leave.[37]

Many communes failed for financial reasons because all resources were pooled without accounts. Inevitably, people were more inclined to withdraw funds than to put money into the cookie jar. Money taken for a frivolous purpose might leave the entire group without money to buy food, or a resident would steal money and flee. To avoid these problems, Twin Oaks had a manager with a bank account in the name of the commune. Residents earned labor credits. Each task brought a certain number of credits, with undesirable tasks rotated among members. Communards who lagged behind in earning credits might be asked to leave. Work assignments were made at a weekly business meeting. When a resident needed clothes, the person applied to the business meeting, which authorized the manager to provide funds to buy specific items at predetermined prices. This level of managerial detail could only work among communards who shared a great deal of trust.[38]

[37] Kinkade, *Walden Two Experiment*, 73, 75, 145, 178, 225–6; Miller, *60s Communes*, 57–8.
[38] Kinkade, *Walden Two Experiment*, 4, 19, 21–4, 45, 50, 171. On labor credits see Barry Newman, "What's This?" *Wall Street Journal*, December 22, 1971, 1, 18.

Despite long hair and jeans, Twin Oaks residents were not so much hippies as rejectionists of the existing industrial capitalist order. Like hippies, Twin Oaks was in retreat from the mainstream. The secular nature of Twin Oaks predicted failure, because few secular communes lasted long. Poor leadership and chaos, including financial meltdowns, usually produced self-destruction. Kinkade and others, however, provided effective leadership. In addition, self-sufficiency was realistic given the size of the farm. Never overly popular, the community always had a dozen or so dedicated permanent residents, and it sometimes reached twenty or thirty adults. Skinner's book provided a philosophical framework. When residents debated policies, they did so within the context of that philosophy. The use of labor credits and tight management of finances mattered. Twin Oaks eventually developed relationships with several other Skinner-inspired rural communes and remained vibrant into the 1990s.[39]

Perhaps the most famous communes were those in the West that were derived from the original hippie community in the Haight. Lou Gottlieb (1923–96) had been the bass player in the Limeliters, a popular folk group during the folk music revival that swept the nation in the late Fifties and early Sixties. Made wealthy by show business, exhausted by touring, and unsettled by an early introduction to LSD, Gottlieb dropped out in 1963 to live in San Francisco. The son of communists, he was a former member of the party. Still a man of the left, he did what any good socialist might do: he bought thirty-one acres of rural land about ninety minutes north of San Francisco near Sebastopol. Gottlieb called the place Morning Star Ranch. In 1966 a few friends camped there, and the following year, after the Diggers publicized the spot as the Diggers Farm, hippies inundated the ranch. Gottlieb did not mind. He recalled, "There were frequently evenings when we had 300 for dinner." Hundreds came to visit, sunbathe nude, take drugs, and experiment with sex. Many chose to stay in this counterculture sanctuary.[40]

[39] Kinkade, *Walden Two Experiment*, 4, 23, 50, 55; Miller, *60s Communes*, 58–9.
[40] Miller, *60s Communes*, 12, 46–8 (quote at 48); Perry, *Haight-Ashbury*, 84–6, 148–9, 169, 217–18; Keltz, *Scrapbook of a Taos Hippie*, 82.

Gottlieb declared Morning Star open land. Rejecting the concept of private real estate and embracing the doctrine of free use, Gottlieb welcomed all comers to live on the property. No one paid rent. Gottlieb inhabited a modest home, which also had the only plumbing. At its peak, a hundred or more hippies resided at Morning Star. A number of residents lived in tents, which worked reasonably well in the summer but proved to be impractical during the winter's heavy rainstorms. Others inhabited old school buses or Volkswagen vans that they drove onto the property. Some constructed shacks out of scrap lumber or other scrounged items. A few built stylish A-frame dwellings, usually just large enough to accommodate two sleeping bags. Some residents cooked alone over campfires or Colman stoves, while others shared cooking in a van that had a built-in stove. Sanitation was a problem. There was little success in keeping latrines and water supplies separate. Realizing the danger, some residents imported bottled water.[41]

"People live here according to the tablets written on the human heart," said Gottlieb. "Once you've abandoned materialistic goals and incentives you develop a very different attitude toward things." He added, "I believe one of the major problems of our time is to teach people to do nothing." The most important activities at Morning Star were nudity, spiritual discussions, psychedelic drugs, and easy sex. Communards rarely wore clothes. In the early period residents read and discussed seriously Eastern religious texts. In 1968 Gottlieb became so inspired that he traveled to India and returned with a holy man, his new guru. Visitors from the Haight often brought drugs, which were sold or given to residents. Rural bucolic beauty was supposed to enhance a trip, and Morning Star was distant enough from city lights that star-bright nights occurred frequently. One resident noted the expectation of free love. "It was pretty interesting," she recalled, "to wake up in the night and find someone in your sleeping bag with you. It was just kind of an assumed thing that everybody wanted to have sex with everybody else."[42]

---

[41] Miller, *60s Communes*, 51–3; Gardner, *Children of Prosperity*, 134–7.
[42] Melville, *Communes in the Counter Culture*, 127 (first quote); Miller, *60s Communes*, 48–50 (second quote at 49).

Because Gottlieb's philosophy did not allow him to bar anyone, it was not long before freeloaders, the mentally ill, rip-off artists, and criminals moved onto the property. Neighbors complained bitterly about stolen (or slaughtered) farm animals. Some of those who moved to Morning Star were anarchists inclined to steal from everyone. "Instant socialism," it was called. A group of hard-bitten winos from San Francisco arrived to extract money and alcohol from visitors in the parking area. Then the Gypsy Jokers motorbike gang carved out a place for themselves at the ranch. They frustrated the communards when they declared part of the property off-limits to others. Morning Star residents begged the sheriff to remove the bikers, but the request was ignored. While Gottlieb's belief in open land prevented him from complaining, the owner was frequently away from the ranch in any case, and when he was in residence, he was often too stoned to make decisions.[43]

Morning Star's population changed over time. It started with a number of single young men who followed Timothy Leary by using LSD in a spiritual quest, as well as loving hippie couples who believed that psychedelics would enhance their relationship. But happy couples soon tired of the busyness of the place, the outbreak of tensions, and freaks on bad drug trips. Committed couples did not stay long, and singles often left when they found partners. Nudists were attracted by the idea of plentiful sunshine without the harassment that came from trying to live without clothes in a city. Teen runaways afraid of being picked up by the police in the Haight also came to Morning Star, which falsely gave the impression of being beyond the purview of authorities. Petty criminals sought sanctuary, as did drug dealers who had ripped off customers. Draft dodgers and AWOL soldiers also passed through. The latter could be spotted easily by their short hair.[44]

Morning Star Ranch came to an all-too-predictable end. Neighbors complained about noise and rising thefts. Sheriff's deputies made sweeps of the ranch looking for drugs, runaways, and draft-age men without current draft cards. During

---

[43] Miller, *60s Communes*, 49–51, 164 (quote); Perry, *Haight-Ashbury*, 204–5, 229, 270. See also Yablonsky, *Hippie Trip*, 181–98.

[44] Miller, *60s Communes*, 47–9, 177–8.

raids, residents with something to hide melted into ravines and crevices where they could not be found. Drugs were commonly buried. As marijuana and LSD gave way to increasing quantities of speed and heroin, filth and squalor bred a variety of preventable diseases. With a surfeit of drug-hazed spontaneous orgies, STDs also soared. Public health officials were probably even more incensed than law enforcement, because the diseases were entirely the product of laziness and lack of judgment. When Gottlieb was repeatedly cited for health and zoning violations, including the erection of illegal and unsafe structures, he ignored the summonses.[45]

As the fines mounted, the owner, perhaps increasingly spaced out on drugs, hired lawyers to defend his property rights – an odd response for a socialist who claimed that he did not believe in private property. When that strategy failed in court, Gottlieb in 1969 legally deeded Morning Star to God, and told officials that they would have to deal with the almighty in court. The local judge was not amused. He declared that God could not be given real estate because he was not manifest. Gottlieb thought it was a grand joke. Finally, the owner's attorneys informed him that if he did not evict everyone from the land (except himself), he would not only lose all of the land due to fines, but he would be jailed as a criminal. Only then did Gottlieb agree to evict the tenants. Many of the hippies, fearing disease and crime, had already fled. The sheriff's department sent in bulldozers, leveled everything, and burned all the abandoned possessions. Those who participated in the raid later recalled the tremendous stench of excrement and decayed vegetable matter.[46]

Some of the remnant fled to nearby Wheeler's Ranch, another open land commune owned by Bill Wheeler, a professional artist. A number of Haight hippies had already settled there. "*Om is where the heart is*," quipped one woman. A black Vietnam veteran said, "I seen enough destruction." He liked the smiling faces. This 360-acre establishment was more remote than

[45] Ibid., 48, 51.
[46] Ibid., 51; Keltz, *Scrapbook of a Taos Hippie*, 87–9.

Morning Star, and it never had the appeal of Gottlieb's place, in part because Wheeler was a large man with whom one did not want to disagree. While he subscribed to open access and did not ban drugs, he wanted residents to respect the property. Campers were welcome, but Wheeler personally approved each site: water and latrines had to be kept separate. Wheeler's Ranch had some communal activities, such as Sunday feasts. "Lots of food, lots of dope," one resident promised a guest. Nudity was routine. Friends of residents were welcome, but total strangers often got the evil eye. Despite Wheeler's precautions, the county opposed the commune, and eventually Wheeler evicted the residents and burned the buildings, which did not meet code.[47]

At Wheeler's, Morning Star, and many other hippie communes, many children were born. These love children were conceived during the sudden upsurge in sex outside marriage. Birth control pills were not yet uniformly available, and counterculture women looked suspiciously upon any new technology, including the pill. "It debases women to use the pill," said Elaine Sundancer. Beliefs also played a role in high birth rates. Many hippie women wanted a child, even though the father might not be part of the child's life. Given the technical difficulty of establishing paternity at that time, women sometimes did not know who had fathered a particular child. Michael Metelica's Renaissance Community believed in reincarnation; each birth was a human spirit returning to life. Because communards lacked money for doctors and hospitals, childbirth usually took place at home using natural methods. Communes often trained midwives to deliver babies. A birth might produce a big celebration. At Black Bear Ranch the residents ritually ate the placenta (afterbirth).[48]

[47] Miller, *60s Communes*, 53–6, 198; Hedgepeth, *Alternative*, 189 (first two quotes); Sara Davidson, "Open Land: Getting Back to the Communal Garden," *Harper's*, June 1970, 91–7 (third quote at 92).

[48] Houriet, *Getting Back Together*, 92 (quote); Lemke-Santangelo, *Daughters of Aquarius*, 81–5; Chelsea Cain, ed., *Wild Child* (Seattle, 1999), 8, 93; Keltz, *Scrapbook of a Taos Hippie*, 183–6; Miller, *60s Communes*, 120–1, 187–8; Cantwell, "Open the Shutters," 173; "Year of the Commune," *Newsweek*, August 18, 1969, 90.

The presence of children meant that hippies were not just rejecting the existing society. In moving to a rural commune and having children, they both gained self-sufficiency and affirmed a commitment to the future. At a time when organized child care was rare, a single woman with a young child found a commune ideal because child care and cooking could be shared. Over time, the percentage of women in communes gradually rose. Thus, raising children in a new way was calculated to produce a new society when the next generation came of age. To express this idea, hippie children were given unusual names: Ken Kesey and Mountain Girl's daughter Sunshine; Frank and Gail Zappa's daughter Moon; and Bill Wheeler and Gwen Leeds's daughter Raspberry. Names were sometimes picked for astrological reasons, or because of a vision on a drug trip. Some names were purposely without gender significance. In an understandable reaction, a good many hippie children later changed their names. Lou Gottlieb's son Vishnu became Bill.[49]

Hippie children ran wild. Mothers allowed the young to work out their problems, which produced resourcefulness, but it also led to a great deal of bullying. Adults transmitted casual attitudes about drugs, nudity, and sex to children, who were treated as adults. In many communes passing around a joint established sociability, and if a child seemed interested, the child, too, could take a toke. (This interest seemed to develop at around age six.) In a few communes it was considered appropriate for children as young as two to take LSD or other psychedelic drugs. These drugs, after all, were seen as aids to creativity and spirituality. Hippie children often wore no clothes. Sometimes the painful truth was that they owned no clothes. Soles of feet were toughened, but the absence of shoes also produced dangerously

[49] Lemke-Santangelo, *Daughters of Aquarius*, 146, 150; Miller, *60s Communes*, 173, 183–5; Cain, ed., *Wild Child*, 30–1; Sundancer, *Celery Wine*, 29, 34–5, 89; Charley M. Johnston and Robert W. Deisher, "Contemporary Communal Child Rearing," *Pediatrics* 52:3 (September 1973), 319–25; Rosabeth M. Kanter, Dennis Jaffe, and D. Kelly Weisberg, "Coupling, Parenting, and the Presence of Others," *Family Coordinator* 24:4 (October 1975), 443–52. On names see Miller, *60s Communes*, 185; Cain, ed., *Wild Child*, xiii, xxiii, 4; Lemke-Santangelo, *Daughters of Aquarius*, 146.

infected cuts. Some adults devoted to free love saw no reason why they should not have sex with children. Parents were often ambivalent about such ideas. While not entirely comfortable with what mainstream society called molestation, hippie adults disliked being called squares.[50]

Few hippie children reached school age until the early 1970s. By then communes had discussed what to do about education. Hostile to public schools, almost all communards were afraid that the establishment would brainwash their children. In some places, attendance laws forced hippie children to attend school, where they often shocked other children. In other places, alternative public schools served counterculture children. Large communes sometimes set up their own schools, or they created home schools. These had varying degrees of success. Iris Keltz, who taught in a counterculture school in New Mexico, suddenly realized that the students came to school stoned every day. Many commune children graduated from college, where they often excelled at writing and the arts. Decades later, commune children who wrote memoirs often expressed frustration at the loose way they had been raised. Almost uniformly, they resolved to give their own children more discipline and more limits.[51]

Further up the coast from Wheeler's Ranch, hippies settled in Mendocino and Humboldt counties, which featured illegal marijuana plantations on government land. Most of these residents were couples who farmed, or two or three couples formed a small rural commune. They were often off the grid and among the first

[50] Lemke-Santangelo, *Daughters of Aquarius*, 143–4, 150–7; Keltz, *Scrapbook of a Taos Hippie*, 67–8, 71, 145; Miller, *60s Communes*, 185–7; Cain, ed., *Wild Child*, 53–7, 135, 138–9, 141; Zicklin, *Countercultural Communes*, 93–118; John Rothchild and Susan B. Wolf, *The Children of the Counter-Culture* (Garden City, NY, 1976), 78–103; Bennett Berger, Bruce Hackett, and R. Mervyn Millar, "The Commune Family," *Family Coordinator* 21:4 (October 1972), 425–7; Bennett M. Berger and Bruce M. Hackett, "On the Decline of Age Grading in Rural Hippie Communes," *Journal of Social Issues* 30:2 (1974), 163–83.

[51] Keltz, *Scrapbook of a Taos Hippie*, 57–64, 77, 109–10, 189–93; Miller, *60s Communes*, 188–9, 239–40; Cain, ed., *Wild Child*, xiv, 17, 95–6, 138; Sundancer, *Celery Wine*, 84–5, 152–3. For recollections see Cain, ed., *Wild Child*; Lisa Michaels, *Split* (New York, 1998).

people to install solar panels to generate electricity. Children were an important part of these isolated communities. Because residences were often inaccessible during winter rains, home schooling sometimes became a necessity. Jentri Anders noted the interactions of hippies with locals near the Eel River. Deeply suspicious of longhairs at first, loggers gradually accepted their new neighbors. Anders herself moved further north into rural Oregon. Elaine Sundancer described rural struggle in one small Oregon commune, High Ridge Farm, that produced a great deal of its own food. As many as sixty hippies settled on Ken Kesey's farm just outside Eugene, but in 1969 an annoyed Kesey told them when they went to Woodstock not to return.[52]

West Coast communards were among the first Americans to put the environment at the center of their lives. Influenced by Henry Thoreau as well as the grandeur of the local landscape, residents of the Eel River area, High Ridge Farm, or other such places were determined both to respect nature and to minimize use of resources. Despite the desire to be self-sufficient in food production, they rejected commercial fertilizer and insecticide and were early proponents of organic farming. They raised their own vegetables, drank herbal teas, and employed Native American plant remedies. "We want to be part of nature," wrote Elaine Sundancer of High Ridge. "I want to drink from the stream. I want to eat unwashed vegetables warm from the sun." Being close to nature also meant getting closer to God, Sundancer thought. These communes used what they called appropriate technology. Following the *Whole Earth Catalog* (1968), High Ridge adopted special outhouses that produced compost fertilizer and erected passive solar buildings.[53]

[52] On marijuana growing see T. C. Boyle, *Budding Prospects* (New York, 1984); *Humboldt County* (2008 film), directed by Darren Grodsky and Danny Jacobs. Jentri Anders, *Beyond Counterculture* (Pullman, WA, 1990); Sundancer, *Celery Wine*. On Kesey's hostility see Miller, *60s Communes*, 19–20, 195; Houriet, *Getting Back Together*, 203–5.

[53] Sundancer, *Celery Wine*, 29, 31, 42–7, 54–5, 76, 102, 119, 125 (quote), 134–9; Miller, *60s Communes*, 77, 122–4, 139–41, 157–8. See also Houriet, *Getting Back Together*, 53–103, 120–7.

One of the earliest rural hippie communes, Drop City, Colorado, was founded in 1965. Drop City got its name in an unusual way. The three founders were artistic hippies from the University of Kansas, who amused themselves by dropping objects from rooftops in downtown Lawrence onto the sidewalk just in front of a pedestrian. They sought to provoke a reaction. This was an example of performance art. Eventually, the bored Droppers, as they styled themselves, left Lawrence to settle in a rural area where they could pursue art, take psychedelic drugs, and create a new civilization. Jo Ann Bernofsky recalled, "We knew that we wanted to do something outrageous, and we knew we wanted to do it with other people." She added, "You had the sense that anything was possible." The organizers imagined an avant-garde artists' colony with individual residences.[54]

The founders paid $450 for six acres of goat pasture south of Denver just off I-25 in Trinidad, Colorado. In sticking with the hippie notion of openness, they allowed anyone to move onto the land. Nor did they have any other rules. What made Drop City interesting was the arrival of Steve Baer, who was committed to the idea of living in geodesic domes. First promoted by Buckminster Fuller as a way to save energy and harmonize with nature, which abhorred straight lines and 90 degree angles, domes were later heavily promoted in Stewart Brand's *Whole Earth Catalog* (1968). Many hippies, however, discovered that Fuller's elegant plans rarely worked in practice. It was hard for inexperienced workers to build precisely all of the odd-angled cuts required by Fuller's designs. In addition, curved walls hampered furniture placement, domes leaked in rainstorms, and heavy winter snow could collapse the flat top at the dome's center.[55]

Baer's genius was to modify the dome concept into a practical hippie abode, which he called a *zome*. Hippies were poor, so found objects were better construction materials than anything

[54] Miller, *60s Communes*, 31–3, 37–8 (quote at 33).
[55] Miller, *60s Communes*, 33–4. See also Alastair Gordon, *Spaced Out* (New York, 2008), 167–94.

bought at a lumber yard. Baer showed that a small modified dome capable of housing one or two people could be built out of a few pieces of purchased lumber and auto rooftops retrieved from junkyards at no cost. A blowtorch was used to cut bright-colored rooftops off of wrecks. Domes popped up all over Drop City, which attracted attention. They could be seen from the freeway, and in 1967 *Time* publicized the domes with a colored picture. Baer's domes were then replicated at other communes. Baer, however, left Drop City. Its small acreage, easy access, and open land had attracted too many deadbeats, rip-off artists, drug addicts, and criminals. Baer moved to Albuquerque, New Mexico, where he promoted his domes throughout the state.[56]

Among the influential long-term residents of Drop City was Peter Rabbit. (Many Droppers took unusual names.) Painfully aware of how addicts and criminals had destroyed Drop City, Rabbit decided to found a new artists' settlement with one major modification: membership would be restricted. To start Libre, Rabbit persuaded a wealthy young heir to buy 360 acres in southern Colorado. In keeping with the avant-garde spirit, Libre featured unconventional architecture. More practically, the whole community had to approve each house site, and no structure could be visible from any other structure. Baer designed Rabbit's dome. All residents lived alone or in nuclear families. Two residents noted, "We are not a commune. We are a community." To avoid transients, there was no central building. In relief, one member wrote, "No more dressing from the communal closet and no more giant pots of inedible lentils." Libre survived into the 1990s with low turnover.[57]

Many hippie communards settled in the Taos area of northern New Mexico. Land was cheap, the rugged landscape appealed to the desire to be close to nature, and the local Indians in the area were willing to share expertise about the use of peyote in religious

---

[56] Miller, *60s Communes*, 34, 38–40, 63, 82; Gordon, *Spaced Out*, 152; "Youth: The Hippies," *Time*, July 7, 1967, 18C.

[57] Houriet, *Getting Back Together*, 217 (first quote); Miller, *60s Communes*, 81–3 (second quote at 82). See also Roberta Price, *Huerfano* (Amherst, MA, 2006).

FIGURE 14. Richard Alpert, Timothy Leary's friend and fellow Harvard psychedelic drug researcher, became a spiritual seeker, visited India, and changed his name to Ram Dass. In the early 1970s, when Allen Ginsberg took this photograph, Dass was helping the Lama commune in New Mexico develop its spiritual mission.

rites. The communes represented a variety of viewpoints. The Lama Foundation was filled with spiritual seekers. The founders, Steve and Barbara Durkee, banned drugs. Lama fell under the influence of Ram Dass (the former Richard Alpert), who made his headquarters there for a time. He had just returned from India and was at that point very influenced by Hindu ideas, which led him to publish *Be Here Now* (1971). Like most of the New Mexico communes, Lama had only limited success with agriculture, but the organization survived as a spiritual study center that took in interested seekers, drawn by Ram Dass's name, at high prices for room and board. The chanting, yoga, and discussions produced positive feedback, which led to more paying visitors.[58]

In contrast, Iris Keltz and her twenty-five to fifty fellow residents at New Buffalo struggled to make ends meet. Building adobe houses was hard physical work, and water problems, which plagued many communes in New Mexico, limited how many people could live on the site and what crops could be grown. Even the goats had trouble thriving. Food supplies often ran short, and residents were left with a grim diet of beans, beans, and more beans. While new arrivals bubbled with enthusiasm, the severely cold winters, blistering summer heat, drought, rats, and insects drove many away. As was often the case, hippie women and their children dominated. Keltz felt that the women dealt with hardships better than men, and they bonded in the kitchen over the stove. The commune's numerous children had a natural excitement that prevented depression, and shared child care benefited single women. Crop failures angered the men, who sometimes responded by leaving to take a job elsewhere.[59]

The hippies at Keltz's commune were nervous about their two dozen counterculture neighbors at the Reality Construction

---

[58] Miller, *60s Communes*, 117–18; Houriet, *Getting Back Together*, 335–43; Keltz, *Scrapbook of a Taos Hippie*, 124, 127–30.

[59] Keltz, *Scrapbook of a Taos Hippie*, 31–6, 39–44, 47–53; Houriet, *Getting Back Together*, 137–200; Miller, *60s Communes*, 64–5, 164. See also Hedgepeth, *Alternative*, 35, 38–45, 50–1, 64–76, 79, 84.

Company (RCC). RCC women rarely appeared off the property, and when the men did so, they wore leather jackets and adopted a tough swagger. Trying to talk with the RCC was a bit like making friends with a rattlesnake. RCC residents were diehard radicals. Hostile to visitors, RCC stationed a guard with a rifle and a walkie-talkie at the entrance to its very long driveway. It was difficult to get permission to visit. "Most of us," said one resident, "are outlaws." Many communards were on the run. At neighboring New Buffalo talk about relocating to Canada ended quickly; half the discussants could not settle in Canada due to criminal records. Oz, in central Pennsylvania, could not appeal an adverse court ruling because some members had violated the draft law. Earth People's Park in Vermont helped draft dodgers get to Canada. The Brotherhood of Eternal Love in Orange County, California smuggled vast quantities of drugs. RCC lasted from 1969 to 1972.[60]

In addition to water problems, all of the Taos communes had bad relations with the local residents, most of whom were poor Hispanics whose ancestors had settled in the area four hundred years earlier. A billboard at the edge of Taos warned, "Hippies – Stay Out or Else." Hispanics were livid. Conservative Catholics, they saw unmarried hippie couples living in sin. Women showed sexual vulgarity by wearing inappropriate clothes, or worse, no clothes at all. Why were these effeminate long-haired men not fighting in Vietnam? Upwardly striving, Hispanics watched in disbelief as middle-class hippies threw off the very culture that Hispanics were desperate to join in order to adopt the folkways of the local Indians, whom Hispanics held in contempt as worthless primitives. When hippies bought land, it drove up prices, which made it harder for Hispanics to buy land, and when hippies signed up for welfare and food stamps, it dried up public funds that Hispanics needed to survive. Hippie children in

[60] Miller, *60s Communes*, 79–80, 131, 178, 206–7, 231; Houriet, *Getting Back Together*, 27, 184 (quote), 198, 354, 366; Keltz, *Scrapbook of a Taos Hippie*, 84, 89, 96, 98.

public school talked dirty, disrespected teachers, and expressed a free-wheeling style that enraged Hispanic parents.[61]

Hippie children were beaten up at school. For communes that had a telephone, harassment was incessant, usually taking the form of sexual pants or blunt warnings to leave the county. Shots were fired at cars, and homes and barns were burned. When hippies left communes to go to town to shop, some storekeepers refused to sell to them. They could not buy meals in town. Going to a bar was dangerous. Because hippies had a reputation for being pacifists, they became easy marks. Men were jumped on the sidewalk, and women were raped. To many locals, a woman who wore a low-cut blouse was enticing men. Law enforcement shrugged. Crimes went unsolved, even when they took place in front of witnesses. No one had seen a thing. Public opinion was clear. People who used illegal drugs, harbored runaways, and were probably draft dodgers did not deserve legal protection.[62]

The hippies did not run. They stayed, partly because they had nowhere to go, partly because they had bought the land where they lived, and partly because a portion of the local business community realized that the hippies, despite their odd dress and habits, could be useful. Real estate brokers knew that the new residents were bringing outside money into a desperately poor county. Hippies were educated, middle-class, and motivated to improve themselves and the community. They could be a source of renewal. One key moment came when Dennis Hopper, already a well-known Hollywood star and director, spent considerable time in Taos. He bought a building, decided to fix it up, and hired local Hispanics to do the work. While largely taking a drug-laden vacation, Hopper spent lavishly on materials and labor. Hopper attracted other wealthy Californians, and residents realized that

---

[61] Keltz, *Scrapbook of a Taos Hippie*, 37, 54, 72–3, 77, 109, 201; Miller, *60s Communes*, 63, 222–3; Melville, *Communes in the Counter Culture*, 139 (billboard); Jon Stewart, "Communes in Taos," in Editors of Ramparts, eds., *Conversations with the New Reality* (San Francisco, 1971), 209–11, 214.

[62] Miller, *60s Communes*, 223–4; Keltz, *Scrapbook of a Taos Hippie*, 68, 83, 92, 96, 195–6, 209; Stewart, "Communes in Taos," 207–9, 212.

some hippies were connected to wealth that could benefit the county.[63]

Over time, most of the Taos communes disbanded, although Lama remained as a spiritual center. There was no revolution, and RCC disappeared. But the hippies largely stayed in the area. A few remained on land that had been part of an original commune, but most residents became monogamous couples, married, had children, and built homes, often on the hillside overlooking the valley. A few continued in agriculture, while others opened businesses in town. Some were restaurants or other concerns that attracted tourists, but mail-order businesses could also be run from Taos. Ever since Mabel Dodge, D. H. Lawrence, and Georgia O'Keeffe had settled in the area decades earlier, Taos had appealed to artists and writers. Some of the long-term counterculture residents painted, wrote, or ran galleries. A number of hippies also became school teachers or worked in government agencies.[64]

Many different types of hippie communes emerged during the late Sixties and early Seventies. Most lasted only a few years, although a few spiritual communes with strong leaders survived into the twenty-first century. While most communards used marijuana, not all used psychedelic drugs. Heavy use of psychedelics usually led to the commune's abandonment. Some groups survived by shifting away from drugs. Even at the beginning, most residents practiced serial monogamy. Over time, this led to many married couples. Although few communes were founded with children, a good many became home to children, who were often raised in wild ways. Single mothers liked living in a commune because of shared child care. In the Sixties gender roles in communes were usually traditional, but feminism increased over time. While men were the dreamers, planners, builders, and spiritual leaders, women were the worker bees who planted gardens, milked goats, cooked meals, tended children, and comforted

[63] Keltz, *Scrapbook of a Taos Hippie*, 77–8, 97, 161, 201, 205.
[64] Miller, *60s Communes*, 78–80, 224; Keltz, *Scrapbook of a Taos Hippie*, 44, 71, 79, 91, 97, 113, 139, 145, 157.

residents. All the communes that thrived had hard-working women.[65]

Rural communes turned out to be the culmination of the hippie movement. When the counterculture began in the mid-1960s, adherents vehemently opposed mainstream culture. Hippies wanted authenticity, which included spontaneity and spiritual seeking. At the same time, freaks expressed individualism. By the late Sixties, however, the love generation found that authenticity and individualism produced a great deal of friction and social fragmentation. The result was a growing desire for community. For various reasons, urban communes provided little sense of community, and hippies then moved to the country. While many rural communes failed, a number survived for decades due either to a religious basis or to unusually gifted leaders. Like psychedelic drugs and easy sex, the concern for authenticity and individualism declined over time, and the counterculture ultimately defined itself around community. Living among the like-minded enabled hippies to transmit values to the next generation while living in a larger society that they continued to find wanting.

---

[65] On women as essential see T. C. Boyle, *Drop City* (New York, 2004; orig. 2003), 60–1; Lemke-Santangelo, *Daughters of Aquarius*, 60–1, 85, 98–9, 159; Miller, *60s Communes*, 212–14.

Conclusion

What, then, was the historical significance of the hippie counterculture that flourished so briefly during the late Sixties and early Seventies? As this book shows, the answer contains quite a bit of ambiguity. Hippies had once believed that their vibrant new culture would be so appealing that the mainstream would disappear, but the reality had proved to be otherwise. While the search for authenticity, including spontaneity and spiritual seeking, had been personally important, the lack of both a robust philosophy and an institutional framework had limited long-term success for the hippie movement. Nor had the embrace of individualism produced much social change, because social structures largely remained untouched. By contrast, the hippie search for community had been very important. Rural communes enabled freaks to grow personally and to thrive inside a society that they found suffocating.[1]

As the counterculture faded during the 1970s, certain hippie ideas and practices permeated mainstream culture. There was a blending. Many hippies, however, felt that their values were co-opted and perverted. However, mainstream conservatives

---

[1] Useful memoirs include Iris Keltz, *Scrapbook of a Taos Hippie* (El Paso, TX, 2000); Roberta Price, *Huerfano* (Amherst, MA, 2006); David Gans, ed., *Conversations with the Dead* (New York, 1991).

believed that the larger society had sold out to the oversexed, drug-using crazies. It is important, therefore, to specify precise ways in which the counterculture helped reshape the mainstream. Three specific hippie legacies can be identified. First, Americans followed the counterculture in expressing a rising individualism. Second, the hippie search for authenticity could be seen in society's changing sexual practices, gender roles, marijuana use, and increased tolerance for diversity, as well as the coarsening and redefinition of popular culture. The counterculture's aversion to authority also spread throughout the society. Third, the hippie desire for community helped launch hippie entrepreneurs, the environmental movement, and the personal computer.[2]

The writer Tom Wolfe referred to the Seventies as the "me decade." Wolfe, who had helped launch the counterculture with his coverage of Ken Kesey's lysergic acid diethylamide (LSD) experiments in *The Electric Kool-Aid Acid Test* (1968), found the next decade sobering. Before dismissing the Seventies as nothing but a hangover from Sixties excess, Wolfe shrewdly observed that the counterculture's penchant for freewheeling individualism had led to an overwhelming sense of the importance of the self. In 1961 John Kennedy had launched the Sixties in his Inaugural Address by urging Americans, "Ask not what your country can do for you – ask what you can do for your country." Perhaps the Vietnam War echoed all too clearly what youth was expected to do for its country, but the war had never been popular, and by the end of the Sixties many of the nation's young concluded that it was wiser to put self before country. Hippie individualism infused itself into mainstream society.[3]

The hippie penchant for authenticity had an even greater impact upon the country. In the area of sexual mores, freaks hated hypocrisy and embraced honesty, so honesty replaced

[2] For overviews see Joseph Heath and Andrew Potter, *Nation of Rebels* (New York, 2004); Thomas Frank, *The Conquest of Cool* (Chicago, 1997).

[3] Tom Wolfe, "The 'Me' Decade and the Third Great Awakening," *New York*, August 23, 1976; Jerrold M. Starr, "The Peace and Love Generation: Changing Attitudes toward Sex and Violence among College Youth," *Journal of Social Issues* 30:2 (1974), 94–7.

much of the hypocrisy that had governed the country's sexual relations. American sexual practices had been changing gradually for a long time, as couples increasingly engaged in discreet premarital sex. Thus, it was relatively easy for mainstream society to accept the hippie idea that committed unmarried couples could live together. Living together, however, was not the same thing as marriage. It lacked even the intent of stability. Freed by the pill from unwanted pregnancies, women were carving out new roles. They trained for their own careers instead of marrying men who had already established careers. The pill also ended the double standard. Few of the women and men who lived together in the mid-Seventies thought of themselves as hippies, even though they had adopted an important counterculture idea.[4]

As another expression of authenticity, hippie women in the late Sixties were the first middle-class women to bear children out of wedlock and raise them on their own. They did so with little help from fathers, who were both poor providers and wanderers. Nor did they have access to organized child care. Usually poorly educated despite a middle-class upbringing, these mothers rarely held paying jobs. Instead, they lived among other women with children in communes where they shared cooking and child care. Often they received welfare checks. The desire to rear a child to spread hippie values seems to have motivated many women to have children. During the Seventies more single middle-class women had babies and decided to raise these children by themselves. Society was far more ambivalent about this new phenomenon than about couples living together, but the idea of a woman raising a child alone became accepted in many parts of the country by the late Seventies.[5]

[4] Beth L. Bailey, *Sex in the Heartland* (Cambridge, MA, 1999), 1–12, 75–104, 126–38, 200–15; Starr, "Peace and Love Generation," 88–90; Bennett M. Berger, *The Survival of a Counterculture* (Berkeley, 1981), 127–32, 143, 148, 151, 159–62.

[5] Chelsea Cain, ed., *Wild Child* (Seattle, 1999), xvi–xviii, xxiii–xxvii, 29–33, 55–7, 62, 95–100; Robert Houriet, *Getting Back Together* (London, 1973; orig. 1971), 61, 66; Timothy Miller, *60s Communes* (Syracuse, NY, 1999), 184–7.

Personal authenticity also meant smoking marijuana. While most hippies had rejected hard drugs, and the use of LSD had fallen after most people concluded that its long-term use did not provide much aid to spiritual seekers, hippies remained heavy pot users. In the Seventies use of marijuana spread into mainstream culture for the first time. This was one way in which counterculture and mainstream blended. Throughout the Seventies, penalties for using marijuana generally declined, and small quantities were often ignored. A generation later, marijuana would begin to be legalized. By 2012 nineteen states and the District of Columbia had authorized medical marijuana. That same year voters in Colorado and Washington State approved initiatives legalizing recreational pot.[6]

Another hippie trait was tolerance. "Do your own thing" had been a Sixties slogan. Part of the hippie penchant for tolerance came from travel to exotic places. In the late Sixties and Seventies cheap international airfares, the high value of the dollar, and the relative safety of much of the world enabled hippies to take many overseas trips. Some travels were in search of natural scenery, with the idea of getting close to God, as Gary Snyder had predicted when introducing Jack Kerouac to backpacking in the High Sierras in California. Some destinations were picked for spiritual reasons, such as standing at the ghats on the Ganges River in India to watch the burning of bodies, or entering a Buddhist retreat in Nepal or Japan. Other places were chosen in search of the perfect high, whether it was Carlos Castaneda's travels in Mexico reported in *The Teachings of Don Juan* (1968), chewing khat (which gave a mild high) in the Middle East, or looking for the perfect cannabis in Marrakesh.[7]

Hippie spiritual seeking had led to widespread borrowing from many of the world's religions. This mishmash lacked any coherent theology, and sometimes the worldview was downright

---

[6] Roger Roffman, *Marijuana Nation* (New York, 2014); Starr, "Peace and Love Generation," 91; National Conference of State Legislatures: ncls.org/research/health/state-medicinal-marijuana-laws.aspx and ncls.org/research/elections-and-campaigns/drug-policy-on-the-ballot.aspx.

[7] Snyder in Jack Kerouac, *Dharma Bums* (New York, 1959; orig. 1958), 77–8.

confusing to outsiders. Inconsistencies, however, did not bother hippies, who rejected ideology as the cause of most of the woes of the twentieth century. They simply took whatever worked for them in expressing outwardly their innermost feelings. One can see this aspect most clearly at the Lama spiritual commune. Because the borrowings were so eclectic, they could (and did) easily evolve, with some elements growing in importance and others cast off over time. While not exactly a form of pantheism, hippie religion tended toward fragmentation as each group embraced its own version – another example of "do your own thing." Pantheistic elements and religious pluralism enabled hippies to express tolerance amid spiritual passions.[8]

Because hippies were tolerant about other cultures, they generally favored immigrants coming to the United States. This positive attitude spread to the larger culture during the Seventies. Americans welcomed immigrants in these years, and immigration soared to the greatest level since the early 1920s. For the first time in American history, large-scale immigration from non-European parts of the world, especially Asia and Latin America, became a hallmark of the country during the Eighties. The face of America changed, and many Americans celebrated multiculturalism, an idea that resonated with the hippie ethos. Immigrants not only changed the country's religious landscape by introducing a large number of practitioners of non-Judeo-Christian faiths, but they also enlarged the country's cultural practices, especially with reference to music, art, style, and food choices. Italian, Greek, Chinese, Indian, and Mexican restaurants were joined by Thai, Peruvian, Moroccan, Afghan, and Ethiopian fare. Pan-Asian and other blends appeared.[9]

The hippie counterculture also played a role in the coarsening of American popular culture. While the overthrow of the

---

[8] William Hedgepeth, *The Alternative* (New York, 1970), 160–5, 172–3; Houriet, *Getting Back Together*, 335–43; Miller, *60s Communes*, 215–16.
[9] Susan B. Carter, et al., eds., *Historical Statistics of the United States* (New York, 2006), 1:557, 573; Richard D. Alba, *Blurring the Color Line* (Cambridge, MA, 2009).

still lingering Victorian prudishness of the Fifties was widely applauded, those old standards of graciousness, formulaic politeness, heavily stylized ritual, and discretely covered bodies had served a social purpose. In the old system, each person had played a carefully delineated role within a commonly encoded system, so that no one mistook anyone's intentions. When the older ways disappeared in favor of, as hippies put it, total truth, brutal honesty, and "letting it all hang out," feelings were all that mattered. In the new calculus, it was difficult to ban any expression or behavior. Not surprisingly, popular culture quickly descended to the lowest common denominator. Nudity on stage could be art, as in the counterculture musical *Hair*, or it could just be voyeuristic audiences (mostly men) ogling naked female bodies. Was bare-breasted table dancing in which breasts, with or without pasties, were shaken in the face of male patrons an act of artistic freedom, or was it just a sexual come on?[10]

The new music produced controversy over references to drugs or raunchy lyrics. In the Sixties, record companies knew that certain words could not be played on the radio. RCA forced Jefferson Airplane to alter or drop three songs from its first album due to offensive references. Later, in "We Can Be Together" on *Volunteers* (1969), the Airplane sang the F-bomb but covered it with so much music it could not be heard clearly. However, the song's lyrics, reprinted inside the album, revealed the truth. The Airplane's success in breaking this barrier enabled the Grateful Dead to include the audible F-word in "Wharf Rat" on *Grateful Dead (Skull and Roses)* (1971). This song, however, could not be played on the radio. Robert Hunter, the lyricist, defended honest language, using the words that people actually spoke, as necessary to artistic freedom. In the long run, artists gained control over lyrics on albums, but Federal Communications Commission rules still inhibited airplay of certain words into the 1990s.

[10] Bailey, *Sex in the Heartland*, 13–104; Caryn James, "Who's That Dancing at My Table?" *New York Times*, March 3, 1995, C12; Bob Morris, "The Age of Dissonance: Tabletopping Exuberance," *New York Times*, August 11, 2002, H3.

Rap and grunge music later challenged the idea of censorship head on.[11]

Did coarsening language, especially in popular recorded music and films, encourage bad behavior? By the Nineties some critics suggested that lyrics that put down women, boasted about rape, or glorified murder were desensitizing young people to violence and brutality. While healthy people distinguished the difference between reality and fantasy and could hear raunchy lyrics as expressions of pain, the mentally ill or confused might hear a command to create real-life violence. The Columbine High School tragedy in 1999 was only one incident that suggested that a nation awash in violent media ran the risk that sickened minds might indulge themselves in spectacular acts of mayhem and sacrifice to gain everlasting fame. The rise of the Internet only made the problem clearer. The gentle hippies of the Sixties could never have imagined such outcomes being derived from their demand for authenticity and honesty.[12]

The counterculture changed popular culture in another way. Traditional society had been rational, scientific, linear in thought, developmentally progressive, and rooted in the printed word, widely available since Gutenberg invented printing with moveable type. The counterculture was emotional, mystical, intuitive, developmentally static, and rooted in expressive experience, whether with drugs, music, or spiritual practices. Religious study that emphasized textual analysis was out; speaking in tongues, ecstatic music, and joyous bodily movement was in. The group dynamic favored collaboration and the gathering of collective opinion over personal study and mastery of a topic. This new approach to life restricted individual intellectual growth, because collective gatherings tended to gravitate to explanations that the entire group could easily understand. The group often stressed rituals, spiritual or otherwise, that put an emphasis upon

[11] Jeff Tamarkin notes to Jefferson Airplane, *Jefferson Airplane Takes Off* (2003 CD; orig. 1966); Robert Hunter interview in Gans, ed., *Conversations with the Dead*, 282–3. "We Can Be Together" and "Wharf Rat" lyrics at azlyrics. com.

[12] Dave Cullen, *Columbine* (New York, 2009).

feelings. Because it was often difficult to organize ideas around feelings, hippies reached conclusions through intuition rather than by using thought. Rational processes gave way to emotions, and magic displaced logic.[13]

The enduring nature of the counterculture was established when twenty thousand hippies attended the first Rainbow Family gathering on federal land in the Colorado Rockies for four days in July 1972. Rainbows held a spiritual service on July 4. They also came together for drugs, nudity, casual sex, rock music, and dancing. Food, drink, and drugs were shared. Participants wanted to recreate the atmosphere of Woodstock, but without the big-name bands or media attention. The event was so success-ful that it became annual, usually staged on federal land in the West. Certain rituals grew up. People routinely hugged strangers. Women often stripped to the waist, and men went naked, except for those who wore skirts, a Rainbow affectation that seemed to promote hypermasculinity. It was considered proper etiquette for a strange man to visit a woman in her tent in the middle of the night to make love. The gatherings have continued into the twenty-first century.[14]

The counterculture also blended into the mainstream, as evi-denced by the young director George Lucas's film, *Star Wars* (1977). Luke Skywalker was an old-fashioned mainstream hero, seldom seen since Gary Cooper shot the bad guy in *High Noon* (1952). The moral ambiguities raised by the Beats and celebrated by the hippies throughout the Sixties had been discarded. A true Jedi knight, Skywalker offered to sacrifice himself for a larger cause. This was an idea that the counterculture could not accept during the Vietnam War. Skywalker, however, embraced some

---

[13] Keith Melville, *Communes in the Counter Culture* (New York, 1972), 15–19, 27–8, 100, 107–12, 197–9.

[14] Cain, ed., *Wild Child*, 105–22; Keltz, *Scrapbook of a Taos Hippie*, 217–22; Anthony Ripley, "Religious Festival Ends with a Meditation Session," *New York Times*, July 5, 1972, 20; William E. Schmidt, "Holdover Hippies Meet for Their Annual Fling," *New York Times*, July 9, 1982, A10; Don Terry, "Arizona Forest Plays Host to a Different Kind of Family Reunion," *New York Times*, July 5, 1998, 8; Kirk Johnson, "34 Years of Hippie Camps, Now in Tinder-Dry Woods," *New York Times*, July 1, 2006, A9.

counterculture traits. He represented intergalactic authority rather than the flag-waving patriotism that had once dominated Hollywood films. No more John Wayne. Skywalker vanquished inhuman foes with his trusty light saber, which the counterculture could accept as appropriate technology. The personal quest fit hippie individualism. The enemy, Darth Vader, turned out to be Skywalker's father, which resonated both with Freud and with the old hippie "generation gap."

Another sign of the evolving influence of the counterculture came with the first Burning Man gathering on a San Francisco beach in 1986. As crowds grew, the rite was moved to the Nevada desert and evolved into a week-long Labor Day art, music, and self-expression extravaganza. Unlike the Rainbow Family, the Burning Man attendees competed to see who wore the most extravagant costumes. The main event was the erection of a forty-foot high wooden figure of a man. Participants danced, shot videos, performed athletic stunts, and otherwise engaged with the wooden structure, which took on the role of a primitive pagan religious symbol. The crude form could be imagined to represent any number of ideas in the minds of the zonked viewers. If the Rainbows merely enjoyed themselves, the Burning Man devotees looked for higher inspiration, while also having a good time with drugs and music. On the final night the wooden sculpture is set ablaze. Everyone then cleans up the desert, which is restored to its natural state. In 2006, 39,100 people attended. Burning Man is popular in the high-tech industry.[15]

The ultimate flowering of counterculture values in popular culture, however, came in 1997, when J. K. Rowling published *Harry Potter and the Philosopher's Stone*. Over the next decade Rowling's seven novels, as well as the blockbuster films that followed, created a world dominated by fantasy, romance,

---

[15] A. Leo Nash, *Burning Man* (New York, 2007); Rick Marin, "The Least Likely Burning Man," *New York Times*, September 10, 2000, ST1, ST3; Abby Ellin, "Out on the Road to Burning Man," *New York Times*, September 17, 2000, BU12; Julia Chaplin, "Burning Man Spreads Its Flame," *New York Times*, November 12, 2006, H1, H6; April Dembosky, "Priming for Burning Man, Flames in Hand," *New York Times*, August 14, 2008, E1, E5.

and magic that went beyond Lucas's more conservative *Star Wars* series. Rowling's main characters consistently strove to create personal identity, develop courage, stay on a moral path, and pursue the truth. In many ways, these novels reinforced traditional culture. However, a school for magic was not an entirely normal place, and the device enabled Rowling to question the devotion to reason, science, linear thought, and the printed word that had provided the underpinnings to traditional culture. At Hogwarts, the printed word sometimes literally jumped off the page. Rowling's moral world was ultimately rooted in magic rather than in reason. It contained logic, but it honored intuition. The popularity of Rowling's books was a triumph for counterculture ideas.

In a different expression of authenticity, the hippie counterculture was deeply hostile to all forms of authority, whether parental, governmental, or corporate. In a reaction against the elders, hippies privileged the self over paternal control. Life experiences shaped this jarring youth rebellion. Both Richard Alpert (Ram Dass) and Jerry Rubin believed that television caused the younger generation to reject parental supervision. Resentment toward government was much worse. Youthful rage against governmental authority grew with the assassinations of John Kennedy, Martin Luther King Jr., and Robert Kennedy. The young, hip or otherwise, entered the Seventies without political heroes. In 1972 Senator George McGovern's old-fashioned populism had little appeal to hippies, who rarely voted. The Watergate scandal, which lasted from 1972 to 1974, confirmed the hippie distrust of government. No one in the counterculture was surprised that President Richard Nixon had harassed his enemies. Attorney General John Mitchell had personally tried to deport John Lennon from the United States. Among hippies, Nixon's forced resignation in 1974 drew a shrug.[16]

---

[16] Alpert interview in Houriet, *Getting Back Together*, 345; Jerry Rubin, *Do It!* (New York, 1970), 90–1, 106, 108; D. Lawrence Wieder and Don H. Zimmerman, "Generational Experience and the Development of Freak Culture," *Journal of Social Issues* 30:2 (1974), 148–9; Nelson W. Polsby, et al., *Presidential Elections* (Lanham, MD, 2012), 257. On Lennon see Jon Wiener, *Come Together* (New York, 1984), 225–71.

In 1979 the social critic Henry Fairlie denounced the way the counterculture had played out politically. He warned that Ayn Rand had prepared a "garden of weeds" for the country. President Ronald Reagan caught the counterculture's skepticism about government authority. At a press conference in 1986, Reagan said, "The nine most terrifying words in the English language are: I'm from the government, and I'm here to help." The wise person, Reagan hinted, resisted. Longhairs had reasons to distrust government authority. They had been routinely busted for drugs, denied concert permits, searched for draft cards, charged with zoning violations, cited for playing loud music, woken from sleeping in a parked car, arrested for distributing business flyers, and prevented from selling underground newspapers. Polling data shows that the federal government never recovered the authority that it lost in the Sixties. In other words, the hippie skepticism about government gradually became the dominant view.[17]

The hippie belief in community played out in several different ways, including the small business boom of the Eighties and Nineties. The first successful hippie entrepreneurs were rock stars, and the listeners did not mind. Hippies, however, were less charitable about record companies, television networks, or retail stores that profited from music. Except for a handful of hippie-owned stores or college co-ops, all of these businesses threatened to choke the bands' creativity and water down content to generate mass sales. The Beatles and the Grateful Dead set up recording companies, but neither proved to be financially successful. Seattle's Sub Pop label, founded in 1986 by Bruce Pavitt and Jonathan Poneman, confronted the majors by signing Nirvana, Soundgarden, and Mudhoney. Co-optation, however, remained the issue. In 1995 Sub Pop's owners sold 49 percent to Warner. In 1999 Shawn Fanning, John Fanning, and Sean Parker

---

[17] Henry Fairlie, "A Decade of Reaction," *New Republic*, January 6, 1979, 15–19 (quote at 18); Reagan News Conference, August 12, 1986, at reaganfoundation.org/Reagan-quotes.aspx. Frank Newport, ed., *The Gallup Poll: Public Opinion, 2012* (Lanham, MD, 2014), 265.

FIGURE 15. By the mid-1970s the hippie vision was often expressed in murals on buildings that housed counterculture businesses or institutions. Nicki Glenn's mural in Madison, Wisconsin depicted fertility and the bountiful resources of nature for the environmentally oriented Whole Earth Learning Community, an alternative day care and education center.

James T. Potter. Wisconsin Historical Society, WHS-36997.

started Napster to allow users to share music files. Napster realized the hippie dream of music freed from either payment or commercialism, but record companies and musicians sued, won, and closed Napster. The result confirmed the hippie belief that big business controlled music.[18]

Co-optation was always the issue. One interesting counterculture business was Celestial Seasonings. Mo Siegel and John Hay started the herbal tea company in the early Seventies, when Siegel picked herbs from the hillsides near Boulder, Colorado. Designed for medicinal as well as nutritional purposes, the teas included ingredients such as chamomile or rose hips. Natural food stores clamored for these teas. By 1982 the company had $27 million in sales, and Siegel was a millionaire. For several years Kraft Foods and then a private equity firm owned the business. In 1991 Siegel, who had founded other businesses, bought the company back. In 1999 the company had $100 million in sales. In 2000, when Siegel sold out, shares were worth $390 million. Hippies complained that Celestial Seasonings was an example of corporate co-optation of the counterculture. This was true, but it also meant that herbal teas moved into mainstream supermarkets, where they joined other counterculture products such as granola, multigrain bread, carrot cake, free-range chicken, tofu, alfalfa sprouts, dried fruit, and organic produce.[19]

Although hippies did not start the environmental movement, which began either with the publication of Rachel Carson's

---

[18] On the Eighties boom see Robert M. Collins, *Transforming America* (New York, 2007), 59–91. On indie rock see Maxim W. Furek, *The Death Proclamation of Generation X* (New York, 2008); Michael Azerrad, *Our Band Could Be Your Life* (Boston, 2001). On Napster see John Alderman, *Sonic Boom* (New York, 2001); Joseph Menn, *All the Rave* (New York, 2003).

[19] Eric Morgenthaler, "Herb Tea's Pioneer: From Hippie Origins to $16 Million a Year," *Wall Street Journal*, May 6, 1981, 1, 16; Laura Landro, "Celestial Seasonings Plans Initial Public Offering," *Wall Street Journal*, September 29, 1983, 53; Thomas C. Hayes, "Celestial Seasonings Pins Its Hopes on More Than Herbal Tea," *New York Times*, April 3, 1983, F6; Stephanie Strom, "Founder Is Rejoining Celestial Seasonings," *New York Times*, August 6, 1991, D3; "Hain Food to Buy Celestial Seasonings," *New York Times*, March 7, 2000, C2.

FIGURE 16. On April 21, 1970, the first Earth Day was celebrated in Madison, Wisconsin with a peaceful march.
David Sandell. © The Capital Times. Wisconsin Historical Society, WHS-48103.

Silent Spring (1962) or with Denis Hayes's organization of the first Earth Day in 1970, the counterculture showed an early green consciousness. In part, this hippie sensibility came from hostility to parental overconsumption as well as a reaction against Madison Avenue's incessant television sales campaigns, which had saturated boomers' psyches when growing up in the Fifties. Hippies' voluntary poverty forced thinking about what items in material culture were absolutely necessary. When hippies moved to the country to retreat from the mainstream, get close to nature, and grow their own food, the list of man-made essentials turned out to be surprisingly short. Safe drinking water was necessary, but composting outhouses replaced flush toilets. Homemade candles substituted for electric lights. Use of cars, trucks, and tractors was limited.[20]

---

[20] Berger, *Survival of a Counterculture*, 19, 91–4, 104–11; Andrew G. Kirk, *Counterculture Green* (Lawrence, KS, 2007), 21, 26–8, 40, 156–60; Houriet, *Getting Back Together*, 34, 91–2; Miller, *60s Communes*, 165. See also Adam Rome, *The Genius of Earth Day* (New York, 2013).

Stewart Brand's *Whole Earth Catalog* (1968) promoted a middle way to advance an environmental ethic. Brand rejected primitivism, such as the New Buffalo commune's decision to copy the Babylonians by harvesting wheat by hand, but he argued that technology should be restricted to items necessary for survival that were consistent with the advancement of environmental stewardship. A water pump to provide safe drinking water or to irrigate crops in a dry climate might be a necessity. Electricity was acceptable to operate a freezer to store home-grown food, but a clothes dryer was an unnecessary indulgence. Brand also advocated new technologies that might prove life transforming. For example, a passive solar design for a home was both ingenious and saved resources. Solar panels to generate electricity off the grid could provide daytime hot water, which was needed for cooking and cleaning. Inventing new devices and using simple methods, Brand thought, were forms of *appropriate technology*, a phrase that the counterculture adopted to describe their practices.[21]

Most communes were committed to environmentalism. Residents often lobbied for nature preserves, routinely opposed logging nearby old-growth forests, and resisted any development that threatened to alter the neighborhood. The idea of living in harmony with nature drove the green outlook. Endangered species drew passionate attention. Later movements, such as Save the Whales, can be traced back to the Sixties counterculture. In later decades, some hippie communes turned out for environmental protests, including the demonstrations that tried to block construction of a nuclear power plant on the New Hampshire seacoast. A few communes were specifically devoted to environmentalism. Paolo Soleri, a former student of Frank Lloyd Wright, opened Arcosanti north of Phoenix, Arizona in 1970. Combining avant-garde architecture with a strong environmental ethic, Soleri planned an eco-village for five thousand people.

---

[21] Kirk, *Counterculture Green*, 1–2, 6–9, 12–15, 30–2, 40–1, 48, 52, 74, 102–3, 105; Houriet, *Getting Back Together*, 213, 215; Elaine Sundancer, *Celery Wine* (Yellow Springs, OH, 1973), 155; Miller, *60s Communes*, 157.

Construction proceeded slowly, and in 2014 Arcosanti's few dozen residents made their living making and selling art.[22]

Hippie women developed their own particular environmental ethic. Because they did not become feminists until the mid-Seventies, they were less hostile to male domination and instead embraced the idea of a unique female relationship with nature. This led to ecofeminism. Borrowing from paganism as well as Native American practices, hippie women stressed being close to the earth, where nature provided food. Marylyn Motherbear Scott said, "My body was one with the earth." Men wanted to conquer nature, but women were part of nature. Sharon Doubiago noted, "Women have always thought like mountains." Pregnancy resembled growing a mountain. Women needed to teach men to get in touch with their feminine side. Ayisha Homolka adopted "earth-based spirituality." In the 1980s Morning Glory Zell worked to save endangered species. Hippie women wrote books that advocated simple living, such as Doris Longacre, *Living More with Less* (1981), Elaine St. James, *Living the Simple Life* (1996), and Cecile Andrews, *The Circle of Simplicity* (2000).[23]

In the Sixties Wendy Johnson became a Buddhist and pioneered organic gardening. Her garden supplied fresh produce to Greens, a San Francisco vegetarian restaurant run by Zen Buddhists. Johnson later helped Alice Waters, the founder of the gourmet restaurant Chez Panisse in Berkeley, set up the first Edible Schoolyard at a Berkeley school. Waters stressed fresh, local ingredients. These organic items were healthier, but eating local food also helped the environment by cutting transportation costs. Because feminism, organic farming, and the hippie back-to-the-land movement coincided in the Seventies, organic food production took off. By 2002, 11 percent of all American

---

[22] Kirk, *Counterculture Green*, 23–4, 98, 130, 133–4, 138–9, 147–8; Miller, *60s Communes*, 139–41, 158. On Save the Whales see Kirk, *Counterculture Green*, 135, 138. On antinuclear protests see Gretchen Lemke-Santangelo, *Daughters of Aquarius* (Lawrence, KS, 2009), 175, 178.

[23] Lemke-Santangelo, *Daughters of Aquarius*, 158, 175–9 (quotes at 176, 177, 177).

farmers were women, and they were more likely to use sustainable agriculture. In Washington State a majority of organic growers were women. Marcia Ostrom explained, "Women enjoy nurturing life in both plants and in the people they're feeding." Women were also more likely to sell produce at farmers' markets, where customers were usually women.[24]

The final and most curious legacy of the hippie counterculture was the role that it played in the development of the personal computer, the rise of the high-tech industry, and the emergence of Silicon Valley, which grew up in the shadow of San Francisco's Haight-Ashbury. The seed was planted, as in so many other cases, by Stewart Brand. While the *Whole Earth Catalog* gave him credibility among hippies, Brand's scientific background, imagination, and insights created a unique vision. He shared the hippie revulsion against large-scale institutions and particularly the counterculture's hostility to big corporations. Hippies felt that gargantuan companies threatened personal freedom. None seemed quite so sinister, because of the combination of wealth, power, and prestige, as IBM, which was huge, modern, elitist, and growing. Hippies were afraid that Big Blue, as it called itself, would soon control everyone and everything through the use of its gigantic mainframe computers.[25]

Brand and a few other young visionaries, all deeply rooted in the Bay Area's hippie counterculture, proposed a different future. Because the price of building a computer was dropping rapidly with no apparent end in sight, why not plan a radically different world in which the individual rather than IBM or other giant corporations that owned expensive mainframes controlled all of the world's computing power? In 1974 Brand announced, "Ready or not, computers are coming to the people." To describe the concept, he coined the term *personal computer*. The personal computer, quickly dubbed the PC, might redress the balance of power and cut into the wealth controlled by giant corporations.

---

[24] Ibid., 179–80 (quote at 180).
[25] Kirk, *Counterculture Green*, 106–7. See also Fred Turner, *From Counterculture to Cyberculture* (Chicago, 2006).

Furthermore, neither IBM nor any other big company had the slightest interest in developing the PC, which, if it were success-ful, would cut profits or perhaps even threaten the existence of big corporations. Thus, the goal was to transform how knowl-edge worked by putting it under the direct control of individuals. The PC was the high-tech version of an idealized hippie world.[26]

The first PC hobby club, ironically called the People's Computer Company, came together in 1966 in a nondescript storefront in Menlo Park, California just a few blocks from where Jerry Garcia had invented the Grateful Dead. The hob-byists were middle-class, white, suburban longhairs who loved both rock music and technology. The high-tech industry emerged in the Seventies out of this improbable location at a time when the valley's pear, apricot, and cherry orchards were being ripped out to build suburban ranch houses. One of the younger hobby-ists was Steve Jobs (1955–2011), who had grown up in the area. The son of a machinist, he had experimented with the tools in his father's well-stocked shop in the family's two-car garage before turning to electronics. In high school, Jobs had long hair and a beard, listened to rock music, took marijuana and LSD, and adopted vegetarianism. After graduation, he moved into a cabin in the hills with his girlfriend. Bowing to parental pressure, Jobs attended Reed College, a counterculture bastion in Portland, Oregon, for a semester in 1972 and then dropped out.[27]

Unimpressed with the family's mainstream Lutheran faith, Jobs was caught up in the Seventies spiritual quest. Influenced by the hippie fascination with the "other" as well as the Bay Area's strong ties to Asia, Jobs traveled in 1974 to India for seven months. He soaked up a radically different culture, adopted Zen Buddhism, meditated frequently, and returned home ready to remake the world. Jobs's technical computer skills were less than stellar, but he had the good fortune to reconnect with Steve

---

[26] Kirk, *Counterculture Green*, 163 (quote); Heath and Potter, *Nation of Rebels*, 300.

[27] John Markoff, *What the Dormouse Said* (New York, 2005), 152, 184–6, 271–3; Walter Isaacson, *Steve Jobs* (New York, 2011), 6–7, 14–20, 31–41.

Wozniak, a true tech wizard. The two, like the earlier duo of Lennon and McCartney, were a great team. Woz could advance the technology, and Jobs was the visionary leader with flashes of brilliant insight. In 1976 they decided to found their own personal computer company. They were stumped with finding a corporate name until Jobs picked Apple. He had been eating many apples. The name was so bizarre and unique that it worked.[28]

There were many twists and turns in the Apple story. A frustrated Woz took a big pile of money and left. Jobs was too hot-tempered to run the company. In 1983 John Sculley, a Pepsi marketing executive, became the CEO. Two years later, Sculley ousted Jobs from Apple. To get back in the game, Jobs used his Apple money to create Next, a computer company that flopped. As serene as the Buddha, Jobs then financed Pixar to make animation films. He personally approved the plot and character development for *Toy Story* (1995), the most successful animation film ever launched. In 1997 Jobs returned to Apple, which was in decline, and soon became the CEO. What followed was the iMac (1998), an elegantly thin computer; iTunes (2001), the first simple system for listening to music; the iPhone (2007), which radically changed how phones were used; and the iPad (2010), best described as a new form of cool. By the time he died in 2011, Jobs had reinvented not just the PC but much of pop culture and how Americans approached the world. The counterculture had arrived.[29]

In the Sixties hippies rebelled against government bureaucracies, large corporations, stodgy mainstream culture, and prudish practices, including widespread censorship. Like the Beats from which they had drawn inspiration, hippies knew much better what they opposed than what they favored. Those hostile to the status quo could temporarily unite, but they often disagreed among themselves on what should come next. While some hippies had leftist instincts, their distrust of authority made

---

[28] Isaacson, *Steve Jobs*, 14–15, 46–8, 52–65.
[29] Ibid., 115, 149–58, 170, 192–228, 232–49, 284–321, 354–5, 382–4, 473–5, 493–4.

them suspicious of socialism or the welfare state, both of which required large bureaucracies. Other hippies were libertarians, although they rarely used that name. Moving to the country to farm one's own land often seemed to be more of a nostalgic retreat than any attempt to create an alternative society that could be a model for the future. Getting back to roots, however, was one way to extricate the self from the establishment. Rural communes were a form of decontamination.

Trying to understand the counterculture is difficult. Not only were hippies inarticulate but media coverage inevitably focused on the glittery, sensational surface, whether outrageously long hair, promiscuous sex, or widespread use of marijuana and LSD. The media often ignored the more important aspects, which were a combination of experimentation and soul searching. Residents of remote rural communes got close to nature and raised food in order to abandon the mainstream and contemplate an alternative. While most communes failed, the communards were sufficiently healed that they were able to reenter society. They did so, however, on new terms. Hippies had gradually given up the counterculture's most self-destructive practices, and they refined their behavior to be less confrontational. At the same time, society became more tolerant. Few hippies continued to believe, as Timothy Leary had once argued, that psychedelic drugs were the instant path to spiritual healing. Wise gurus knew better.

Business found it easy to market the counterculture style, even if doing so meant that the counterculture was being co-opted. Hippies set out despising business, but, ironically, many hippies ended up opening successful small companies. Because hippies were independent-minded and did not want to work for other people inside a large organization, setting up a business was an excellent way to make a living. Alice Waters opened Chez Panisse, Berkeley's first gourmet restaurant, after studying in France, where she became so enamored of French food that she attended cooking school. Later, Waters wrote cookbooks to spread her idea that people should eat local, fresh food, and she cultivated the next generation through her school garden project.

Business could both provide a family with financial support and advance a counterculture agenda.

Hippie communes often preached and practiced living in harmony with nature. Those parts of the United States where the Sixties counterculture was strongest, including the West Coast and Vermont, often have been in the forefront of environmental issues. Being green is a civic virtue in such places, and Green Party candidates have occasionally won elections in former hippie strongholds. Libertarians, too, have often polled well in these areas. The hippie influence on high tech was rooted in distrust of large corporations and a desire to empower the average person, but the hippie love of the "other" could also be seen in the large immigrant workforce in the tech industry, and the early push for global sales of American tech products. In addition to generous stock options, high-tech companies were among the first to innovate flextime, employee child-care, free employee bus service, and health benefits for gay partners. Tech companies abandoned dress codes, celebrated the body with free workouts, and sponsored music or art on-site to stimulate creativity.

Hippies launched a *cultural revolution* that helped change American society. Cruder language, casual sex, and a certain amount of drug use gained a kind of acceptance in large segments of the country. Hair and dress, as well as tattoos, became personal expressions of the self not subject to government or social regulation. Rock music became socially acceptable, but musical taste exploded in many different directions, in part because technology made it possible for each person to have personal music. Multiculturalism flourished amid rising immigration, as religions, languages, cultural productions, and food proliferated. The complexity sometimes dazzled, and sometimes it became bewildering, but there was no denying that America was, in fact, a diverse nation. The hippie cultural revolution remains a work in progress. The values and practices of the Sixties are still percolating through the society, which is still evolving. It remains to be seen where this will end, or indeed if it ever will. Perhaps change itself is the permanent new dynamic.

Index